Death Dictionary

ALSO BY CHRISTINE QUIQLEY
AND FROM MCFARLAND

Conjoined Twins: An Historical, Biological and Ethical Issues Encyclopedia (2003; paperback 2006)

Skulls and Skeletons: Human Bone Collections and Accumulations (2001; paperback 2008)

Modern Mummies: The Preservation of the Human Body in the Twentieth Century (1998; paperback 2006)

The Corpse: A History (1996; paperback 2005)

Death Dictionary
Over 5,500 Clinical, Legal, Literary and Vernacular Terms

CHRISTINE QUIGLEY

McFarland & Company, Inc., Publishers
Jefferson, North Carolina, and London

The present work is a reprint of the library bound edition of Death Dictionary: Over 5,500 Clinical, Legal, Literary and Vernacular Terms, *first published in 1994 by McFarland.*

LIBRARY OF CONGRESS CATALOGUING-IN-PUBLICATION DATA

Quigley, Christine, 1963–
  Death dictionary : over 5,500 clinical, legal, literary and vernacular terms / by Christine Quigley.
       p.   cm.
  Includes bibliographical references.

  ISBN 978-0-7864-6715-0
  softcover : 50# alkaline paper

  1. Death — Dictionaries. I. Title.
HQ1073.Q54 2011
306.9'03 — dc20   93-28817

BRITISH LIBRARY CATALOGUING DATA ARE AVAILABLE

© 1994 Christine Quigley. All rights reserved

No part of this book may be reproduced or transmitted in any form or by any means, electronic or mechanical, including photocopying or recording, or by any information storage and retrieval system, without permission in writing from the publisher.

Front cover image: Musculature and bones of the forearm and hand, Gerard de Lairesse (National Library of Medicine)

Manufactured in the United States of America

McFarland & Company, Inc., Publishers
  Box 611, Jefferson, North Carolina 28640
  www.mcfarlandpub.com

For you, Katina

CONTENTS

Preface
ix

Introduction
1

Symbols and Abbreviations
11

The Dictionary
13

Thesaurus
167

Bibliography
193

PREFACE

Although the phrase "Memento Mori" is not often heard today, the *Death Dictionary* gives readers no choice. It offers the disturbing news that murder comes in at least seventy-six distinct shapes and sizes, suicide in twenty-five — including *completed,* a suggested alternative to *successful.* With this resource, readers can be mindful of a possible negative patient care outcome or beware of the big jump, the bow out, the heavy fall.

The *Dictionary* provides the means to compare *metaphorical death* to *symbolic death.* On a more practical level, it assists in deciphering epitaphs and wills (living or otherwise). With the *Death Dictionary* we can arm ourselves with the knowledge that to encounter a *necrophagist* is to bump into a cannibal, and that if that cannibal speaks of *bakolo* (or *long pig* or *two-legged mutton*), we may be on the menu.

Although several dictionaries of unusual words have been published in recent years, none has so unified a theme as the *Death Dictionary.* The *Dictionary* cuts across professions, economic classes, and historical eras. Words have been collected from sixty-five cultures, nine religions, and twenty fields. The *Dictionary* opens the door on jargon used by police officers, funeral directors, and medical personnel. It documents the informal language of death row and the morgue and it explains the formal language of grief counselors, euthanasia supporters, and the proverbial life insurance salesman.

While some of us may not want to admit it, death is something that all five billion of us — with the possible exception of the cryonically preserved — have in common. Whether it be by *gasphyxiation, autoerotic asphyxia,* or *spontaneous human combustion,* we will each experience it.

The *Death Dictionary* is a collection of words and phrases the editor has come across in over a thousand death education texts, slang and specialized dictionaries, funeral industry journals, true crime annals, death row and consolation literature, and the memoirs of archeologists, medical examiners, criminologists, doctors, and disaster victims.

The *Dictionary* is intended as an informative, objective reference work. Definitions are concise and, except for usage notes, are not editorialized. Alphabetization is letter by letter, so *A.L.A.C.P.* precedes *à la mort* despite spacing and punctuation. Within each entry, definitions and variants are alphabetized by part of speech, so nouns are preceded by adjectives and followed by verbs. All words are related directly to the process or description of death, thus *mourning clothing* and *widow's weeds* are included, but *jet* (black ornamentation often found on mourning jewelry or clothing) is not. Similarly, if a word has meanings other than the death-related definition, they have been excluded without being expressly noted.

While varied spellings are cross-referenced within the text, synonyms are more accessible in the thesaurus at the back of the book. The thesaurus groups words under forty main categories, including Afterlife, Corpse, Execution, Funeral, Grief, Murder, Suicide, Terminal Illness, and Will. The largest grouping has been split into Dead, consisting solely of synonyms; Dying, which adds descriptions of the dying process; and Death, further broken down into Announcements of, Fear of, Gods/Goddesses of, Omens of, Synonyms, and Types.

Words and phrases are designated as slang, archaic, obsolete, or idiom. In addition, they may also be professional jargon or euphemism without being noted as such, for instance *casketed,* which is both. With a handful of exceptions (most of them Latin), all entries are in English. Etymology is limited for the most part to eponymous words, such as *burking*. Entries are arranged as follows:

SAMPLE ENTRY

word part of speech. plural form **words.** Style. Language. Culture. Field. Religion. Definition; secondary definition [usage or etymology]. variant, part of speech.

A list of symbols and abbreviations precedes the text. The *Death Dictionary* borrows translated expressions from thirty modern and extinct languages, including Greek, German, Old

English, Aramaic, and the Romance languages. The mythology, customs, and dialects of over sixty cultures have provided an international and panhistoric scope to the *Dictionary,* juxtaposing current Canadian slang with ancient Babylonian mythology. Most mythological entries are of ancient rather than modern origin. *Indian* indicates language from the continent of India, while entries from the Indians of North America are designated *Aztec, Mayan,* or *Native American.*

Words from the major Western religions are augmented by the occasional entry from Buddhism or Shintoism. And the formal and informal language of twenty disciplines and professions is represented. Fields range across, for example, Archeology, Cryonics, Law (including Law Enforcement), Theology, Theater and the Military.

While every effort has been made to avoid inaccuracies, the editor welcomes clarification and suggested additions. Please write in care of the publisher.

Christine Quigley
August 1993

INTRODUCTION

Why a dictionary of death?

Because the vocabulary exists and the words needed collecting.
Where else can you look up the meanings of *thanatropism, thanatognomonic, thanatomimesis,* and *thanatopsis,* not to mention *Thanatos,* whose names gives life (and death) to these words? What other reference book can you consult to find thirty synonyms for the electric chair or to sort out the difference between *patricide* and *parricide*? How many other dictionaries divulge the meaning of *psychopomp* and offer the reader a twenty-letter word for the study of martyrs (*philotheopareptesism*)?

Words, even about death, have a certain poetry. A *noyade* sounds somehow less threatening than a mass drowning and *la fosse* less excruciating than live burial. To die *commorient* sounds almost as romantic as having a *myriologue* composed. Who would guess that *sky burial* was a Tibetan custom of disposing of the body by cutting it up and throwing it to the birds or that to *turn into the wind* was a revenge technique in which the Chinese left their slain enemies where they fell? Even scientific terms can be surprising: long-buried bodies leave a vestige known to archaeologists as a *soil silhouette.* Foreign words and phrases have their own mystique, even when never spoken aloud. Latin catchphrases like *acerbitas mortis, memento mori,* and *Sic transit gloria mundi* echo in the inner ear, and pride is felt by the layperson at knowing the difference between *algor mortis* and *livor mortis.* Words for their own sake are worthy of collection, but the subject of death provides a cross-section of time, emotions, and cultures and yet is narrow enough to consist of several specific vocabularies—medical, philosophical, and psychological among them.

Thanatologist Robert Kavanaugh wrote twenty years ago: "A

2 Introduction

major barrier against open discussion of death is our lack of an American folk language in which all can communicate comfortably about every aspect of human mortality.... In our futility, we grasp at strands of the three professional vocabularies Americans are still compelled to use when speaking of death: the medical, the religious and the language of funeral directors."[1] In the meantime, both the professional and popular lexicons have grown enormously. The last words of the dying are no longer recorded for posterity, but neither are the words of their caretakers systematically defined. *Consolation literature* has given way to death education texts, but even these do not offer the everyday language of those in the death professions. In fact, references to the death professions usually omit such fields as *marantology, sindonology,* and *forensic odontology,* each of which has a place in the *Death Dictionary.*

This book hopes to capture without prejudice the language of the hospital and the hospice, the memorial service and the morgue, the suicide prevention center and the city streets. It aspires to point out further implications of words we thought we knew—words like *necrophilia,* which can be both *sexual* and *nonsexual,* and *cannibalism,* which is somehow more socially acceptable when it is *nonrecurrent* than when it is *societal.* The *Death Dictionary* is by no means a how-to manual, but it does make plain some of the linguistic mysteries which continue to cloak both the theory and practice of death.

Because death is a dramatic subject.

While all deaths are momentous, individually or collectively, certain deaths—*accidental death, sudden death, premature death*—are by their very nature more momentous than others. Such deaths seem unjust and provoke questions, often self-directed, about prevention, even though many of our efforts are already directed at preventing, controlling, or at least warning of accidents, disease, and natural catastrophes. There are even people who think *natural death* itself may be preventable and actively make provisions for *post-suspension counseling* to follow their *cryopreservation.* Death is an ongoing battle between two warring sides—one spreads epidemics and doles out disasters, the other vaccinates its children, disaster-proofs its dwellings, and patents new life-saving techniques.

"To die would be an awfully big adventure," says Peter Pan,

although few but the *death-welcomer* look forward to it like he does. Death is associated with pain and punishment and *appropriate deaths* are in the minority. Most deaths — if they give any warning — are raged against, denied or defied, anything but resigned to. Choices like *pregnancy reduction* and *active euthanasia* are agonized over in the courts, in the media, and at home. The *right to life* and the *right to die* are both in dispute. What is *death with dignity* to some is *geronticide* to others. What some term *therapeutic abortion* is condemned by others as *child-murder*. But whether or not a death is of our making, and regardless of how long or full the life, it is still mourned and counted as a loss, sometimes annually (*anniversary phenomenon*). As the members of the *A.R.L.S.* (Association for Recognizing the Life of Stillborns) will testify, the grief over death which gave rise to the practice of *wailing* is still as strong, if not as loud.

Today, the *duel* has become the drive-by shooting. America's largest cities trade off the title *murder capital* as national membership grows in *P.O.M.C.* (Parents of Murdered Children). It is perhaps a symptom of our society that the synonyms for murder number more than three hundred, from *abbreviate* to *zotz*. In fact, *Homo necans* (human killer), has been suggested as a species name to replace *Homo sapiens*. And yet *crimes of passion* and *serial killings* inspire miniseries, organized crime *hits* continue to make headlines, and *assassination* still has the potential to unite a country in grief. Death is an injustice when it occurs naturally. When it is taken from us by another human, it is grounds for outrage. Outrage against those who would blame the victim, outrage against the courts for freeing violent offenders, outrage against the ever-cheapening value of life exhibited by the killers. The ultimate insult is the nuclear threat of *omnicide*. We now must fear not only the *homicidal,* but the *mundicidal* maniac.

Suicide is drama, too, but unlike murder it is statistically underrepresented. While law enforcement officers have been quick to pick up signs of *autoerotic asphyxia* in cases of death by hanging, *autocides*—car accidents which are really disguised suicides—often go undiagnosed. We have come a long way from classifying a suicidal person as a "felon against himself" (*felo-de-se*) and calling *completed* suicides "successful," to conducting *psychological autopsies* in order to understand such deaths and to further suicide prevention. Being familiar with terms like *suicide gesture* and mnemonic

4 Introduction

devices like *3-Ds* is one step toward saving a life. Knowing the characteristics of a *suicide cluster* may save many.

Because death is both individual and universal. While there are those who dispute the widespread claim that death is democratic, there is no denying (*cryonics* aside) that it is common to all humans. The causes may change (*overlaying* has become archaic in light of *SIDS*) and the ratios (*death rate* and *volume of death*) may vary, but the fact of death remains constant throughout time. Death happens to all of us, but it usually happens one at a time. It may give identity to the dead (*martyrs* and *cadavers*) or to the living (*widows* and *Gold Star Mothers*). It may fall into a conventional category (*drowning*) or its cause may remain undetermined (*five-day case*). It may be expected (*near and certain death*) or it may strike without warning (*act of God*). But it is certain that there are as many deaths as there are personalities.

In addition to each death's being unique, a single death may be many things to many people. The course of a terminal illness may be experienced as *social disengagement* by the patient, *suspicion awareness* by the hospital staff, and *anticipatory death* by his or her survivors. "To die and to lose one's life are much the same thing," says an Irish proverb. True, the resulting lack of life is unanimous, but some go out with a bang and others with a whimper. In some cases, the body knows how to die (*heart death*), but the mind rebels against it, allowing successful *resuscitation;* in others, the mind precedes the body (*cerebral death*). It is the manner in which we die—mentally and emotionally—which sets us apart. There are more than the five broad stages of death—*rage and anger, denial, bargaining, depression,* and *acceptance*—outlined by Elisabeth Kübler-Ross, as she is the first to admit. The etiquette of death taught in the *ars moriendi* period is now given over to achieving *closure,* a highly individuated process.

Death is a solo experience, though it follows many precedents. And the way we imagine ourselves facing death may change abruptly when put to the test. It is certainly easier to think of death in the abstract than to assess our own *personal death awareness.* But as Victor W. Marshall states, "The first stage in coming to terms with death is to recognize that death is a personal possibility."[2] Within these pages, you may determine whether you are a *death-experimenter,* a *death-ignorer,* or a *death-initiator.* You may decide whether you subscribe to *religious immortality* or to *biological immortality* (or both). We are not all atheists, but neither do we all find comfort in the promise of *Abraham's bosom*. An *awareness of finitude* allows us to plan our time wisely, whether we believe in an *afterlife,* an *underworld,* or neither.

Because death can never be defined by the living.
While there are thousands of ways to describe death, in actuality we know not what it is. Our descriptions, other than those of *near-death experiences* or ecstatic visions, are based on observations of the dying, on the physical characteristics of death, and on *postmortem changes.* Family, friends, and occasional passers-by once gathered around the *deathbed,* even though the center of attention could never tell them what they really wanted to know. As Virginia Woolf commented in a letter to Vita Sackville-West, death is "the one experience I shall never describe." Today, the art of dying allows for even less rehearsal. We can speculate, assume, or hope, but "The best, and perhaps the only, way to understand death is to die...."[3]

Short of that, there is nothing wrong with arming ourselves with knowledge. To label and identify the components of death does not mean to condone them (*thanatophilia*), but to better fortify ourselves against the inevitable (*thanatophobia*). For those who work with (against) death everyday, a corpse is an *unconscious person* until proven otherwise. Compassion must give way to more immediate needs: motorcycles become *donorcycles* to those who harvest organs for transplantation. Health professionals have an informal vocabulary (*O-sign* and *Q-sign*), which must be viewed in context of the life-and-death decisions they take part in every day (*extraordinary means* and *no code*). Ironically, it is when death is carefully monitored, such as in a hospital, that the moment it occurs becomes increasingly difficult to pinpoint. Life and death are no longer mutually exclusive. As surgeon Richard Selzer muses:

> You do not die all at once. Some tissues live on for minutes, even hours, giving still their little cellular shrieks, molecular echoes of the agony of the whole corpus. Here and there a spray of nerves dances on. True, the heart stops; the blood no longer courses; the electricity of the brain sputters, then shuts down. Death is now *pronounceable*. But there are outposts where clusters of cells yet shine, besieged, little lights blinking in the advancing darkness. Doomed soldiers, they battle on until death has secured the premises all to itself.[4]

6   Introduction

Rigor mortis may be an unequivocal means of determining the death of the body, but the continued existence of the soul is yet to be scientifically determined, however widely believed. Who would not rather be *enskied* than simply *entombed*? Except through *symbolic death,* the state or "statelessness" of death cannot be pre-experienced. Most of us fear the unknown, as well as the means by which we may be thrust into it. But F.J. Sheed claims, "Death itself, apart from the pain that might precede it and the punishment that might follow, does not bother me."[5] Whatever promise death may hold, it also includes the threat of nonexistence in the earthly world, except through *reincarnation.* Those suffering from *annihilation anxiety* often hedge their bets with posterity by influencing a *social heir* or by creating or procreating to ensure *significant survival.* Our language of the soul indicates that most of us hope for more than just the *big sleep,* although even this expression hints at one day being awakened.

Because death has a long history, which the language reflects.
Jerry Robinson, imprisoned for life in Auburn, New York, for killing two police officers, petitioned for his release, claiming that he had completed his natural life sentence when his heart stopped for two minutes during open-heart surgery. One hundred years ago, the name *slip-string* may have applied, but that was before death had become such a complex issue. The hangman need only be familiar with the *patent drop* to avoid a mess. Prisoners had few rights, except to say a few *last words* to the crowd from the gallows. If a public hanging were not on the calendar, a public *lynching* — usually of a racial minority — would commonly be carried out. Discrimination is still accused of the U.S. Courts, but it is a far cry from 18th-century France's class-conscious *high block* and *low block.* Away from shore, a mutineer did not need to know the difference between *keelhauling* and *keelraking* to suffer the same consequence either way. Today, rather than a raucous *tumbrilitis,* the condemned are offered candlelight vigils. It is more than likely they would trade them in for a *lifeboat* — a *commutation,* a *reprieve,* even a short *stay of execution.* Jerry Robinson should consider himself lucky.

The *Death Dictionary* has a "Hall of Infamy" which includes *Cain* and *Bluebeard,* both immortalized by the murders they committed. It explains the *Werther effect,* an expression which takes its name from Goethe's fictional character. It offers *Brodie,* whose posthumous fame rests on his survival of his suicide attempt. Readers will learn that the bodysnatcher *Rolfinck* suffered the same eponymous fate as his more famous counterpart *Burke*. They will be introduced to English hangman *Jack Ketch* and they will shake hands with Egyptian *Anubis,* Greek *Charon,* and twenty-four more cultural equivalents of the *Grim Reaper,* including Mexico's *Clean and Peeled One.*

Just as there will always be names for death's deities, we will always need words for the disposal of the dead and those who carry it out. Although bodies are still *laid out,* we no longer *lay up in lavender.* Few remember that *R.I.P.* stands for *Requiescat in pace,* not the popular translation. While some have grown up with the custom, others have never heard of the *Kiss of Peace.* Before present-day funeral directors made their own mark on the language, funerals were carried out by *upholders* and *undertakers.* Today, funeral establishments offer complete *funeralization* of the dead, often including *bereavement counseling* for surviving family members, rather than the gloomy *hatchments* and *palls* of yesterday. Hearses are no longer drawn by horses, and the deceased may now require air transport in a *human remains case* before being *casketed.*

The *Death Dictionary* gives evidence of the evolution of the title *crowner* to *coroner* to *medical examiner.* It compares the old *death-throe,* noted in deathbed accounts, with the new *instantaneous cadaveric spasm,* noted in autopsy reports. It supplies writers of historical fiction with customs like the *ordeal of the bier* and crime writers with technical terms like *suggillation* (post-mortem bruising). Along the way, it clarifies the frequently misunderstood nuance of *corpus delecti* and modern concepts of *preneed.* While it may change the reader's mind about burial to know that the body may undergo *saponification* or that it might wait out the season with the rest of the *winter bodies,* consumer information is not a new idea. Years before Jessica Mitford's tirade against the *sealer casket,*[6] the *willow coffin* was offered as a sound environmental alternative. "Dust to dust ," in light of cremation statistics, seems to be taken increasingly literally.

Because current usage mirrors our culture.

In this age of information, it helps to be able to distinguish between *medicide* and *marantology.* This book does so without reference to proponents of either one. It is useful to know the difference, if you are in the market for it, between *term* and *whole life* insurance. This book provides a quick reference, rather than an exhaustive comparison between the two. It is informative to know, especially if you are a *beneficiary under a will,* the subtle difference between *per capita* and *per stirpes* distribution of an estate. This book gives you that and more, from *abatement of a legacy* to *ultimogeniture.* If the word—or idiom or abbreviation—has relation to death by being a cause, a description, a synonym, or a result of it, you will find it defined within.

The inclusion of *ouranophobia* (fear of heaven) and *hadephobia* (fear of hell) may remind the reader of the apocryphal epitaph of an atheist: "All dressed up, no place to go." But the *Death Dictionary* offers seventy other possible destinations. It confirms the use of *first-* and *second-degree murder, manslaughter,* and *nonnegligent homicide,* as well as offering alternatives, including the old standby *rub out:*

> When asked if she had killed her husband, Ruth Snyder objected to the word "kill" because "it sounds so cruel and I don't like to use it." When asked if that was not what she had done, she said, "Yes, but I don't like to use that term." When asked what she would prefer, she suggested "get rid of him."[7]

Ask twenty people the meaning of death and you will receive twenty different, though not entirely dissimilar, answers. Those answers may be couched in colloquial language (*call it quits*) or the words of the church (*call of God*). The question may elicit analogies as far removed as the mythical *pale horse* and the military *taps.* The *Death Dictionary* encompasses a wide selection of metaphors, in addition to the physical realities of death, from *constructive death*—the opposite of *technological death*—to the *second death,* a reminder that we are all living on *borrowed time.*

This book is not just for language lovers or for those in the *death professions,* although it is hoped that both groups will make use of it. It is for all mortals, particularly those who seek to put death in context. Whether it is spelled with a *d* or a *D,* death is both knowable and unknowable, sometimes good—sometimes bad, an end for some—a beginning for others. At the same time, death is rarely black and white . The *Death Dictionary* defines *brain death, cardiac death,* and over sixty other shades of gray. As we "dig deeper" into the phenomenon of death, and as our society offers more services for the dead and the bereaved, we create more labels. It is these labels — official and unofficial — which the *Death Dictionary* proposes to document.

REFERENCES

1. *Facing Death*. Baltimore: Penguin Books, 1972, p. 69.
2. *Last Chapters: A Sociology of Aging and Dying*. Monterey, California: Brooks/Cole, 1980.
3. Monika Hellwig. *The Meaning of the Sacraments*. Dayton: Pflaum Press, 1972, p. 92.
4. *Mortal Lessons: Notes on the Art of Surgery*. New York: Simon & Schuster, 1976, p. 136.
5. *Death into Life: A Conversation*. New York: Arena Lettres, 1977, p. 131.
6. *The American Way of Death*. New York: Simon & Schuster, 1963.
7. Wenzell Brown. *They Died in the Chair*. New York: Popular Library, 1958, p. 36.

SYMBOLS AND ABBREVIATIONS

+ and
abbrev. abbreviation
adj. adjective
adv. adverb, adverbial
Ar. Arabic
Anthropol. anthropology
Archeol. archeology
B.C. before Christ
Biol. biology
c. century
Christian. Christianity
CIA Central Intelligence Agency
Eccles. ecclesiastical
Egypt. Egyptian
esp. especially
exclam. exclamation
FBI Federal Bureau of Investigation
fem. feminine.
Fr. French
Gael. Gaelic
Ger. German, Germanic
Gk. Greek
Heb. Hebrew
intr. intransitive
Ir. Irish
Ital. Italian
Japan. Japanese
L Latin
Lat. Latin
lit. literally
Med. medicine
Mil. military
myth. mythology
n. noun
obs. obsolete
orig. origin, originally
Pathol. pathology
phr. phrase
pl. plural
Port. Portuguese
p.part. past participle
pr.part. present participle
pref. prefix, prefer
prep. prepositional
prob. probably
Psychol. psychology
Rom. Roman
Rom. Cath. Roman Catholic
Scand. Scandinavian
Sociol. sociology
Sp. Spanish
st. saint
suff. suffix
Theol. theology
tr. transitive
transl. translation
U.S. United States
v. verb
var. variant

THE DICTIONARY

A

A *abbrev.* Accidental death.
A.A. *abbrev.* Alternatives to Abortion.
A.A.A. *abbrev.* Americans Against Abortion.
aaal *abbrev.* Abolish all abortion laws.
A.A.C. *abbrev.* Association of American Cemeteries.
A.A.C.S. *abbrev.* Association of American Cemetery Superintendents.
A.A.D.N.C. *abbrev.* Apostolate to Assist Dying Non-Catholics.
A.A.I. *abbrev.* Alternatives to Abortion International.
Aalu or **Aaru** *n. Egypt. myth.* The land of the dead in which embodied souls work and relax.
A.A.R.C. *abbrev.* Assassination Archives and Research Center.
Aaru see **Aalu**
A.A.S. *abbrev.* Alternatives to Abortion Society; American Association of Suicidology.
ab *abbrev.* Abortion.
ab. *abbrev.* Abort; abortion.
Abaddon *n. Hebrew myth.* Death; the lowest part of Sheol where sinners are punished.
abatement by death *n. phr. Law.* Dismissal of a criminal case due to the death of the defendant.
abatement of a legacy *n. phr. Law.* The reduction in amount of or the extinction of a legacy to a beneficiary by the payment of debts owned by the grantor of the legacy.
Abattur see **Abatur**
Abatur or **Abattur** *n. Mandean myth.* A god of death who weighs souls at the Last Judgment.
abbreviate *intr. v. slang.* Kill; murder. *var.* abbreviated, abbreviating, abbreviates, *v.*
ABC *abbrev. Mil.* Atomic, biological, chemical warfare.

A.B.C.C. *abbrev. Mil.* Atomic Bomb and Casualty Commission.
ABCW (abcw) *abbrev. Mil.* Atomic, biological, chemical warfare.
A.B.F.S.E. *abbrev.* American Board of Funeral Service Education.
A.B.F.S.E.C. *abbrev.* American Board of Funeral Service Education Commission.
abiosis *n.* Absence of life. *var.* abiotic, *adj.*, abiotically, *adv.*
A.B.M.C. *abbrev.* American Battle Monuments Commission.
abort *intr. v.* To give birth to a stillborn child; to terminate pregnancy. *tr. v.* To terminate a pregnancy. *var.* aborter, *n.*, aborted, aborting, aborts, *v.*
aborticide *n.* Destruction of a fetus in the uterus. *var.* aborticidal, *adj.*
abortifacient *adj.* Causing abortion. *n.* A drug that causes abortion.
abortion *n.* The termination of a pregnancy before the fetus is able to sustain independent life; premature expulsion of an embryo or fetus; an aborted embryo or fetus.
abortionist *n.* One who performs abortions.
Abraham's bosom *n. phr. Christian.* Resting place of the souls of the faithful in Heaven.
absent from the body *adj. phr.* Physically dead but having a disembodied living soul.
abwik *abbrev. Law.* Assault and battery with intent to kill.
A.C.A. *abbrev.* American Cemetery Association.
acceptance *n.* A stage of terminal illness in which the patient is psychologically and emotionally prepared for death.
accessory to murder *n. phr. Law.* One who aids indirectly in killing a person.
accidental death *n. phr.* Death by other than natural causes; death caused by an act of God.
A.C.C.I.P.K.A. *abbrev.* American Citizen's Committee of Inquiry into President Kennedy's Assassination.
A.C.C.M. *abbrev.* Advisory Committee on Cemeteries and Memorials.
account for *v. phr.* To enumerate as dead; to kill. *var.* accounted for, *adj. phr.*
aceldama *n.* A battlefield; a place associated with bloodshed [the name of the field purchased with the money received by Judas for betraying Christ].
ace of spades *n. phr. slang.* Widow.
acerbitas mortis *idiom. Lat.* The bitterness of death.
Acheron *n.* or **Acherusian Bog** *n. phr. Gk. myth.* The river of woe over which Charon ferried the souls of the dead to Hades.
Acherusian Bog see **Acheron**
A.C.H.S.W. *abbrev.* American

ACK • administration 15

Committee on the History of the Second War.

ACK *abbrev.* Accidentally killed.

ack *adj. slang. Law.* Accidentally killed.

acknowledgment card. *n. phr.* A card sent in recognition of an expression of sympathy after a death.

A.C.M.A. *abbrev.* American Certified Morticians Association.

A.C.M.C. *abbrev.* American Cemetery-Mortuary Conference; American Cemetery-Mortuary Counsel.

across the river *prep. phr. slang.* Dead.

acroteriazein *n. Gk.* The practice of severing the feet, hands, nose, and ears of a corpse and tying them to its elbow to prevent it becoming a vampire.

A.C.S. *abbrev.* American Cryonics Society.

active euthanasia *n. phr.* Causing the death of a terminally ill person, usually at his or her request, to prevent further suffering.

active voluntary euthanasia *n. phr.* Any act to terminate life carried out by a rational person who has been medically determined to experience intractable pain and debasement of the human condition.

act of God. *n. phr.* Sudden death caused by any unavoidable physical force; loss of life which is beyond human control.

actuary *n.* One who estimates life expectancy, esp. for an insurance company. *var.* actuarial, *adj.,* actuarially, *adv.*

acute disaster *n. phr.* A disaster which strikes suddenly.

acute suicide *n. phr. Psychol.* Purposeful suicide with a high completion rate.

A.C.W.A. *abbrev.* American Civil War Association.

ad & d *abbrev.* Accidental death and dismemberment.

Adapa *n. Akkadian myth.* The first man, through whose actions humans remain mortal and suffer disease and death.

A.D.E.C. *abbrev.* Association for Death Education and Counseling.

ademption *n. Law.* The disposal of specific property bequeathed in a will in a way which invalidates the bequest; the intentional extinction or withdrawal of a bequest in a will by the testator.

adipocere *n.* A brown, fatty, waxlike substance that forms on bodies which decompose in a moist environment. *var.* adipocerous, *adj.*

Adlivun *n. Eskimo myth.* The place where the dead are purified before continuing the journey to the Land of the Moon.

administer *tr. v. Law.* To manage and dispose of the estate of a deceased person. *var.* administered, administering, administers, *v.*

administration *n. Law.* The management and disposal of

the estate of a deceased person.

administration cum testamento annexo *n. phr. Law.* Administration granted when an executor is not named in a will or when the executor named is incompetent, unwilling, or deceased.

administration de bonis non *n. phr. Law.* Administration granted to manage and dispose of goods of the deceased which were not administered by the former executor or administrator.

administration durante in absentia *n. phr. Law.* Administration granted during the absence of the executor.

administration durante minore aetate *n. phr. Law.* Administration granted during the minority of the executor.

administrator *n. Law.* A person legally appointed to manage and distribute the estate of a person who has died without a will or without naming an executor.

administratrix *n. Law.* A female administrator.

admix *abbrev. Law.* Administratrix.

admx *abbrev. Law.* Administratrix.

Adraste *n. British myth.* Goddess of war.

ADW *abbrev. Law.* Assault with a deadly weapon.

adw *abbrev. Law.* Assault with a deadly weapon.

AE *abbrev.* Years of life.

Aecus *n. Gk. myth.* One of the three judges of the dead.

A.E.F. *abbrev.* American Euthanasia Foundation.

Aesculapius *n. Gk. myth.* A deified physician struck down by Zeus because of his ability to resuscitate the dead.

A.F.D.A. *abbrev.* Advertising Funeral Directors of America.

A.F.D.E.A. *abbrev.* American Funeral Directors and Embalmers Association.

A.F.D.S. *abbrev.* Associated Funeral Directors Service.

A.F.D.S.I. *abbrev.* Associated Funeral Directors Service International.

afterlife *n.* An existence which follows death.

afterworld *n.* A place which the dead enter and inhabit.

agathanasia *n.* A good death; death with dignity.

aged in wood *adj. phr. slang.* Buried.

age-specific death rate *n. phr.* The number of deaths within a given age category per one thousand people.

aggravated assault *n. phr. Law.* Serious bodily injury intentionally brought about, attempted, or threatened by a person armed with a deadly weapon.

aggravated murder *n. phr. Law.* Premeditated homicide.

agonal *n.* A tale of suffering and death; the agony of death.

agonal breath *n. phr.* Final respirations of a dying person.

agonal heartbeat *n. phr.* Final contractions of the heart before death.

A.G.S. *abbrev.* The Association for Gravestone Studies.

A.H.A. *abbrev.* Association for Humane Abortion.

Ahpuch see **Hunhau**

Ahriman *n. Persian myth.* An embodiment of all evil, who brings sickness and death into the world.

Aiakos *n. Gk. myth.* God of the underworld and judge of the dead.

A.I.B. *abbrev.* Assassination Information Bureau.

A.I.C.A. *abbrev.* American Institute of Commemorative Art.

A.I.D.B. *abbrev.* Abortion Information Data Bank.

airdance *n. slang.* Execution by hanging.

air injec *abbrev.* Air injection.

air injection *n. phr.* Death brought about by injecting air into a vein.

air jig *n. phr. slang.* Execution by hanging.

air polka *n. phr. slang.* Execution by hanging.

air rhumba *n. phr. slang.* Execution by hanging.

Akephalos *n. Gk. + Egypt. myth.* The headless ghost of a person beheaded for a criminal offense which is addressed in magic rituals.

Aker *n. Egypt. myth.* A god representing the entrance and exit of the underworld by means of two lions at either end of a narrow strip of land.

akh *n. Egypt. myth.* The state in which the dead exist after death.

Ala *n. Nigerian myth.* Goddess of the duel aspects of fecundity and death.

A.L.A.C.P. *abbrev.* American League to Abolish Capital Punishment.

à la mort *prep. phr. Fr.* To the death; mortally.

alc *abbrev.* Approximate lethal concentration [used of a drug or poison].

alcoholic murderer *n. phr. Sociol.* A killer in whom aggressiveness is triggered by drinking.

A.L.E.F. *abbrev.* Alcor Life Extension Foundation.

algor mortis *n. phr.* The temperature of a corpse, esp. used to determine time of death.

Alignak *n. Eskimo myth.* Deity protective of orphans and the disinherited.

Allatu *n. Babylonian myth.* Goddess of the netherworld.

all bets off or **call all bets off** *idiom.* Dead.

alleged murder *n. phr. Law.* A homicide which is unproven or unsolved.

all off *idiom.* Dead.

All Souls' Day *n. phr. Rom. Cath.* November 2, a day of prayer for souls in purgatory.

all up or **all up with** *idiom.* Doomed to die.

all up with see **all up**

all washed up *idiom.* Dead.

A.L.R.A. *abbrev. British.* Abortion Law Reform Association.

Al-Sirat *n. Islamic myth.* The sharp and narrow bridge to paradise.

altarage *n.* Payment for masses for the dead.

altruistic suicide *n. phr. Sociol.* Suicide committed by an individual closely integrated into a group for the welfare of that group; one who commits altruistic suicide.

A.M. *abbrev.* Ars Moriendi.

A.M.A. *abbrev.* American Monument Association.

Amam *Egypt. myth.* The beast which waits at the base of the scales to eat the hearts of the dead who fail to pass judgment.

ambiotic *adj.* Causing abortion. *n.* A drug that causes abortion.

amblosis *n.* Abortion.

amblotic *adj.* Causing abortion.

Amentet see **Amenti**

Amenti or **Amentet** *n. Egypt. myth.* The place to which the souls of the dead are brought to be judged; the west, where the dead assembled to await the sun-god Ra to pass; goddess and receiver of the dead at the entrance to the underworld.

Ameretat *n. Persian myth.* God of immortality, representing the reward awaiting the faithful.

America's Hot Seat *n. phr. slang.* The electric chair.

amicicide *n.* Murder of a friend; one who murders a friend.

Amkihiu *pl. n. Egypt. myth.* The souls of the blessed who have gained admission into the boat of the sun-god Ra.

Ammit *n. Egypt. myth.* A god who devours sinners on the day of judgment.

amort *adj.* At the point of death; as if dead; spiritless.

anabiosis *n.* Restoration of life after apparent death; resuscitation; reanimation.

anabiotic *adj.* Apparently but not irreversibly dead.

anagoge or **anagogy** *n.* The decipherment of mystical allusions to heaven or the afterlife. *var.* anagogic, anagogical, *adj.*, anagogically, *adv.*

anagogy see **anagoge**

Anaitis *n. Asian myth.* Goddess of immortality and fertility.

anamnesis *n. Rom. Cath.* The memorial of Christ's sacrifice; part of the Canon of Mass in which Christ's action at the Last Supper is commemorated.

anastasis *n. Christian.* The resurrection of Christ; resurrection of the dead.

anatomical embalming *n. phr.* Preservation of the body without cosmetic adjustment and cavity aspiration; complete immersion in preservative solutions, esp. for dissection.

anatomy room *n. phr.* The classroom in a medical school in which cadavers are dissected.

ANC *abbrev.* Arlington National Cemetery.

ancestor *n. Law.* One who has preceded another in possession of an inheritance.

ancient writings *n. phr. Law.* Wills more than thirty years old.

Andarta *n. Gallic myth.* Warrior goddess.

Andraste see **Adraste**

androphagous *adj.* Cannibalistic.

androphomania *n.* Homicidal mania; insanity marked by homicidal tendencies. *var.* androphomaniac, *n.*

anele *tr. v. archaic.* To anoint, esp. in administering extreme unction. *var.* aneled, aneling, aneles, *v.*

anesthesiological death *n. phr.* Death resulting from anesthetization during surgery.

angelito *n. Sp.* A dead child.

angel makers *pl. n. phr. obs.* Women who take in foster children for a flat fee and mistreat them until they die.

animo testandi *adj. phr. Law.* With the intention of making a will.

annihilate *tr. v.* To destroy completely; put out of existence. *var.* annihilable, *adj.*, annihilator, *n.*, annihilated, annihilating, annihilates, *v.*

annihilation *n.* The act or process of putting out of existence; complete destruction.

annihilation anxiety *n. phr. Psychol.* Dread of complete extinction; fear of becoming nothing.

anniversary phenomenon *n. phr.* Heightened grief at the time of the yearly anniversary of a loss, sometimes accompanied by suicidal tendencies.

Annwn or **Annwyn** *n. Celtic myth.* The kingdom of the dead.

Annwyn see **Annwn**

anointing of the sick *n. phr. Rom. Cath.* The seventh and last sacrament [replaces **last rites** and **extreme unction**].

anomic grief *n. phr.* A state of bereavement in which mourning customs are unclear due to an inappropriate death and the absence of prior bereavement experience.

anomic suicide *n. phr. Sociol.* Suicide resulting from normlessness or social and personal disintegration.

ante mortem *adj. phr. Lat.* Before death.

antethumous *adj. slang.* Before death.

anthro *abbrev.* Anthropophagy.

anthropoid coffin *n. phr.* A casket made to conform to the shape of a body.

anthropolite see **anthropolith**

anthropolith or **anthropolite** *n. Archeol.* Petrified human remains.

anthropological death *n. phr. Sociol.* Separation from one's usual area of living and working, esp. through expatriation or exile.

anthropomancy *n.* Divination by the entrails of human beings; necromancy.

anthropophagus *n., pl.* **anthro-**

pophagi A cannibal. *var.* anthropophagic, anthropophagous, *adj.*, anthropophagist, anthropophagite, *n.*

anthropophagy *n.* Cannibalism. *var.* anthropophagism, *n.*

anticipation *n.* Alertness to the real possibility of the death of oneself or others.

anticipatory bereavement or **anticipatory grief** *n. phr.* Grief experienced before a death actually occurs; griefwork aimed at loosening attachment to the dying, making loss less painful when it occurs.

anticipatory grief see **anticipatory bereavement**

antidysthanasia *n. Psychol.* Avoidance of death that comes in a difficult way.

antilapse statute *n. phr. Law.* A law allowing the heirs of a legatee who predeceases the testator to be substituted as the recipients of the legacy.

anti-submarine warfare *n. phr. Mil.* The detection, identification, tracking, and destruction of hostile submarines.

Anubis *n. Egypt. myth.* A mortuary god and patron of embalming and funeral rites who leads the dead to judgment and guards tombs.

A.N.W.P.P. *abbrev.* Accidental Nuclear War Prevention Project.

à outrance *prep. phr. Fr.* To the death.

AOW *abbrev. Mil.* Articles of war.

A.P.F.S.C. *abbrev.* Academy of Professional Funeral Service Commission.

A.P.F.S.P. *abbrev.* Academy of Professional Funeral Service Practitioners.

A-pill *abbrev.* Abortion pill.

Apis *n. Egypt. myth.* A god of fertility and the dead.

apocarteresis *n.* Suicide by starvation.

apotheosis *n., pl.* **apotheoses** *Gk.* The deification of mortals after death. *var.* apotheosize, apotheosized, apotheosizes, apotheosizing, *v.*

apparent death *n. phr.* A reversible condition exhibiting many of the classic signs of death.

appropriate death *n. phr.* Death experienced without suffering, and preceded by autonomy, acceptance, and the closure of important relationships; a death suitable for a person's age, lifestyle, situation, and significant others.

A.R.A. *abbrev.* Abortion Rights Association.

Ara see **Aray**

Aralez *n. Armenian myth.* A dog-like creature believed to resurrect those killed in battle by licking their wounds.

Arallu see **Aralu**

Aralu or **Arallu** *n. Sumerian + Babylonian myth.* An underworld inhabited by the winged shadows of the dead.

Araru *n. Armenian myth.* God of war.

Arawn *n. Celtic myth.* The

ruler of the netherworld of Annwn.

Aray see **Ara**

architectural cemetery *n. phr.* [A proposed term for] a cemetery characterized by the composition of groups of graves separated by hedges, trees, and terraces.

arcosolium *n.* A niche containing a tomb in a catacomb.

Areimanios see **Arimanius**

Ares *n. Gk. myth.* God of war.

Arimanius or **Areimanios** *n. Persian myth.* A god of the underworld and embodiment of Hades.

A.R.L.S. *abbrev.* Association for Recognizing the Life of Stillborns.

A.R.M. *abbrev.* Abortion Rights Mobilization.

Armaiti or **Armati** *n. Hindu myth.* Goddess of the earth and of the dead who have returned to it.

Armati see **Armaiti**

armed propaganda *n. phr.* Acts of political violence, esp. assassinations and bombings.

armed robbery *n. phr. Law.* The act of taking, or attempting to take, property in another's immediate possession by using or threatening to use a deadly or dangerous weapon.

ars moriendi *pl. n. Rom. Cath.* Medieval religious guide books on the art of dying, instructing readers on how to make a good death and enter heaven.

articulated *adj. Archeol.* Of bones found in the same position in which they occur in life.

artificial death *n. phr.* Death by other than natural causes.

artificial mummification *n. phr.* Preservation of the body by means of evisceration, smoking, or embalming.

artuate *tr. v. obs.* To tear limb from limb. *var.* artuation, *n.*, artuated, artuating, artuates, *v.*

A.S.A. *abbrev.* Association for the Study of Abortion.

ascension of the soul *n. phr.* The entering of the soul into Heaven after death.

ashes *pl. n.* Human remains, esp. after cremation.

asleep in the deep *idiom.* Dead.

Asphodel Meadows *n. phr. Gk. + Rom. myth.* The place where all souls await judgment.

asphyxia *n.* Death or unconsciousness resulting from lack of oxygen.

asphyxiate *tr. v.* To deprive of oxygen; smother. *intr. v.* To smother; suffocate. *var.* asphyxiator, *n.*, asphyxiant, *n.* + *adj.*

asphyxiation *n.* Death due to lack of oxygen; execution carried out in a gas chamber; suicide committed by breathing a lethal gas.

assassin *n.* A murderer, esp. of a public figure.

assassinate *tr. v.* To murder, esp. a public figure. *var.* assassinative, *adj.*, assassinator, *n.*, assassinated, assassinating, assassinates, *v.*

assassination *n.* The murder of a public figure, esp. a politician.
assassrep *abbrev.* Assassination report.
assault with a deadly weapon *n. phr. Law.* The act of unlawfully and intentionally causing, attempting, or threatening to cause injury or death with a deadly weapon.
assault with intent to kill *n. phr. Law.* The act of unlawfully and intentionally attempting to inflict death with a deadly weapon.
Asto Vidatu *n. Persian myth.* A god of death and personification of the disintegration of bodies.
astral body *n. phr. Theol.* Semi-spiritual body which accompanies the physical body in life and survives it at death; soul.
ASW *abbrev. Mil.* Anti-submarine warfare.
asw *abbrev. Mil.* Anti-submarine warfare.
asw/aaw *abbrev. Mil.* Anti-submarine warfare/anti-air warfare.
Ataecina *n. Hispanic myth.* Goddess of death and the underworld.
at death's door *idiom.* Very near death; dying.
athanasia or **athanasy** *n.* Immortality; everlasting life.
athanasy see **athanasia**
Athena *n. Gk. myth.* Goddess of war and wisdom.
at home with the Lord *idiom.* Dead and with God in heaven.
atomy *n. archaic.* A skeleton.
at peace *idiom.* In a restful state of death.
at rest *idiom.* In the repose of death.
Atropos *n. Gk. + Rom. myth.* One of the three fates, responsible for cutting the thread of life.
attainder *n. Law.* The extinction of the civil rights of a person condemned to death for treason or felony.
attaint *tr. v. Law.* To deprive of civil rights by sentence of attainder. *var.* attainted, attainting, attaints, *v.*
attempted murder *n. phr. Law.* An intentional attempt to kill another person.
attempted suicide *n. phr.* An instance in which a person has tried but failed to take his or her own life; incomplete suicide.
attest *tr. v. Law.* To witness the final execution of a will. *var.* attestant, attester, attestor, *n.* attested, attesting, attests, *v.*
attestation *n. Law.* The final execution of a will in the presence of witnesses.
at the end of one's rope *idiom.* Near death; dying.
autocide *n.* An accidental death believed to be a disguised or unconscious suicide, or the victim of such a death; the killing of a person with a motor vehicle. *var.* autocidal, *adj.*
auto-da-fé *n. pl.* **autos-da-fé**

autoerotic asphyxia • ba   23

The public announcement of the sentences imposed on heretics tried by the Inquisition; the public execution of those sentences by the secular authorities, esp. burning at the stake [lit., act of the faith].

autoerotic asphyxia or **autoerotic death** *n. phr.* Accidental death by strangulation as a result of hanging oneself for sexual pleasure.

autoerotic death see **autoerotic asphyxia**

auto-icon *n. archaic.* The preserved body of a person publicly displayed as a memorial to him or her [from the philosophy of Jeremy Bentham (1748–1832)].

autolysis *n.* Decomposition of body tissue due the activity of enzymes released after death.

automania *n.* Preoccupation with suicide. *var.* automaniac, *n.*

automorguemobile *n. obs.* A hearse.

autop *abbrev.* Autopsy.

autophonomania *n.* Preoccupation with suicide. *var.* autophonomaniac, *n.*

autopsy *n.* A post-mortem examination of a body to determine the cause of death. *tr. v.* To examine a body to determine cause of death. *var.* autopsic, autopsical, *adj.*, autopsist, *n.*, autopsied, autopsying, autopsies, *v.*

autosacrifice *n.* The sacrifice of oneself; ritual suicide. *v.* autosacrificial, *adj.*

a.v. *abbrev.* Length of life.

Avalon *n. Welsh myth.* The paradisical island of the dead in the Western Seas.

avenging murderer *n. phr. Sociol.* A killer who murders in response to the withdrawal of sexual interest by a partner.

AW *abbrev. Mil.* Articles of war.

awareness of finitude *n. phr.* A state of mind in which a person recognizes the amount of time left before death.

AWWWII *abbrev.* American Widows of World War II.

ax-murder or **axe-murder** *n.* A murder carried out with a hatchet, ax, or similar weapon.

Azrael *n. Hebrew myth.* The angel who separates the soul from the body at death.

B

B. *abbrev.* Bereaved.
ba *n. Egypt. myth.* An aspect of the soul released at death which roams during the day but returns to the tomb at night.

back-door exit or **back-gate exit** *n. phr. slang.* Death in prison.
back-door parole or **back-gate parole** *n. phr. slang.* Death in prison.
B.A.C.S. *abbrev.* Bay Area Cryonics Society.
bacteriological warfare *n. phr. Mil.* Armed conflict using bacteriological weapons; germ warfare.
Badb or **Badb Catha** *n. Celtic myth.* The "battle raven," a war goddess who haunts the battlefield, inciting and confusing the warriors with her magic.
Badb Catha see **Badb**
Baiame or **Daramulun** or **Nurundere** *n. Australian myth.* Master of life and death.
bakolo *n.* Human flesh prepared for consumption by cannibals.
baldachin *n.* A canopy over the tomb of an illustrious person.
balefire *n.* Funeral pyre.
bale tomb *n. phr.* A chest tomb in which the covering stone is curved.
ballistophobia *n.* Fear of being shot. *var.* ballistophobic, *adj.*, ballistophobe, *n.*
bane *n. archaic.* Fatal injury; murderer. *n.* A cause of death or disaster; deadly poison. *tr. v.* To kill, esp. with poison. *var.* baneful, *adj.*, banefully, *adv.*, banefulness, *n.*, baned, baning, banes, *v.*
bang off *v. phr. slang.* To shoot and kill.

banns *pl. n. archaic.* A public announcement of a death.
banshee *n. Gael. myth.* A female spirit whose appearance or wailing was believed to presage a death in the family [lit., woman of the fairies].
Barastaer see **Barastir**
Barastir or **Barastaer** *n. Caucasian myth.* Mortuary god who escorts souls to paradise or to the underworld.
barbecue stool *n. phr. slang.* The electric chair.
Bardos *pl. n. Tibetan myth.* The intermediate states between death and rebirth.
bargaining *n.* A stage of terminal illness in which patients psychologically and emotionally accept death, but negotiate with themselves, with others, or with God for more time.
barghest *n.* An evil spirit appearing as an omen of death or misfortune.
Baron Samedi *n. phr. Haitian myth.* Lord and guardian of the cemetery.
barrow *n. Archeol.* A large mound of earth or stones marking a grave; tumulus.
bascule *n.* The movable wooden plank on which the condemned is positioned in preparation for guillotining.
basic thanatomimetic narrative *n. phr.* The experience during apparent death; the stages of the near-death experience.
basketed *adj. slang.* Dead and buried.

baste *tr.* + *intr. v. slang.* Kill; murder. *var.* basted, basting, bastes, *v.*
batt. *abbrev. Mil.* Battle.
battue *n.* A massacre of helpless persons.
B.C. *abbrev.* Bereavement Center.
b-c kit *abbrev. Mil.* Battle-casualty kit.
B.C.P. *abbrev.* Bereaved Children's Program.
be among the immortals see **join the immortals**
bear *n. archaic.* A hand stretcher on which an uncoffined body was carried to the grave.
bearers *pl. n. archaic.* Four senior pallbearers, relieved during the procession by underbearers.
beatification *n. Rom. Cath.* Declaration by the Pope that a deceased person is blessed in heaven and worthy of veneration.
beatify *tr. v. Rom. Cath.* To proclaim a deceased person to be one of the blessed in heaven and worthy of veneration. *var.* beatified, beatifies, beatifying, *v.*
be cancelled *v. phr. slang.* To die; be killed.
become a landowner *v. phr. slang.* To die.
become filling for a casket *v. phr. slang.* To die.
be cut down *v. phr. slang.* To die; be killed.
bed-board *n.* A grave marker consisting of a board over the length of the grave supported by a post at each end.
be death on *v. phr. slang.* To cause the death of.
bed-head *n.* A grave marker consisting of a board over the length of the grave supported by a post at each end.
bed of clay *n. phr.* Grave.
bedside coffin *n. phr. obs.* A container, usually wooden, placed next to the corpse or in the parlor.
beggar's cross *n. phr. Hungarian.* A grave marker consisting of two boughs tied together with string.
Beg-tse *n. Tibetan myth.* God of war.
behead *tr. v.* To sever the head of; decapitate. *var.* beheadal, beheading, *n.*, beheaded, beheading, beheads, *v.*
behind the scenes *prep. phr. slang.* Dead.
be in Abraham's bosom see **rest in Abraham's bosom**
Belatu-Cadros *n. Gallic myth.* God of the destruction of enemies.
Beletseri *n. Babylonian myth.* Clerk of the underworld.
Beli *n. Celtic myth.* A god of the abode of the dead.
bellicism *n.* War-mindedness. *var.* bellicose, *adj.*
belligerent *adj.* Making war. *n.* A person or nation engaged in warfare. *var.* belliferous, *adj.*, belligerence, belligerency, *n.*
bellipotent *adj.* Powerful in war.
Bellona *n. Rom. myth.* Female personification of war.

bell the cat *idiom.* To face danger or possible death for the welfare of the majority.

belly puncturer *n. phr. archaic.* Practitioners of cavity embalming, considered inferior to arterial embalming [derogatory].

belly up *prep. phr. slang.* Dead.

be measured for a new overcoat *idiom.* To be buried.

bemoan *tr. v.* To mourn over; express pity for. *intr. v.* To grieve. *var.* bemoaner, *n.*, bemoaned, bemoaning, bemoans, *v.*

beneath *prep. slang.* Dead and buried.

beneficiary *n. Law.* The person named in an insurance policy or will to receive funds, property, or other benefits from the estate of the deceased.

beneficiary under the will *n. phr. Law.* The person named in a will to receive certain property.

benemortasia *n.* Euthanasia.

benign *adj.* Of a hospital ward in which death, usually unexpected, is experienced by the staff as tragic and shocking.

be packed up *v. phr. slang.* To be buried.

be put to bed with a shovel *idiom.* To die.

beqt. *abbrev.* Bequest.

bequeath *tr. v. Law.* To leave personal property to another by means of a will. *var.* bequeathal, bequeather, bequeathment, *n.*, bequeathed, bequeathing, bequeaths, *v.*

bequest *n. Law.* A gift of personal property left by will.

bereave *tr. v.* To deprive of a loved one by death. *var.* bereaved, bereaven, *adj.*, bereavement, bereaver, *n.*, bereaved, bereaves, bereaving, *v.*

bereaved *n., pl.* **bereaved** One who suffers the death of a loved one.

bereavement counseling *n. phr. Psychol.* Consultation begun after a death to address the physical, emotional, and social impact it has had on survivors.

bereavement team *n. phr.* A group in a hospice made up primarily of volunteers who counsel the family after a patient dies.

bereft *adj.* Suffering the death of a loved one; bereaved.

be salted away *idiom.* To die.

be sewed in a blanket *idiom.* To be buried.

be spilled in the drink *idiom.* To drown.

be stopped *v. phr. slang.* To be shot to death.

be thrown for a loss *idiom.* To die.

Beulah Land *n. phr.* A land beyond the Valley of the Shadow of Death characterized by perpetual spring and peacefulness [from John Bunyan, *Pilgrim's Progress*, 1678].

beyond *n.* Afterlife.

bfcy. *abbrev.* Beneficiary.

Bhagwan *n. Indian myth.* Supreme deity responsible for judging the dead.

BID *abbrev. Med.* Brought in dead.
bid. *abbrev. Med.* Brought in dead.
bidder *n. archaic.* A person employed to announce a funeral and invite attendance.
bier *n.* A support on which a corpse or coffin is placed prior to burial for viewing or procession to the grave.
big jump *n. phr. slang.* Death.
Big Sleep *n. phr. slang.* The gas chamber.
big sleep *n. phr. slang.* Death.
bilge *tr. v. slang.* Kill; murder. *var.* bilged, bilges, bilging, *v.*
biocide *n.* The destruction of life. *var.* biocidal, *adj.*
bioemporium *n.* [A proposed term for] a facility in which neomorts would be housed and maintained to harvest organs for transplant.
biological death *n. phr.* The cessation of cellular activity in the organs and tissues of the human body; the state from which resuscitation of the body as a whole is impossible by currently known means.
biological immortality or **biosocial immortality** *n. phr.* Living on through one's children, tribe, nation, or species; immortality through reproduction.
biological philanthropy *n. phr.* The donation of organs for transplant after death.
biological survival *n. phr.* The relief of pain, physical maintenance, and adaptation to limitations of the terminally ill.
biological warfare *n. phr. Mil.* Armed conflict carried out with disease-producing weapons.
biometry *n.* The study of the probable length of human life. *var.* biometric, biometrical, *adj.*, biometrically, *adv.*, biometrician, biometrics, *n.*
bioscopy *n. Med.* Physical examination of a body to determine death.
biosocial immortality see **biological immortality**
biowar *abbrev. Mil.* Biological warfare.
bite the dust *idiom.* To be killed in battle; to die.
bi-unit method *n. phr.* A method of pricing a funeral which includes one charge for professional services and a second charge for the casket.
black *n.* Mourning clothing.
black-bottle *tr. v. slang.* To poison. *var.* black-bottled, black-bottles, black-bottling, *v.*
black cap *n. phr.* The headpiece worn by British judges when pronouncing a death sentence.
black comedy see **black humor**
Black Death or **Black Plague** *n. phr.* An epidemic of bubonic plague which swept through Europe and Asia in the 14th century [from the black spots appearing on the skin of its victims].
Blackhead *n. Chinese.* A

member of a Taoist sect who conducts funeral services.
black humor or **black comedy** *n. phr.* Grim or grotesque satire, esp. as a literary genre [pref. **gallows humor**]. *var.* black humorist, *n.*
Black Master *n. phr. obs.* A carriage owner who supplied a hearse for funerals.
Black Plague see **Black Death**
Blade of Eternity *n. phr. slang.* The guillotine.
blast *tr. v. slang.* To shoot and kill. *var.* blasted, blasting, blasts, *v.*
blast off *v. phr. slang.* To shoot and kill.
blessed or **blest** *adj. Rom. Cath.* Enjoying the happiness of heaven [used of beatified persons]. *var.* blessedness, *n.*
blest see **blessed**
blindfold act *n. phr. slang.* Execution by hanging; execution by firing squad.
blitz *n.* A heavy air-raid, esp. the series of German air-raids on London during World War II. *tr. v.* To bomb from the air. *var.* blitzed, blitzes, blitzing, *v.*
blitzkrieg *n. Ger.* Sudden devastating attack [lit., lightning war].
block *n.* A solid piece of wood upon which condemned persons are beheaded.
blood *n.* Bloodshed; murder. *tr. v.* To initiate into war. *var.* bloody, *adj.*, blooded, blooding, bloods, *v.*
blood bath *n. phr. slang.* A savage slaughter; massacre.

bloodguilt *n.* Remorse resulting from murder or bloodshed.
bloodless *adj.* Dead.
bloodletting *n.* Killing; slaughter. *var.* bloodletter, *n.*
blood money *n. phr. obs.* Money paid as compensation to the next of kin of a murder victim. *n. phr.* Money gained at the cost of another's life; a fee paid to a hired assassin.
bloodshed *n.* Killing; slaughter.
bloodstained *adj.* Guilty of murder.
bloodthirsty *adj.* Eager for bloodshed; murderous. *var.* bloodthirstily, *adv.*, bloodthirstiness, *n.*
bloody-minded *adj.* Liking bloodshed.
blooey *adj. slang.* Dead.
blot *tr. v.* or **blot off the map** *v. phr. slang.* To kill; murder. *var.* blotted, blotting, blots, *v.*
blot out *v. phr. slang.* To kill.
blotting *pr.part. slang.* A murder.
blow away *v. phr. slang.* To shoot and kill.
blown across the creek or **blown over the creek** *idiom.* Having died of unnatural causes.
blown away *v. phr. slang.* was killed.
blown over the creek see **blown across the creek**
blowoff *n. slang.* Death.
blow one's brains out *v. phr. slang.* To commit suicide by shooting oneself in the head.
blow one's head off or **blow**

one's top off *v. phr.* To shoot and kill.

blow one's lights out *v. phr. slang.* To shoot and kill; murder.

blow one's top *v. phr. slang.* To commit suicide by shooting oneself in the head.

blow out *v. phr. slang.* To shoot and kill; murder.

blow the gizzard out of *v. phr. slang.* To shoot and kill.

Bluebeard *n.* A murderer [from Charles Perrault's "Barbe Bleu," 1697].

blue glow *n. phr. slang.* A situation in which the victim is aware of impending death, esp. due to accident or disaster [after an accident in 1964 at the Los Alamos Scientific Laboratory in New Mexico, where a momentary blue glow indicated a lethal dose of radiation].

BM *abbrev.* Bishop and martyr.

body *n.* A corpse.

body bag *n. phr.* A zippered rubber or plastic bag used to transport a corpse. *n. phr. Mil.* A plastic bag used to transport the dead from the battlefield.

body bequest program *n. phr.* A plan which permits a person (prior to death) or a person's family (after death) to donate his or her body to a medical institution.

body cot *n. phr.* A stretcher on which a corpse is removed from the place of death.

body count *n. phr.* The number of fatal casualties in a disaster or battle.

bodysnatch *intr. v.* To steal a corpse. *var.* bodysnatched, bodysnatches, bodysnatching, *v.*

bodysnatcher *n.* Grave robber; resurrectionist. *n. slang.* An undertaker [derogatory].

bodysnatcher's stone *n. phr. obs.* A large stone placed upon a grave to deter graverobbers.

body-stone *n.* A large stone laid across a grave between the headstone and footstone; horizontal gravestone.

bold one *n. phr. slang. Mexican.* Death in personified form.

bomb *n. slang.* A lethal dose of a drug.

bone box *n. phr. slang.* A hearse; casket.

bone factory *n. phr. slang.* A cemetery.

bone house *n. phr. slang.* A casket.

bone-orchard *n. slang.* A cemetery.

bones *pl. n.* The skeleton; mortal remains.

bone-vase *n. Chinese.* The final resting place in which the cleaned bones of a relative are deposited two years after death.

boneyard *n. slang.* A cemetery.

bony one *n. slang. Mexican.* Death in personified form.

booked *p.part. slang.* Near death; dying.

Book of the Dead *n. phr. Egypt. myth.* A collection of

writings about life after death buried with the mummy to help the deceased in the afterlife.

boothill *n. slang. Canadian.* A graveyard.

borough English *n. phr. archaic. Law.* A custom in which the youngest son inherits all the property of a decedent father.

borrowed time *idiom.* The period of survival after an episode that could have been fatal.

bottle up *v. phr. slang.* Kill; murder.

bought it or **bought one** *v. phr. slang.* Was killed, esp. in military action.

bought one see **bought it**

bound for glory *idiom.* Dying; very recently dead.

bourreau *n. Haitian.* Executioner.

bow off or **bow out** *v. phr. slang.* To die [used among actors].

bow out see **bow off**

bow-out *n. slang.* Death.

box *n. slang.* A casket. *intr. v. slang.* To bury. *Med.* To die. *var.* boxed, boxes, boxing, *v.*

boxed up *adj. phr. slang.* Dead and buried.

B.P. *abbrev.* Bereaved Parents.

b.q. *abbrev. Lat.* May he or she rest well.

Brahmanicide or **Brahminicide** *n.* The killing of a Brahmin; one who kills a Brahmin.

brain death *n. phr. Med.* Death determined by the absence of central nervous system activity, specifically by unreceptivity and unresponsivity, no movements or breathing, no reflexes, and a flat electroencephalogram. *var.* braindead, *adj.*

brains *pl. n. slang.* The leader of an organized assassination ring.

brambling *n. archaic.* The custom of pegging brambles over a grave to protect it from grazing sheep and cattle.

Branab Llyr *n. phr. Celtic myth.* God of the dead who is able to restore humans to life.

brandea *pl. n. Rom. Cath.* Cloths considered to be relics after lying in contact with the remains of holy apostles.

break it off *idiom.* To die.

break one's clay pipe *idiom. Fr.* To die.

breathe one's last *v. phr.* To die.

brodie *n. slang.* A suicidal leap, esp. one that is survived [after Stephen Brodie, who jumped from the Brooklyn Bridge July 23, 1886, and lived].

broken pitcher *n. phr. slang.* Corpse.

brush off *v. phr. slang.* To kill; murder.

bubbling *pr.part. slang.* Killing by injecting air bubbles into the veins.

buck-toothed *n. slang. Mexican.* Death in personified form.

buggy ride *n. phr. slang.* Gangster-style murder.

bullet entrance wound *n. phr.* The small round hole made by a bullet entering the body or head of a victim.

bullet exit wound *n. phr.* The often ragged large hole made by a bullet leaving the head or body of a victim.

bump off *v. phr. slang.* To kill a person, esp. violently; assassinate.

bump-off *n. slang.* Death.

bump oneself or **bump oneself off** *v. phr. slang.* To commit suicide.

bundle burial *n. phr. Anthropol.* Grave in which the bones are mixed together as the result of decomposition or reburial.

bur. *abbrev.* Buried.

burculacas *n. Gk. myth.* The body of a wicked person who visits at night, calling out names of those who will die the following day.

burial *n.* Interment of a dead body.

burial allowance *n. phr.* The amount of money allocated for burial in an insurance policy.

burial bundle *n. phr. Native American.* A corpse dressed and wrapped in a number of robes.

burial case *n. phr. archaic.* A burial receptacle.

burial casket *n. phr. archaic.* A rectangular burial receptacle.

burial clothing *n. phr.* Garments in which a corpse is dressed for interment.

burial club see **burial guild**

burial enclosure *n. phr.* A burial vault.

burial goods *pl. n. phr. Anthropol.* Objects placed with a corpse in the grave.

burial ground or **buryingground** *n. phr.* A graveyard.

burial guild or **burial club** *n. phr.* A Medieval group formed to defray heavy funeral expenses and to perpetuate the memory of dead members through the payment of dues, attendance of funerals, and prayer.

burial insurance *n. phr.* The payment of premiums during life to cover the cost of one's interment, funeral, or both after death.

burial laws *pl. n. phr.* Federal, state, or local statutes regarding interment of the dead.

burial-place *n.* A graveyard; grave.

burial position *n. phr. Archeol.* The attitude in which a corpse is found in the grave.

burial programs *pl. n. phr. Anthropol.* Multiple steps used in burying people of different statuses in a single culture.

burial robe *n. phr. archaic.* A garment, usually of wool, in which the deceased was buried.

burial safe *n. phr. archaic.* A vault, often bolted, in which a casket was buried to deter grave robbers.

burial statistics *pl. n. phr.* The ratio of burial to cremation or other means of disposal.

burke *tr. v.* To kill by suffocation or strangulation to obtain an intact body to be sold for dissection [after William Burke (1792-1829)].

burking mania *n. phr. archaic.* The widespread fear of graverobbing common in the 19th century.

burkiphobia see **burkiphoby**

burkiphoby or **burkiphobia** *n. phr. archaic.* The widespread fear of graverobbing common in the 19th century.

burkism *n. archaic.* Murder for the purpose of obtaining bodies to sell for dissection.

burn *intr. v. slang.* To die in the electric chair. *tr. v. slang.* To execute in the electric chair. *var.* burned, burning, burns.

burn at the stake *v. phr.* To execute by fire.

burn in effigy *v. phr.* To conduct a mock execution in which the likeness of a public enemy is set on fire.

burn off *v. phr. slang.* To shoot and kill.

burn slowly *v. phr. archaic.* To die.

bury *tr. v.* To deposit a dead body in a grave, a tomb, or in the sea; inter with funeral rites. *slang.* To kill; murder. *var.* buried, buries, burying, *v.*

burying-ground see **burial ground**

the business *n. phr. slang.* Murder.

butcher *n.* One who enjoys killing. *tr. v.* To kill brutally or with enjoyment. *slang.* To kill; murder. *var.* butcherer, *n.*, butchered, butchering, butchers, *v.*

butchery *n.* Cruel or wanton killing; slaughter.

button man *n. phr.* A low-ranking member of a crime syndicate given the tasks of murder and beating.

buy a packet or **buy it** *idiom.* To be shot down in combat; to become a casualty.

buy it see **buy a packet**

buy the farm *idiom.* To be killed, esp. in military action; to die.

BV *abbrev.* He/she lived a good life.

BW *abbrev. Mil.* Bacteriological warfare; biological warfare.

bw *abbrev. Mil.* Biological warfare.

bw-cw *abbrev. Mil.* Biological warfare-chemical warfare.

BWL *abbrev. Mil.* Biological warfare laboratory.

BWRC *abbrev. Mil.* Biological warfare research center.

C

C *abbrev.* Coffin.
C. *abbrev.* Condemned.
C.A. *abbrev.* Cryonics Association.
C.A.A. *abbrev.* Cremation Association of America.
C.A.C.O. *abbrev.* Casualty Assistance Call Office; Casualty Assistance Call Officers.
cad. *abbrev.* Cadaver.
cadav *abbrev. slang.* Cadaver.
cadaver *n.* A corpse, esp. one intended for dissection. *var.* cadaveric, *adj.*
cadaveric spasm *n. phr.* A stiffening of the arms or hands at the time of death, often clutching a gun or knife; rigor mortis.
cadaverous *adj.* Suggestive of death; corpselike. *var.* cadaverously, *adv.*, cadaverousness, *n.*
caducity *n. Law.* Lapse of a legacy through the later birth of an heir.
cafe coronary *n. phr. slang. Fr.* A choking death due to an obstruction of food in the windpipe.
C.A.F.M.S. *abbrev.* Continental Association of Funeral and Memorial Societies.
Cain *n.* A murderer [after the oldest son of Adam and Eve who killed his brother Abel].
cairn *n.* A mound of stones raised as a memorial. *var.* cairned, *adj.*
caisson *n.* The wagon on which the casket is carried in a funeral with full military honors.
calamity *n.* An event characterized by disaster and loss of life. *var.* calamitous, *adj.*, calamitously, *adv.*, calamitousness, *n.*
call *n. slang.* Death.
call all bets off see **all bets off**
called away *idiom.* Died. *adv. phr.* Dead.
called home *idiom.* Dead and with God in heaven.
call it a day or **call it a job** *idiom.* To die.
call it quits *idiom.* To die.
call of God *idiom.* Death.
C.A.L.M. *abbrev.* Citizens Against Legalized Murder.
calvarium *n., pl.* **calvaria** or **calvariums** An incomplete skull, esp. one without a lower jaw.
Calvary *n. Christian.* The place where Christ was crucified; a sculptural depiction of Christ's crucifixion.
Camaxtli *n. Aztec myth.* God of warriors slain in battle and victims offered in human sacrifice.
C.A.N.A. *abbrev.* Cremation Association of North America.
canari *n. Haitian.* A clay jar used in Haiti to shelter the

soul and broken during the funeral rites.

cancel one's account *idiom.* To die.

cancel one's Christmas *idiom.* To kill.

cannibal *n.* A person who eats human flesh. *var.* cannibalistic, *adj.*, cannibalism, *n.*

cannibalize *tr. v.* To eat the human flesh of.

cannon *tr. v. slang.* To shoot and kill. *var.* cannoned, cannoning, cannons, *v.*

cannon fodder *n. phr.* Soldiers treated as expendable materials of warfare.

cannonize *tr. v. Rom. Cath.* To formally recognize a deceased person as a saint. *var.* canonization, cannonizer, *n.*, cannonized, cannonizes, cannonizing, *v.*

canopic jar *n. phr.* or **canopus** *n.* A container used by the ancient Egyptians to entomb the viscera of the dead [after Canopus, a city of ancient Egypt].

canopus see **canopic jar**

can't ever get well *v. phr. slang.* Is marked for death.

C.A.N.W. *abbrev.* Citizens Against Nuclear War; Campaign Against Nuclear War.

caoine *n. Ir.* A traditional death song.

capital *adj.* Involving execution; punishable by death.

capital crime or **capital offense** *n. phr. Law.* A criminal offense punishable by death.

capital murder *n. phr. Law.* A homicide punishable by death.

capital offense see **capital crime**

capital punishment *n. phr.* The death penalty imposed for the commission of certain crimes.

capun *abbrev.* Capital punishment.

carbon-copy killing *n. phr.* A murder inspired by a previous murder. *var.* carbon-copy killer, *n.*

carcase see **carcass**

carcass or **carcase** *n. archaic.* A human corpse.

cardiac death *n. phr. Med.* Cessation of heartbeat and breathing, esp. verified by electrocardiogram.

Cariociecus *n. Hispanic myth.* A god of war.

carnage *n.* A slaughter; massacre. *n. obs.* Corpses, esp. of soldiers killed in battle.

carnifex *n.* A public executioner, esp. in ancient Rome.

carnificial *adj.* Associated with a public executioner.

carrion *n.* Dead and decaying flesh.

carry a tree *idiom.* To be crucified.

carry off *idiom.* To cause the death of.

carry out *idiom. Lat.* + *Gk.* To conduct a funeral.

carve up *v. phr. slang.* To perform an autopsy.

cas. *abbrev.* Casualty.

cascan *abbrev.* Casualty cancelled.

cascor *abbrev.* Casualty corrected.

cash in one's checks or **cash in one's chips** *idiom.* To die [from the game of poker, in which a player may quit at any time and exchange chips for cash].
cash in one's chips see **cash in one's checks**
casket *n.* A coffin. *tr. v.* To place a corpse in a casket, esp. for viewing.
casket-bearer *n.* Pallbearer.
casket-burial case *n. phr. archaic.* A grave vault.
casket-case *n. archaic.* A grave vault.
casketeer *n. slang.* A racketeer undertaker who persuades the bereaved to purchase needlessly expensive caskets and funeral ceremonies [derogatory].
Cas Reps *abbrev.* Casualty reports.
castored *p.part. slang.* Killed with a pellet shot from the tip of a cane or umbrella at close range.
casualty *n.* A fatal accident; a person killed in an accident; a soldier who is killed in action during war.
casus belli *n. phr. Lat.* Justification for declaring war.
catabythismomania *n.* An impulse to commit suicide by drowning. *var.* catabythismomaniac, *n.*
catacomb *n.* or **catacombs** *pl. n.* An underground chamber with recesses for graves; a subterranean cemetery.
catacomb burial *n. phr.* The deposit of a body in subterranean cemetery.
catacombs see **catacomb**
catafalco see **catafalque**
catafalque or **catafalco** *n.* The ornamental structure upon which a casket rests during a funeral or while a body lies in state; a funeral car.
catastrophe *n.* An unexpected disastrous event. *var.* catastrophic, *adj.*, catastrophically, *adv.*
catch it where the chicken got it *idiom.* To be killed.
catch the tide *idiom.* To die.
causa mortis *adj. phr. Law.* In anticipation of approaching death.
C.A.W.A.W.L. *abbrev.* Crusade to Abolish War and Armaments by World Law.
cbrw *abbrev. Mil.* Chemical, biological, radiological warfare.
CBW *abbrev. Mil.* Chemical and biological warfare.
cbw *abbrev. Mil.* Chemical-biological warfare.
C.C. *abbrev.* Centering Corporation.
cc *abbrev.* Condemned cell.
C.C.M.S. *abbrev.* California College of Mortuary Science.
CCRN *abbrev. Med.* Critical care registered nurse.
CCS *abbrev.* Casualty clearing station.
C.C.S.A. *abbrev.* Clergy Consultation Service on Abortion.
C.C.S.C. *abbrev.* Cemetery Consumer Service Council.
CCU *abbrev. Med.* Critical care unit.

C.D. *abbrev.* Concern for Dying.
cd. *abbrev.* Condemned.
CDC *abbrev.* Cadaver disposal center.
C.D.E.R. *abbrev.* Center for Death Education and Research.
cdv *abbrev.* Cadaver.
ceased *p.part. slang.* Deceased.
cebar *abbrev.* Chemical, biological, radiological warfare.
Cecrops *n. Gk. myth.* A snake deity who taught the inhabitants of Athens to bury the dead.
C.E.D. *abbrev.* Committee for the Elimination of Death.
celestial air force *n. phr. slang.* The collective dead in heaven.
cellular death *n. phr.* Irreversible degeneration of the cells of the body.
cellular/molecular death *n. phr.* The death at different rates of all the cells in the human body.
cellu-vegetative death *n. phr.* Death considered to be an incomplete process because of the ability to keep some cells alive outside of the body indefinitely.
cem. *abbrev.* Cemetery.
cement city *n. phr. slang.* A cemetery.
cement coffin *n. phr. slang.* A method of murder associated with crime syndicates in which the victim is thrown into a body of water with feet and legs weighted.
cemeterian *n.* A cemetery owner; member of a cemetery association.
cemetery *n.* A burial ground; graveyard.
cemetery lot *n. phr.* A plot of land purchased in a graveyard.
cenotaph *n.* A monument erected in honor of a person buried elsewhere; an empty tomb. *var.* cenotaphic, *adj.*
centesimation *n.* The execution of one out of every one hundred persons in a group, esp. soldiers.
cephalophore *n. Rom. Cath.* One of the martyrs who carried their severed heads to their places of burial.
Cerberus *n. Gk. myth.* The three-headed guard dog at the entrance to Hades.
cere *tr. v.* To wrap in cerecloth; shroud. *var.* cered, ceres, cering, *v.*
cerebral death *n. phr. Med.* Brain death.
cerecloth or **cerement** *n.* Cloth coated with wax and used to wrap a dead body.
cerement see **cerecloth**
cerements *pl. n.* Burial clothes; shroud.
ceremonial weeping *n. phr.* A ritual display of grief.
cessation *n.* The progressive extinction of autonomy and consciousness prior to death.
C.F. *abbrev.* Compassionate Friends.
C.F.D. *abbrev.* Concern for Dying.
C.F.S.E.B.U.S. *abbrev.* Conference of Funeral Service Examining Boards of the United States.

C.G. *abbrev.* Connecticut Gravestones.

C.G.I.S. *abbrev.* Council of Guilds for Infant Survival.

chair *n. slang.* The electric chair.

chamber *n. slang.* The gas chamber.

chance-medley *n. Law.* An unpremeditated homicide for which the killer is partially to blame.

chantry *n. Eccles.* An endowment for saying masses and prayers, usually for the soul of the founder; a chapel endowed for the saying of masses and prayers for the soul of a benefactor.

chapel see **funeral service room**

character of death *n. phr. Anthropol.* Features typical of death in a society, esp. typical age at death and leading causes of death.

charnel *n.* or **charnel house** *n. phr.* A structure in which the bones or bodies of the dead are deposited.

charnel house see **charnel**

charogne *n. archaic.* A cadaver.

Charon *n. Gk. myth.* The ferryman who conveyed the souls of the dead to Hades over the river Styx.

Charontes *pl. n. Etruscan myth.* Male and female demons of death.

charopalevi *idiom. Gk.* Dying [lit., fighting Charon].

Charun *n. Etruscan myth.* A demon of the underworld who escorts the dead and watches over graves.

cheat the chair *v. phr. slang.* To commit suicide, escape, or die naturally before one is due to be executed by electrocution.

cheat the gallows *v. phr. slang.* To die before one is due to be executed by hanging.

check out *idiom.* To die; commit suicide. *v. phr. slang. Med.* To die in the hospital.

chemical warfare *n. phr. Mil.* Armed conflict using chemicals other than explosives.

chem war *abbrev. Mil.* Chemical warfare.

chested *p.part. archaic.* Buried in a coffin.

C.H.I. *abbrev.* Connecticut Hospice Institute.

Chicagoed *p.part. slang.* Killed; murdered.

Chicago overcoat *n. phr. slang.* A coffin.

Chichuateteo *pl. n. Mayan myth.* Women who die in childbirth and become demons who devour children at crossroads.

child destruction *n. phr. British.* The killing of a child capable of being born alive; infanticide.

childhood bereavement *n. phr.* The temporary role of children who are adjusting to the death of one or both parents.

child-killer *n.* A serial murderer whose victims are juveniles.

child-murder *n.* Abortion; the murder of a juvenile.

38 chill • civil death

chill *tr. v. slang.* To kill; murder.
Ch'i-you *n. Chinese myth.* God of war and weapons.
C.H.M.A. *abbrev.* Casket Hardware Manufacturers Association.
choke *tr. v.* To stop or interrupt the normal breathing of. *intr. v.* To be suffocated. *n.* The act of choking. *var.* choked, chokes, choking, *v.*
choker *n. slang.* A garrotter.
Chontamenti or **Chonti-amentiu** *n. Egypt. myth.* A god of the dead represented as a crouching dog or jackal.
Chonti-amentiu see **Chontamenti**
chop off *v. phr. slang.* To shoot and kill.
chrestos *n. Gk.* The collective dead [lit., excellent].
chrisom *n.* or **chrisom child** *n. phr.* A child that dies within a month of birth.
chrisom child see **chrisom**
Christicide *n.* The killing of Christ.
chronic care *n. phr. Med.* Hospitalization of persons with life-threatening diseases at various stages of incapacitation.
chronic disaster *n. phr.* A long-term threat to life.
chronic suicide *n. phr.* Ambivalent suicide with a low completion rate.
chthonian or **chthonic** *adj.* Pertaining to or inhabiting the underworld; ghostly.
chthonic see **chthonian**
church suffering *n. phr. Rom. Cath.* The souls of Christians in purgatory.
church triumphant *n. phr. Rom. Cath.* The souls of Christians in heaven.
churchyard *n.* Land adjacent to a church used as a burial ground.
C.I.A. *abbrev.* Committee to Investigate Assassinations.
CICU *abbrev. Med.* Coronary intensive care unit.
-cide *suff.* Killer; act of killing. *var.* -cidal, *adj.* combining form.
Cihuateto *n. Aztec myth.* The souls of women who die in childbirth and are rewarded with eternal life.
cinerarium *n., pl.* **cineraria** A repository for the ashes of cremated bodies. *var.* cinerary, cinereal, *adj.*
C.I.N.W. *abbrev.* Committee for Immediate Nuclear War.
circle the drain *idiom. Med.* To be near death.
cist *n. Archeol.* A neolithic or Bronze Age burial chamber lined with stone and covered with stone slabs. *var.* cistic, *adj.*
Citipati *pl. n. Tibetan myth.* The skeletal lords of the graveyard.
city of the dead *n. phr.* Cemetery.
city of the silent *n. phr.* A cemetery.
Ciuapipiltin *pl. n. Mexican myth.* The spirits of women who die in childbirth.
civil death *n. phr. Law.* The status of a living person

which is legally equal to death, esp. the loss of civil rights.

civil defense *n. phr. Mil.* Protective measures and emergency relief undertaken by organized civilians in the case of a natural disaster or enemy attack.

CL *abbrev. Med.* Critical list.

clay *n.* The human body as distinct from the spirit.

clean and peeled one *n. slang. Mexican.* Death in personified form.

clean-out *n.* A massacre conducted as part of a pogrom.

clean up on *idiom.* To kill; murder.

clemency *n.* Mercy in meting out the death penalty.

cleronomy *n.* Inheritance.

click it *idiom.* To die.

clinical death *n. phr. Med.* The determination of death based upon physical examination with the assumption of potential revival; cessation of spontaneous heartbeat and respiration.

clip *tr. v. slang.* To kill. *var.* clipped, clipping, clips, *v.*

C.L.L.T. *abbrev.* Center for Loss and Life Transition.

close call or **close shave** *idiom.* A narrow escape from being killed.

closed awareness *n. phr.* A situation in which the hospital staff and relatives know that a patient is dying, but the patient is not told.

close shave see **close call**

close up one's accounts *idiom.* To die.

closure *n.* The completion of relationships with loved ones by the terminally ill.

Clotho *n. Gk. myth.* One of the three fates who spins the thread of human life.

cluster suicides *pl. n. phr. Sociol.* Groups of three or more completed suicides, closely related in time and space; a suicide epidemic.

c.m. *abbrev. Lat.* By reason of death.

C.M.A.A. *abbrev.* Casket Manufacturers Association of America.

CMO *abbrev. Med.* Comfort measures only [used to designate terminal patients who should be allowed to die].

Coatlicue *n. Aztec myth.* Goddess of earth and death.

Cocidius *n. Celtic myth.* A god of war.

cock up one's toes *idiom.* To die.

Cocytus *n. Gk. myth.* A river bordering Hades, along which the unburied dead were required to wander for one hundred years.

code *n. Med.* The attempt to resuscitate a clinically dead patient. *tr. v.* To attempt to restore pulse and blood pressure to a clinically dead patient. *var.* coded, coding, codes, *v.*

codicil *n. Law.* A supplemental modification of an existing will. *var.* codicillary, *adj.*

codl. *abbrev. Law.* Codicil.

coffin *n.* A box or chest in which a corpse is buried. *tr. v.* To place in a coffin [pref. **casket**].

coffin-case *n. archaic.* A grave vault.

coffin furniture *pl. n. phr.* Ornamental metal plates attached to the exterior of a casket.

coffin-maker *n.* One who handcrafts caskets, usually out of wood.

coffin-plate *n.* A metal plaque engraved with the name of the deceased and attached to his or her casket.

coffin silhouette *n. phr. Archeol.* Discoloration of the soil of a grave as a result of the decay of the corpse and the casket.

coffin torpedo *n. phr. archaic.* An explosive device buried with a coffin to deter grave robbers.

co-heir *n. Law.* One who inherits the same property together with another person.

coil up one's cable or **coil up one's rope** *idiom.* To die.

coimetrophia *n.* Fear of cemeteries.

coin. *abbrev. Mil.* Counterinsurgency-anti-guerrilla warfare.

cold *adj. slang.* Dead.

cold-bed *n.* The bed of the deceased.

cold meat *n. phr. slang.* Dead body or bodies.

cold-meat box or **cold-meat crate** *n. phr. slang.* A casket; coffin.

cold-meat crate see **cold-meat box**

cold-meat party *n. phr. slang.* A funeral; burial.

cold-meat shed *n. phr. slang.* An execution shed.

cold meat ticket *n. phr. slang. Mil.* A disk worn for identification if killed.

cold mud *n. phr. slang.* A grave.

cold pig *n. phr. slang.* A corpse.

cold room *n. phr. slang.* A morgue, esp. in a hospital.

collateral inheritance tax *n. phr. Law.* A property tax levied after the death of the owner.

collation *n. Law.* Return to an estate of property received in advance by an heir so that the whole may be divided equally.

columbarium or **columbary** *n.* A structure containing niches for cinerary urns; a niche in a columbarium.

columbary see **columbarium**

combat fatality *n. phr. Mil.* A death occurring during battle.

come into *idiom.* To receive after another's death; inherit.

come to a sticky end *idiom.* To be murdered.

COMEX *abbrev. Mil.* Combat expendable.

commemorate *tr. v.* To honor the memory of a person, esp. ceremonially. *var.* commemorative, commemoratory, *adj.*, commemoration, commemorator, *n.*, commemorated, commemorating, commemorates, *v.*

commiserate *tr. v.* To feel or express sorrow for; condole with. *intr. v.* To feel or express misery. *var.* commiserative, *adj.*, commiseratively, *adv.*, commiseration, commiserator, *n.*

commit *tr. v.* To perpetrate [used of murder]; to inter or entomb. *var.* commitment, *n.*, committed, committing, commits, *v.*

commit sideways *v. phr. slang.* Commit suicide.

committal *n.* Burial; deposit of human remains in a place of final disposition.

committal service *n. phr.* A brief, optional continuation of the funeral service held at the cemetery or in the chapel of a crematory in which the remains are interred or deposited.

common grave *n. phr.* A mass grave for the burial of the poor, indigent, or unidentified.

commorient *n.* A person killed in a disaster that claimed other lives. *adj.* Dying together.

communal property *n. phr. Law.* Collectively owned property disposed of in a will.

commutation *n.* or **commutation of sentence** *n. phr. Law.* Substitution of life imprisonment for the death penalty, usually by the governor or state pardoning board.

commutation of sentence see **commutation**

companion spaces *pl. n. phr.* A pair of adjacent burial plots, esp. one on top of the other, usually for the interment of husband and wife.

competent behavior *n. phr.* The ability of the terminally ill to solve daily problems and to carry out limited customary tasks.

complete autopsy *n. phr.* The examination after death of the organs of the abdomen, chest, and head.

completed suicide *n. phr.* A suicide which has resulted in death.

comploration *n.* Wailing and weeping together.

compound disposal or **secondary disposal** *n. phr. Anthropol.* Disposal of a dead body by several methods over a period of time.

compulsory suicide *n. phr.* A form of punishment in which a noble is allowed to die at his own hand rather than by the sword of the public executioner.

concealment of birth *n. phr.* The secret disposition of the body of an infant who died before, at, or after birth.

conclamatio mortis *n. phr. Lat.* A ceremonial farewell paid to the dead in ancient Rome, usually by hired mourners [lit., the calling out of the dead].

concrete overcoat *n. phr. slang.* A method of murder associated with crime syndicates in which the victim is thrown into a body of water with feet and legs weighted.

condemn *n. Law.* To sentence a person to death upon conviction of a capital offense. *var.* condemnatory, *adj.*, condemnation, *n.*, condemned, condemning, condemns, *v.*

condemned *p.part.* A person sentenced to death.

conditional bequest *n. phr. Law.* A bequest which takes effect or continues depending on the occurrence or nonoccurrence of a particular event.

conditional immortality *n. phr. Theol.* Eternal life granted to those whose actions are judged to be worthy.

condole *intr. v.* To express grief or sympathy. *obs.* To grieve. *tr. v. archaic.* To grieve or lament. *var.* condolatory, *adj.*, condoler, *n.*, condoled, condoles, condoling, *v.*

condolence *n.* Sympathy with another person's grief or misfortune; an expression of sympathy. *var.* condolent, *adj.*

confessio *n.* A crypt beneath an early Christian altar containing the relics of a martyr.

confirmed kill *n. phr. Mil.* An enemy casualty attributed to a particular soldier.

conflummox *intr. v. slang.* To die. *var.* conflummoxed, conflummoxes, conflummoxing, *v.*

Congressional Assassination Act *n. phr. Law.* A statute which makes killing or plotting to kill a member of Congress a federal crime.

conk *v.* or **conk out** *v. phr. slang.* To die. *var.* conked, conking, conks, *v.*

consolation literature *n. phr.* An often sentimental literary genre which includes obituary poems and memoirs, mourner's manuals, and books about heaven.

console *tr. v.* To give comfort or solace to in time of grief. *var.* consolable, consolatory, *adj.*, consolingly, *adv.*, consolation, consoler, *n.*, consoled, consoles, consoling, *v.*

consort *n. archaic.* A woman who predeceases her husband [used on gravestones].

construction proceeding *n. phr. Law.* A case brought in court to interpret and apply provisions of a will which are unclear or ambiguous.

constructive death *n. phr.* The date on which an ill or injured person would have died if physicians had not intervened to keep him or her alive by technological means.

content *adj. slang.* Dead.

contract *n. slang.* An agreement to murder a person in exchange for money or as repayment of a favor.

conventional warfare *n. phr. Mil.* Armed conflict without the use of nuclear weapons.

cook *intr. v. slang.* To die in the electric chair. *var.* cooked, cooking, cooks, *v.*

cooked *p.part. slang.* Dead.

cook one's goose *idiom.* To kill.

cooling board • coup de grace 43

cooling board *n. phr. archaic.* A device which covers and cools the torso of a body to delay decomposition; an embalming table.
cop *intr. v. slang. Mil.* To die. *var.* copped, copping, cops, *v.*
cop a packet or **stop a packet** *v. phr. slang. Mil.* To be wounded, esp. fatally.
coparcenary *n.* Joint heirship.
coparcener *n.* A joint heir in an estate.
cop it *v. phr. slang. Mil.* To die.
cop-killer *n.* The murderer of a police officer.
copycat killing *n. phr.* A murder inspired by a recent or famous murder. *var.* copycat killer, *n.*
cor. *abbrev.* Coroner.
coroner *n.* A public officer whose principal duty is to investigate the causes and circumstances of any accidental or suspicious death within his or her jurisdiction [pref. **medical examiner**]. *var.* coronership, *n.*
coroner's jury *n. phr.* A group of people summoned to attend an inquest to determine the cause of an accidental or suspicious death.
corp *n. slang. Nautical.* A corpse.
corpse *n.* The dead body of a human being. *tr. v. slang.* To kill; murder. *var.* corpsed, corpses, corpsing, *v.*
corpse cooler or **corpse preserver** *n. phr. obs.* A device which covered and cooled the torso of a body to delay decomposition.
corpse gate *n. phr.* A cemetery structure which protects pallbearers from the weather while waiting for the burial service to begin.
corpse preserver see **corpse cooler**
corpse silhouette *n. phr. Archeol.* Discoloration of the soil of a grave due to organic decay.
corpus *n. archaic.* A corpse.
corpus delicti *n. phr., pl.* **corpora delicti** *Law.* Objective proof or material evidence that a crime has been committed, esp. the discovery of a murder victim [lit., the body of the crime].
corruption of blood *n. phr. Law.* Incapacity to inherit or bequeath property, usually because of attainder.
corse *n. archaic.* A corpse.
cortege *n.* A funeral procession.
cottonwood blossom *n. phr. slang.* The hanged victim of a lynch mob.
count daisies or **push up daisies** *v. phr. slang.* To be dead and buried.
count out *v. phr. slang.* To kill; murder.
count worms *v. phr. slang.* To be buried.
coup de grace *n. phr. Fr.* A death blow or finishing stroke administered to end the misery of a person who is mortally wounded [lit., stroke of mercy].

C.P.N.W. *abbrev.* Committee to Prevent Nuclear War.
C.P.P. *abbrev.* Capital Punishment Project.
C.R.A. *abbrev.* Committee to Resist Abortion.
crack down *v. phr. slang.* To shoot and kill.
crack off *v. phr. slang.* To shoot and kill.
crape *n.* A black band worn on a hat or sleeve as a sign of mourning.
crapehanger *n. slang.* Mortician; undertaker [derogatory].
crap out *v. phr. slang.* To die.
crate *tr. v. slang.* To bury. *var.* crated, crates, crating, *v.*
crawl one's hump *v. phr. slang.* To kill by stealth.
crease *tr. v. slang.* To kill. *var.* creased, creases, creasing, *v.*
creative death *n. phr.* Death caused in a spectacular manner, esp. as portrayed in horror movies.
creative immortality *n. phr.* Living on after death through one's works or influence on others.
crem. *abbrev.* Cremation.
cremains *pl. n.* Cremated remains.
cremate *tr. v.* To incinerate a corpse. *var.* crematist, cremator, *n.*, cremated, cremates, cremating, *v.*
cremation *n.* Disposal of the dead by incineration; killing by setting on fire; suicide by setting oneself on fire.
crematorium *n.* A furnace or establishment for the incineration of corpses.
crematory *n.* A furnace or establishment for the incineration of corpses. *adj.* Of or pertaining to cremation.
cremo *abbrev.* Crematorium.
crib death *n. phr. Med.* Sudden infant death syndrome.
crime of passion *n. phr.* Murder incited by the infidelity of a lover or mate; murder committed in the heat of anger, or other passionate outburst.
criminal agency *n. phr. Law.* A criminal act by one person which results in the death of another person.
criminal homicide *n. phr. Law.* Killing a person without excuse or justification; killing committed during commission of a crime.
criminal negligence *n. phr. Law.* The unintentional death of an individual brought about by the carelessness or neglect of another.
critical *adj.* Involving possible or probable loss of life.
critical care *n. phr. Med.* Treatment given to a person with a possible or probable fatal condition.
critical illness *n. phr. Med.* A condition likely to be fatal at any time.
critical list *n. phr. Med.* The roster of patients under critical care in a hospital.
Crnobog or **Crnoglav** *n. Slavic myth.* God of the dead.
Crnoglav see **Crnobog**
croak *intr. v. slang.* To die. *tr. v. slang.* To kill a person.

var. croaked, croaking, croaks, *v.*
croak act *idiom.* Death.
croaker *n. slang.* A corpse.
croak oneself *v. phr. slang.* To commit suicide.
cromlech *n.* A prehistoric tomb or monument.
cross *n.* A structure consisting of an upright and a crosspiece used by the ancient Romans for execution; the cross or a symbolic representation of the cross on which Jesus was crucified.
crossbones *pl. n.* A representation of two bones placed crosswise, usually under a skull, symbolizing danger or death.
cross of the cemetery or **cross of the dead** *n. phr. Hungarian.* A cross standing above the graves in a cemetery to indicate the denomination of those buried.
cross of the dead see **cross of the cemetery**
cross over *v. phr. slang.* To die.
crouch *n. archaic.* Cross.
crowbait *n. slang.* A corpse.
crowner *n. archaic.* Coroner.
C.R.T.I. *abbrev.* Center for the Rights of the Terminally Ill.
crucifix *n.* A representation of Christ on the cross.
crucifixion *n.* The act of putting to death on a cross; the execution of Christ.
crucify *tr. v.* To execute a person by nailing or binding the hands and feet to a cross. *var.* crucifier, *n.*, crucified, crucifies, crucifying, *v.*
crude death rate *n. phr.* The number of deaths in a given period per one thousand people.
cruel and unusual punishment *n. phr. Law.* A penalty that is considered torturous, grossly excessive, unfair, or shocking by people of reasonable sensitivity [used of the death penalty].
cruentation *n. obs.* The bleeding of wounds signifying the presence of the murderer.
crux commissa *n. phr. Lat.* A cross with three arms.
crux decussata *n. phr. Lat.* A Greek cross.
crux humilis *n. phr. Lat.* An assembled Roman cross.
crux immissa *n. phr. Lat.* A cross with four arms.
cry *intr. v.* To make sounds of grief; weep or lament.
cryogenic interment or **cryopreservation** *n. phr.* The ongoing storage of a cryonically preserved corpse.
cryonaut *n. slang.* A person in cryonic suspension.
cryonics *pl. n.* The process of freezing and storing the newly dead to prevent tissue decomposition and allow resuscitation after the development of new medical cures. *var.* cryonic, *adj.*, cryonically, *adv.*
cryonic suspension *n. phr.* The frozen storage of a corpse for potential future revival.
cryopreservation see **cryogenic interment**

crypt *n.* An underground burial vault beneath a church; a concrete chamber in a mausoleum into which a casket is placed. *var.* cryptous, *adj.*
C.S.A.C. *abbrev.* Coalition for Safety of Abortion Clinics.
C.S.C.A. *abbrev.* Central States Cemetery Association.
C.S.C.A.S. *abbrev.* Conference of State Cemetery Association Secretaries.
C.S.C.M. *abbrev.* Committee to Stop Children's Murder.
C.S.I.I. *abbrev.* Computer Systems for the Interment Industry.
C.S.L. *abbrev.* Center for Sibling Loss.
C.S.N.A. *abbrev.* Cremation Society of North America.
C.S.S.D. *abbrev.* Cryonics Society of San Diego.
C.S.S.L.T.B. *abbrev.* Center for the Study of Suicide and Life-Threatening Behavior.
c.t.a. *abbrev. Law.* With the will annexed.
cubiculum *n.* A tomb or burial chamber.
Culsu *n. Etruscan myth.* A female demon at the portal to the underworld.
cult of the dead *n. phr. Anthropol.* The practice of communicating with and making offerings to the dead.
curb-stone undertaker *n. phr. archaic.* A funeral director who rents all of his or her equipment [derogatory].
curl up and die *intr. v. phr. slang.* To retreat and die.

curl up one's toes *v. phr. slang.* To die.
curtain call *n. phr. slang. Theater.* Death.
curtains *pl. n. slang.* Death.
curtesy *n. Law.* The right of a husband, upon the death of his wife, to a certain minimum share of the estate she possessed during their marriage.
cut adrift *adj. phr. slang. Nautical.* Dead.
cut down *v. phr. slang.* To kill; murder.
cut off *v. phr. slang.* To kill; murder. *idiom.* Killed, esp. prematurely; disinherited.
cut one's cable or **cut one's stick** *idiom.* To die.
cutter *n.* An ancient Eyptian who opened the body during the preparation of a mummy.
cutthroat *adj.* Murderous. *n.* A murderer.
CVN *abbrev. Mil.* Casualty vulnerability number.
CW *abbrev. Mil.* Chemical warfare.
cw-bw *abbrev. Mil.* Chemical warfare–biological warfare.
C.W.C. *abbrev.* Center on War and the Child.
CWGC *abbrev.* Commonwealth War Graves Commission.
cwik *abbrev. Law.* Cutting with intent to kill.
C.W.P.S. *abbrev.* Center for War/Peace Studies.
czaricide *n.* The killing of a czar; one who kills a czar.

D

D *abbrev.* Disaster; death.

d. *abbrev.* Died; dead; deceased.

dacnomania *n.* A mania for killing. *var.* dacnomaniac, *adj.* + *n.*

D.A.D. *abbrev.* Dignity After Death.

Dagda or **Dagde** *n. Celtic myth.* A warrior-god who is master of life and death.

Dagde see **Dagda**

DAI or **dai** *abbrev.* Death from accidental injuries.

dai see **DAI**

damnation *n. Theol.* Condemnation to eternal punishment after death; eternal punishment of the soul.

damned *pl. n. Theol.* Souls doomed to eternal punishment. *p.part.* Condemned, esp. to eternal punishment. *var.* damnable, damnatory, *adj.*, damn, damning, damns, *v.*

damnosa hereditas *n. phr. Law.* Burdensome inheritance.

damnum fatale *n. phr. Law.* Fatal damage; loss of life which occurs from a cause beyond human control.

danake *n. Gk. myth.* Boat fare for Charon.

dance *intr. v.* To die by hanging; to be executed by hanging. *var.* dancer, *n.*, danced, dances, dancing, *v.*

dance hall or **dance-hall** *n. phr. slang.* The passageway in a prison leading to the electric chair; the cell to which a condemned prisoner is taken on the day of the scheduled execution.

dance-hall see **dance hall**

dance of death or **danse macabre** *n. phr.* A symbolic dance presided over by a skeletal personification of death who leads the dead of all ages, conditions, and ranks to the grave; an artist's representation of such a dance, esp. paintings and woodcuts from the 14th century *slang.* Hanging.

dance of the skeletons *n. phr.* Dance of Death.

dance on air *idiom.* To be hanged.

danger list *n. phr. Med.* A list of patients believed to be near death, maintained by the hospital staff and reported to family and administration.

dangerous weapon *n. phr. Law.* An instrument used, or attempted to be used, which has the potential to endanger life.

dangle in the sheriff's picture frame *idiom.* To be executed by hanging; to die by hanging.

danse macabre see **dance of death**

Danu *n. Ir. myth.* Goddess of death.

Daramulun see **Baiame**

Davey Jones's Locker or **Davy Jones's Locker** *idiom. Nautical.* The bottom of the ocean, esp. as the grave of all who perish at sea.

Davy Jones's Locker see **Davey Jones's Locker**

day of judgment see **Judgment Day**

day of reckoning *n. phr.* The day of death or of final judgment, on which it is believed one will have to render an account of one's life and conduct to God.

db *abbrev.* Dead body.

d&b *abbrev.* Dead and buried.

dc *abbrev.* Death cell.

d&c *abbrev. Med.* Dilation and curettage [a method of abortion in which a curette is used to scrape the uterus].

d'd *abbrev.* Deceased.

ddw *abbrev. Law.* Displaying deadly weapon.

dead *adj.* No longer alive; having the physical appearance of death. *slang.* Marked for certain death. *n.* One who has died; those who have died. *var.* deadness, *n.*

dead and gone *v. phr. slang.* Long dead.

dead as a doornail *idiom.* Undoubtedly dead.

dead as a herring *idiom.* Very dead.

dead-board *n. archaic.* A wooden grave marker consisting of two posts and a board which extends lengthwise from head to foot.

dead body *n. phr.* A corpse.

deadborn *adj.* Stillborn [pref. **stillborn**].

deader *n. slang.* A corpse, esp. a recent one; funeral or burial.

dead goner *n. phr. slang.* A corpse; one marked for death.

dead hand *n. phr. Law.* The prevention of a person's actions after one's death through the conditions of a will.

deadhouse *n. slang.* Morgue.

deadly *adj.* Causing or capable of causing death; suggestive of death; desiring or trying to kill. *adv.* So as to suggest death. *var.* deadlier, deadliest, *adj.*, deadliness, *n.*

deadly weapon *n. phr. Law.* An object, instrument, or weapon capable of producing death or serious bodily injury.

dead man *n. phr. slang.* A male prisoner condemned to be executed.

dead meat *n. phr. slang.* A corpse.

dead on arrival *adj. phr. Med.* Unable to be resuscitated after being transported to a hospital.

deanimation *n.* Legal death followed by cryonic preservation with the assumption of potential resuscitation.

Death *n. myth.* A personification of the destroyer of life, esp. as a skeleton.

death *n.* The act of dying or

the state of being dead; cause or manner of dying; murder, killing, or execution.

death agony *n. phr.* A struggle which may precede death. *Psychol.* The universal tendency to physiologically struggle for life and to suffer resulting anxiety.

death anxiety or **death fear** *n. phr. Psychol.* A preoccupation with the death of the self, the deaths of significant others, the dying process, and the state of being dead.

death bed *n. phr. slang. Med.* A seriously ill or dying patient intentionally located near a nurses' station in a hospital.

deathbed *n.* The bed on which a person dies; the last hours before death.

deathbed confession *n. phr.* A guilty revelation made just before death, esp. to clear one's conscience.

deathbed hallucinations *pl. n. phr.* A near-death experience; visions seen by a dying person, esp. deceased relatives.

deathbed marriage *n. phr.* A wedding ceremony in which one of the partners faces impending death.

deathbed vision *n. phr.* A near-death experience; deathbed hallucinations.

deathbed words *pl. n. phr.* The last utterance of a dying person; last words.

death-bell *n.* A bell which announces a death; the sound of a tolling or tinkling bell, said to presage the death of those who hear it.

death benefits *pl. n. phr.* Payment made to a beneficiary according to the terms of a life insurance policy.

deathblow *n.* A blow or stroke that causes death; a fatal event or occurrence.

death by degrees *n. phr. slang.* A prolonged process of dying.

death camp *n. phr.* A prison or compound in which many people are confined and executed.

death-capitulator *n. Psychol.* One who resigns oneself to death.

death cell *n. phr.* The cell in which a condemned person is housed prior to execution.

death certificate *n. phr. Law.* A document by which a death is legally recognized and which is permanently filed with the state or district health department.

death chamber *n. phr.* The room in which an execution is carried out.

death-chancer *n. Psychol.* One who takes chances with his or her life which involve a realistic risk.

death-chill *n.* The cooling of the body which occurs after death.

death control *n. phr.* Social measures offered or imposed to restrict overpopulation, esp. euthanasia and abortion.

death crier *n. phr. archaic.* One

who publicly announced the death of an illustrious person.

death cult *n. phr. Anthropol.* Rituals associated with death and burial within a culture, esp. religious rites.

death-damp *n.* The cold, clammy sweat which may cover the body prior to death.

death-darer *n. Psychol.* One who risks his or her life in situations of a relatively low probability of survival.

death day *n. phr.* The day on which a person dies; the anniversary of one's death.

death-dealing *adj.* Causing or capable of causing death.

death-duties *pl. n.* The laying out of the dead; funeral service.

death-experimentor *n. Psychol.* One who lives on the brink of death in a state of semi-consciousness brought about by alcohol or drug abuse.

death fear see **death anxiety**

death feigning *n. phr.* Mimicry of death.

death-fire *n.* The appearance of a luminous apparition or flame believed to presage death.

death-gurgle *n.* Death rattle.

death house *n. phr.* A cell block or area of a prison in which condemned prisoners are housed until execution.

death-ignorer *n. Psychol.* One who denies the fact that termination always involves cessation.

death-initiator *n. Psychol.* One who believes he or she will die in the near future and determines to avoid it.

death instinct *n. phr. Psychiatry.* Impulses toward destruction or death; inclination to suicide.

death knell *n. phr.* The tolling of a bell at a death or funeral.

deathlike *adj.* Having the appearance or qualities of death.

deathly *adj.* Descriptive of death; causing death. *adv.* Deathlike.

deathly ill *adj. phr.* Suffering from a life-threatening sickness or disease.

death mask *n. phr.* A cast of a person's face made after death.

death-money *n. Chinese.* Worthless paper money which is burned for use by the dead in the afterlife.

death notice *n. phr.* Obituary. *obs.* A handbill or advertisement of a public execution.

death penalty *n. phr.* The legal punishment of execution.

death-point *n. Biol.* The length of time one can survive in a certain degree of heat or after immersion in water at a temperature of 212 degrees Fahrenheit.

death profession *n. phr.* A career which involves frequent contact with the dead, esp. medicine and funeral service.

death rate *n. phr.* The ratio of total deaths to total population in a specified community;

the number of deaths per thousand of population.
death rattle *n. phr.* A gurgling or other noise made in the throat of a dying person.
death-related *adj.* Associated with death.
death rite *n. phr.* A funeral.
death roll *n. phr.* Death toll.
death room *n. phr.* The chamber in which a death has or will soon take place. *obs.* The parlor of a house in which the dead were laid out.
death row *n. phr.* The cell block or area in a prison in which condemned prisoners are housed until execution.
death scene *n. phr.* The specific location in which a death has taken place; portrayal of a climactic death in film or theater.
death-seeker *n. Psychol.* One who wishes for an end to all conscious experience and acts in a way designed to achieve it.
death sentence *n. phr.* The order of punishment by execution. *slang.* Imminent death, esp. by disease.
death's-head *n.* The human skull or a representation of it symbolizing mortality.
death ship *n. phr.* A vessel containing crew or passengers which is deliberately destroyed, esp. to collect insurance money.
deathsman *n. archaic.* An executioner.
death-sough *n.* The last heavy breath or sigh of a dying person.
death statistics *pl. n. phr.* The quantity or ratio of deaths in a country or society; numerical comparison of causes of death.
death-struck *adj. slang.* Dead.
death switch *n. phr.* The mechanism by which the electric chair is activated.
death tax *n. phr.* Inheritance tax.
death threat *n. phr.* A communicated intention to kill a person.
death-throe *n.* The struggle which accompanies death.
death-token *n.* Something which indicates approaching death.
death toll *n. phr.* The number of people killed in a disaster; the ringing of a bell slowly and regularly to mark a death.
death trap *n. phr.* A structure or situation that is potentially dangerous to life.
death valley *n. phr. slang. Med.* The intensive care unit in hospitals for the elderly.
death vigil *n. phr.* A wake.
death warrant *n. phr. Law.* An official order authorizing a person's execution.
death watch *n. phr. archaic.* The public announcer of a death.
deathwatch *n.* A vigil kept beside a dying or dead person; one who guards a condemned person before execution.
death-welcomer *n. Psychol.*

One who anticipates death eagerly.

death wish *n. phr. Psychiatry.* A desire for one's own death or the death of another.

death with dignity *n. phr.* Death without exhaustive resuscitation methods.

de bonis non administratis *adj. phr. Law.* Of an administrator appointed when the former administration is left unfinished through death or through the removal of the previous administrator.

debt of nature *idiom.* Death.

dec. *abbrev.* Deceased; decompose.

decani *pl. n.* Overseers of the members of medieval burial builds during preparation for a funeral.

decap *abbrev.* Decapitation.

decapitate *tr. v.* To sever the head of; behead. *var.* decapitation, decapitator, *n.*, decapitated, decapitates, decapitating, *v.*

decd. *abbrev.* Deceased.

decease *n.* Death. *intr. v.* To die. *var.* deceased, deceases, deceasing, *v.*

deceased *n. Law.* One who has died; the victim of a homicide.

decedent *n. Law.* The deceased.

decedents' debts *pl. n. phr. Law.* Notes owed by deceased persons.

decimate *tr. v.* To destroy; to execute every tenth person chosen by lot. *var.* decimation, *n.*, decimated, decimates, decimating, *v.*

declaration of war *n. phr. Mil.* Formally stated intentions of a country to fight or invade another.

declic *n.* The lever on a guillotine which releases the blade.

decollate *tr. v.* To behead. *var.* decollation, *n.*, decollated, decollates, decollating, *v.*

decomposed room *n. phr.* A specially ventilated room in a morgue or mortuary in which decayed bodies are examined, autopsied, or embalmed.

decomposition *n.* The decay of the human body. *var.* decompose, decomposed, decomposes, decomposing, *v.*

decorate a cottonwood *idiom.* To be executed by hanging.

Decoration Day *n. phr. archaic.* Memorial Day.

decree of distribution *n. phr. Law.* Court approval of the work of the executor which allows him or her to distribute the assets of the estate to beneficiaries or heirs.

dedolence *n. archaic.* The absence of sorrow. *var.* dedolent, *adj.*

deep end *idiom.* Death.

deep mourning *n. phr. obs.* The first six months after a death during which the bereaved abstained from social or recreational activities.

deep 6 see **deep-six**

deep-six *tr. v. slang.* To jettison a corpse at sea; to dispose of a corpse; to murder. *n.* Burial at sea; grave. *var.* deep-sixed, deep-sixes, deep-sixing, *v.*

deesis *n. Orthodox.* The depiction of Christ enthroned at the Last Judgment with St. Mary the Virgin and St. John the Baptist on either side pleading for souls.

def. *abbrev.* Defunct.

defenestration *n.* Suicide by throwing oneself out the window; the act of throwing someone out a window.

defossion *n.* Execution by being buried alive; live burial.

defunct *adj.* Having ceased to live or exist. *var.* defunctness, *n. slang. n.* A corpse.

defunctive *adj.* Pertaining to dead people.

defusion *n. Psychoanalysis.* The distinction between the instinct to live and the death instinct.

deicide *n.* The killing of a god, esp. Jesus Christ; one who kills a god. *var.* deicidal, *adj.*

demise *n.* Death; the transfer of a ruler's authority by death or abdication. *Law.* The transfer of an estate by will. *tr. v.* To transfer by will; to transfer sovereignty by abdication or will. *intr. v.* To be transferred by will or descent; to die. *var.* demisable, *adj.*, demised, demises, demising, *v.*

dempster or **doomster** *n. archaic.* Public executioner in Edinburgh, Scotland, who had the duty to pronounce sentence in a capital crime.

denial *n.* A stage in terminal illness in which the patient psychologically and emotionally rejects the idea of his or her death; an initial stage of grief in which survivors may be unable to believe a death has occurred.

deny *tr. v.* To reject death as a possible outcome.

deodand *n. archaic.* The object which caused a death and which was forfeited to the crown in English law.

depart *intr. v.* To die. *var.* departure, *n.*, departed, departing, departs, *v.*

departed *p.part.* Dead.

depersonalization *n. Psychol.* A pathological state in which a person feels non-existent or dead.

deposit *tr. v.* To bury or entomb, esp. temporarily. *var.* deposited, depositing, deposits, *v.*

deposited with the parent earth *idiom.* Buried.

depression *n.* A stage in terminal illness in which the patient mourns past and future losses, experiences anticipatory grief, and begins the process of letting go of family and friends; a stage of grief in which a survivor remains despondent about the death.

derrick *n.* The gallows [after Godfrey Derick or Derrick, 17th c. hangman at Tyburn].

descent *n. Law.* The acquisition of property from a decedent without the use of wills; intestate succession.

desert warfare *n. phr. Mil.* Armed conflict carried out under arid conditions.

designator *n. archaic.* The director of an ancient Roman funeral procession.
dessication *n.* The dehydration of human tissues; mummification. *var.* dessicate, dessicated, dessicates, dessicating, *v.*
Dessounin *n. Haitian myth.* A ritual performed to separate the spirit of the dead from the body.
destroy *tr. v.* To kill; obliterate. *var.* destruction, *n.*, destroyed, destroying, destroys, *v.*
determination of death *n. phr. Law.* The tests required to legally pronounce a person dead.
deuterogamy *n. Law.* A second legal marriage following the death or divorce of a first spouse.
devise *n. Law.* A gift of disposition of lands or other real property made by a will.
devisee *n. Law.* The person to whom a disposition of lands or other real property is made by a will.
devisor *n. Law.* A person who disposes of lands or other real property by a will.
devotio *n. archaic.* A form of emperor worship in which illustrious individuals vowed to die on his behalf.
dial-a-mation *n.* A telephone service offering cremation.
Diancecht *n. Celtic myth.* God of healing who restores humans to life.
die *intr. v.* To cease existing, esp. over time; to experience agony or suffering of death. *var.* died, dies, dying, *v.*
die all at once *idiom.* To die suddenly.
die before one's time *v. phr.* To die before one's time of productivity has ended.
die by inches *idiom.* To die slowly.
die by one's own hand *idiom.* To commit suicide.
die game *idiom.* To die valiantly.
die in a horse's nightcap *idiom.* To be executed by hanging.
die in harness *idiom.* To die while working.
die in one's boots see **die with one's boots on**
die in one's shoes see **die with one's boots on**
die in the hot seat *v. phr. slang.* To be executed in the electric chair.
diener see **mortuary diener**
die off *v. phr.* To participate in a sudden decline in population; to die in turn until few are left.
die of lead poisoning *idiom.* To be shot to death.
die of the measles *idiom.* To be murdered but made to appear as if one died from natural causes.
die of throat trouble *idiom.* To be executed by hanging.
die on *v. phr. slang. Med.* To die under the care of.
die out *v. phr.* To die off; to become extinct.
Dies Irae *n. Christian.* A medieval Latin hymn describ-

ing the day of judgment, used in requiem masses and sung on All Souls' Day [lit., day of wrath (the first words of the hymn)].

die with one's boots on or **die in one's boots** or **die in one's shoes** *idiom.* To be killed rather than die in bed; to die while still active in one's work; to die suddenly.

die without issue *v. phr. Law.* To fail to have children during life.

digamy *n.* Remarriage after the death or divorce of one's first spouse.

dilation and curettage *n. phr. Med.* A method of abortion in which the wall of the uterus is scraped through the vagina and cervix.

di Manes *pl. n. phr. Rom. myth.* The souls of the dead who reign in the underworld.

dim one's lights *idiom.* To kill; murder.

dina *abbrev. Law.* Found dead in an automobile; found dead in an airplane.

dinb *abbrev. Law.* Found dead in bed.

dire *adj.* Of a hospital ward housing terminal patients who are known, loved, and mourned by the staff.

direct action *n. phr.* Assassination [used by the CIA].

direct disposer *n. phr.* An individual or firm engaged solely in providing cremation services.

direct disposition *n. phr.* Cremation and disposition of human remains without rites and ceremonies.

dirge *n. Music.* A funeral hymn; a mourning song. *var.* dirgeful, *adj.*

dirt-bag murder *n. phr. slang. Journalism.* A murder which is not sensational enough to report.

disappear *intr. v.* To be murdered without a trace. *var.* disappearance, *n.*, disappeared, disappearing, disappears, *v.*

disarticulate *intr. v.* To separate during the process of decay [used of the bones of the skeleton]. *tr. v.* To disassemble the bones of a skeleton. *var.* disarticulation, *n.*, disarticulated, disarticulates, disarticulating, *v.*

disaster *n.* An event which causes widespread destruction and loss of life; a grave misfortune. *var.* disastrous, *adj.*, disastrously, *adv.*

disembody *tr. v.* To free the spirit from the physical body. *var.* disembodiment, *n.* disembodied, disembodies, disembodying, *v.*

disengagement *n.* or **social disengagement** *n. phr. Sociol.* The process by which the aged or terminally ill withdraw from society in anticipation of death.

disentomb *tr. v.* To remove from a tomb. *var.* disentombment, *n.*, disentombed, disentombing, disentombs, *v.*

dish *intr. v. slang.* To murder; kill.

dished *p.part. slang.* Dead.

disinheritance *n. Law.* The act by which a donor dissolves the right of a person to inherit property to which he or she previously had a right; the termination of a person's right to inherit. *var.* disinherit, disinherited, disinheriting, disinherits *v.*

disinter *tr. v.* To remove from a grave or tomb; exhume. *var.* disinterment, *n.*, disinterred, disinterring, disinters, *v.*

dismal trade *n. phr. obs.* The profession of undertaking or gravedigging.

Dis manibus *prep. phr. Lat.* Dedicated to the souls of the dead.

dispatch *tr. v. slang.* To kill; murder. *n.* Murder. *var.* dispatched, dispatches, dispatching, *v.*

Dis Pater *n. phr. Rom. myth.* God of the underworld corresponding to Hades.

display room or **selection room** *n. phr.* A showroom for caskets in a funeral home.

disposition *n.* The entombment, burial, or cremation of the dead; final placement of human remains. *n. Law.* Distribution of an estate by will.

dissect *tr. v. Med.* To cut apart, esp. for anatomical study; to autopsy. *var.* dissectible, *adj.*, dissector, *n.*, dissected, dissecting, dissects, *v.*

dissecting fee *n. phr. Med.* The price for which a medical cadaver may be obtained.

distancing *n.* The attempt of professional caregivers to be as honest and giving with terminal patients as possible, limited only by other responsibilities.

distant and certain death *n. phr.* Death as inevitable for everyone.

distant and uncertain death *n. phr.* Death as a denied eventuality.

diw *abbrev. Law.* Dead in the water.

Di-zang *n. Chinese myth.* Ruler of hell from which he rescues souls.

DL *abbrev. Med.* Danger list.

DM *abbrev. Lat.* Dis manibus.

dn *abbrev.* Died near.

DNR *abbrev. Med.* Do not resuscitate [used to designate dying patients who should be allowed to expire].

do *tr. v. slang.* To murder; kill. *var.* did, does, doing, *v.*

DOA or **D.O.A.** or **doa** *abbrev. Med.* Dead on arrival. *n. slang.* A person who is dead on arrival at a hospital.

doa see **DOA**

do a blackout or **do a fadeout** *idiom.* To die.

do a croak *idiom.* To die.

do a dance in midair *idiom.* To be executed by hanging.

do a fadeout see **do a blackout**

do a fold or **do a fold-up** *idiom.* To die.

do a fold-up see **do a fold**

do a perisher *idiom. Australian.* To die from dehydration.

do away with *idiom.* To kill; murder.

do away with oneself *idiom.* To commit suicide.
do business for or **do one's business for** *v. phr. slang.* To kill; murder.
DOD or **dod** *abbrev.* Date of death; died of disease.
dod see **DOD**
do for *idiom.* To kill.
dog meat *n. phr. slang.* A dead person [used as a threat].
doi *abbrev. Law.* Died of injuries.
do in *idiom.* To kill; murder.
dokhma *n. Persian.* The stone wall on which Parsee dead are exposed.
dole *n. archaic.* Grief.
doleful *adj.* Associated with grief; mournful. *var.* dolefully, *adv.*, dolefulness, *n.*
dolent *adj.* Grieving; mournful.
dolor *n. archaic.* Grief. *var.* dolorous, *adj.*
doloroso *adj. Music.* Mournful. *adv.* Mournfully.
D.O.M. *abbrev. Lat.* To God the best and the greatest [used as an inscription for the dead].
domestic homicide *n. phr.* The murder of a spouse or family member.
Doms *pl. n.* Members of a hereditary caste in India who arrange cremations.
Donatists *pl. n.* Members of a 4th-c. sect who considered themselves apostles of death and tried to commit suicide daily by jumping from cliffs, burning themselves alive, or forcing others to kill them.
done for *idiom.* Dead; doomed; dying.
done on toast *idiom.* Dead.
done to death *v. phr. slang.* Murdered.
done under *idiom.* Dead.
done up *idiom.* Dead.
don filial piety *idiom.* To dress in mourning clothing when parents or near relatives die.
Dong-yo Da-di *n. Chinese myth.* A god who determines the times of birth and death for all creatures.
donor *n. Med.* One who makes a gift of all or part of his or her body for transplant, research, or education.
donor-cycle *n. slang. Med.* A motorcycle [because many donated organs are obtained from the bodies of motorcycle accident victims].
dood *n. Dutch.* Death.
doole *n. archaic.* A black mourning garment, esp. when given away.
doom *n.* A mural or stained glass window depicting the Last Judgment, esp. over the west door of a church.
doomed *p.part.* Of death which may occur at any time, esp. as a result of terminal illness; destined to die.
doomsday *n.* The day of the Last Judgment; the day in the future on which the world will end.
doomster see **dempster**
do one's bit *slang. Mil.* To die in service to one's country in wartime.
do one's business for see **do business for**

do oneself in *idiom.* To commit suicide.

door badges *pl. n. phr. archaic.* A colored ribbon hung on the door by a 19th-c. undertaker to denote a death.

dormantory *n.* [Proposed term for] a storage facility for bodies in cryonic suspension.

dormitio *n.* A depiction of the death of the Virgin Mary.

dormition *n.* A peaceful and painless death.

dormitory facilities *pl. n. phr.* The room in which bodies are stored in a funeral home.

DOS *abbrev. Law.* Dead on the scene.

do the croak act see **do a croak**

do the Houdini *idiom.* To dispose of a corpse so as to eliminate any chance of its discovery or evidence of a murder.

do the job for *idiom.* To kill; murder.

doubled up *idiom.* Dead.

double indemnity *n. phr.* A clause in an insurance policy which doubles the face value of the contract in case of accidental death.

double murder *n. phr.* The killing of two people at the same time by a single person.

douse *intr. v. slang.* To die. *tr. v. slang.* To murder.

douse one's lights or **douse the lights** *idiom.* To commit suicide; murder.

douser *n. slang.* Murder.

DOW or **dow** *abbrev. Law.* Died of wounds.

dow see **DOW**

dowager *n.* A widow who holds the title or property of her dead husband.

dower *n. Law.* The part of a deceased's real estate allotted by law to his widow for her lifetime, one-third under common law. *tr. v.* To assign a dower to. *var.* dowered, dowering, dowers, *v.*

dower right *n. phr. Law.* The principle that a wife may not be disinherited; a wife's minimum share of her husband's inheritance.

down for the long count *idiom.* Dead.

down there *n. phr. slang. Gk.* Hades; hell.

dowry *n. archaic.* A dower.

drag a lake *v. phr.* To search a body of water for an accident or murder victim.

draw a blank *idiom.* To die.

drawing and quartering *n. phr.* A method of execution in which the condemned is half-hanged, disemboweled, dismembered, and exposed; a method of execution in which the arms and legs of the condemned are tied to four horses forced to pull in opposite directions. *var.* drawn and quartered, *v.*

draw the curtain or **draw the curtain for** *idiom.* To kill; murder.

draw the curtain for see **draw the curtain**

drive rivets into the coffin of *idiom.* To kill; murder.

dromos *n.* A passage to an ancient subterranean tomb.

drop *n.* The distance of the fall in an execution by hanging which is usually calculated to break the neck. *tr. v. slang.* To kill. *var.* dropped, dropping, drops, *v.*
drop-dead list *n. phr. slang.* A hit list [often used figuratively].
drop everything *idiom.* To die.
drop into Kingdom Come *idiom.* To kill; murder.
drop off *idiom.* To die.
drop off the hook *idiom.* To die.
drop one's leaf *idiom.* To die.
drop the curtain *idiom.* To die.
drop the curtain on *idiom.* To kill; murder.
drown *intr. v.* To die by suffocating in water or other liquid. *tr. v.* To kill by suffocating in water or other liquid. *var.* drowned, drowning, drowns, *v.*
drowning *pr.part.* An instance of death by suffocation in water or other liquid.
dry burial *n. phr. Anthropol.* A method of interment among the ancient Egyptians in which bodies were wrapped in coarse cloth and laid upon beds of charcoal under six or more feet of sand.
dry funeral *n. phr. Anthropol. Indian.* A second ceremony held on All Souls' Day one or two years after a funeral.
dry-gulch *tr. v. archaic. slang.* To kill sheepherders and burn their wagons. *var.* dry-gulched, dry-gulches, dry-gulching, *v.*

dry tree *n. phr. slang.* The gallows.
d.s.p. *abbrev. Lat.* Died without issue.
d/t *abbrev.* Total ratio of deaths.
Duat *n. Egypt. myth.* The afterworld.
duel *n.* A prearranged fight with deadly weapons between two people wishing to settle a dispute. *intr. v.* To settle a dispute in a prearranged fight, esp. to the death.
dump *tr. v. slang.* To kill; murder. *var.* dumped, dumping, dumps, *v.*
dumping *n. slang. Law.* The practice of or an instance of moving a body after death to avoid a police investigation or publicity.
durable power of attorney *n. phr. Law.* A document giving one the legal authority to discontinue treatment of a terminal illness if the patient is unconscious or incompetent.
durgah *n. Hindu.* The tomb of a Mohammedan saint.
dust *n. lit.* Human remains. *tr. v. slang.* To kill.
dustbin *n. slang.* The grave.
dusting *pr.part. slang.* Murder.
dust-off *n. slang.* Murder.
dust off *v. phr. slang.* To kill; murder.
Dutch act or **Dutch cure** or **Dutch route** *n. phr. slang.* Suicide.
Dutch cure see **Dutch act**
Dutch route see **Dutch act**
d.v.m. *abbrev. Lat.* Died during his or her mother's lifetime.

d.v.p. *abbrev. Lat.* Died during his or her father's lifetime.

DWA *abbrev. Law.* Deadly Weapon Act.

dying *adj.* Nearing death; completed just before death. *pl. n.* The collective or a specific group of terminally ill people.

dying day *n. phr.* The day of one's death [used figuratively].

dying declaration *n. phr.* or **dying declarations** *pl. n. phr. Law.* A statement made by a person facing impending death; a statement concerning the cause of death made by the victim of a homicide who was conscious of dying and felt death was immediate and inescapable.

dying words *pl. n. phr.* The final communications of a dying person.

E

early fetal death *n. phr. Med.* Fetal death occurring within the first twenty weeks of pregnancy.

earth bath *n. phr. slang.* A burial; grave.

earth burial *n. phr.* Interment underground.

earthquake fever *n. phr. slang.* Anxiety attacks characterized by a sense of helplessness and sudden consciousness of mortality.

Easter *n. Christian.* A feast observed on the first Sunday after the full moon on or after March 21st to commemorate the resurrection of Jesus Christ after his crucifixion.

easy *adj. slang.* Dead.

eat dandelions by the root *idiom. Fr.* To be dead and buried.

ebb out *idiom.* To die.

ebenezer *n. archaic.* A memorial stone, esp. one which commemorates divine assistance.

e by i *abbrev. Law.* Execution by injection.

ecbolic *adj. Med.* Causing abortion. *n. Med.* Something which causes abortion.

E.C.M.A. *abbrev.* Embalming Chemical Manufacturers Association.

ed *abbrev. Mil.* Enemy dead.

E.E.C. *abbrev.* Euthanasia Education Council.

E.E.F. *abbrev.* Euthanasia Education Fund.

E.F.D.A. *abbrev.* European Funeral Directors Association.

ego death *n. phr.* The liberating annihilation of all previous physical, emotional,

intellectual, moral, and transcendental reference-points.
egoistic suicide *n. phr. Sociol.* Suicide resulting from the lack of integration with other members of society.
eigne *n. archaic.* Heir apparent.
Ekei *n. Gk. myth.* The world of the dead.
Ekimmu *Assyrian myth.* The spirit of an unburied body.
ekphora *n. archaic. Gk.* Conveyance to the place of burial.
E.K.R.C. *abbrev.* Elisabeth Kübler-Ross Center.
election under the will *n. phr. Law.* The principle that to receive under a will is to conform to all of its provisions; the choice of accepting the benefit given under the will and relinquishing a claim to property which the will disposes of to another.
electric chair *n. phr.* A device in which one under sentence of death is electrocuted; execution by electrocution; sentence of death by electrocution.
electric cure *n. phr. slang.* The electric chair; electrocution.
electrocute *tr. v.* To kill using electricity; to execute using electricity. *var.* electrocution, *n.*, electrocuted, electrocuting, electrocutes, *v.*
electrocution chamber *n. phr.* The room in a prison which houses an electric chair.
electrolethe *n.* [A proposed name for] the electric chair.

electronic warfare *n. phr. Mil.* Armed conflict using electronic systems and devices.
elegiac *adj.* Associated with an elegy; mournful. *var.* elegiacal, *adj.*, elegiacally, *adv.*
elegize *intr. v.* To compose an elegy. *tr. v.* To compose an elegy about. *var.* elegized, elegizing, elegizes, *v.*
elegy *n.* A poem, song, or other lament composed for the dead.
eleventh hour *idiom.* The last moment before death.
eliminated *p.part. slang.* Killed.
éloge *n. Fr.* Eulogy; funeral oration, esp. a laudatory one.
elogy *n.* Éloge; obituary, esp. a laudatory one.
elysian *adj.* Associated with Elysium.
Elysian Fields see **Elysium**
Elysium *n.* or **Elysian Fields** *n. phr. Gk. myth.* Abode of the blessed after death; heaven.
E.M. *abbrev.* Bishop and martyr.
embalm *tr. v.* To preserve a corpse, esp. with chemicals. *var.* embalmer, embalmment, *n.*, embalmed, embalming, embalms, *v.*
embalming fluid *n. phr.* A liquid, usually formaldehyde-based, used to preserve the dead.
emergency care *n. phr. Med.* Hospitalization designed for the rapid treatment of accidental injury and sudden critical illness; life-saving services.

emergent *adj. Med.* Life-threatening [a category of hospital triage]; in imminent danger of dying; of a hospital emergency ward or intensive care unit in which death is common and the staff-patient relationship is shortlived, precluding mourning.

Emma-O or **Emma-ten** *n. Buddhism.* The king of hell who records the sins of those condemned to purgatory and determines the extent of their punishment.

Emma-ten see **Emma-O**

empty the uterus *v. phr.* To abort an entire multiple pregnancy; to perform or undergo an abortion.

encharnelled *p.part.* Deposited for burial, esp. in a charnel house.

encoffin *tr. v.* To enclose in a coffin.

end *n.* The termination of existence; death.

end it all *v. phr. slang.* To commit suicide.

endocannibalism *n. Anthropol.* Cannibalism practiced only upon relatives.

end of life *n. phr.* Death.

endophagy *n. Anthropol.* Cannibalism practiced only upon friends or members of the same tribe.

endow *tr. v. obs.* To provide with a dower. *var.* endowment, *n.*, endowed, endowing, endows, *v.*

end sealer *n. phr. obs.* A burglarproof vault in which a casket was placed before burial in the early 19th c.

end up *v. phr. slang.* To die; be killed.

Enoch Arden *n. phr. Law.* A proceeding which permits the dissolution of a marriage when one spouse disappears and is presumed dead after a designated period of time, usually seven years.

enshroud *tr. v.* To wrap in a winding-sheet. *var.* enshrouded, enshrouding, enshrouds, *v.*

ensky *tr. v.* To make immortal. *var.* enskied, enskies, enskying, *v.*

entail *tr. v. Law.* To settle an estate on a person and all or certain of his or her descendants. *n.* An estate settled in this way; a line of succession.

entomb *tr. v.* To deposit in a chamber or grave; to function as a tomb for. *var.* entombed, entombing, entombs, *v.*

entombment *n.* The deposit of a casket within a sealed crypt.

Enyo *n. Gk. myth.* Goddess of war.

EOL *abbrev.* End of life.

epd *abbrev. Sp.* Rest in peace.

epicede *n.* A dirge.

epicedium *n., pl.* **epicedia** Elegy; dirge. *var.* epicedial, *adj.*

epid. *abbrev.* Epidemic.

episcopicide *n.* The killing of a bishop; one who kills a bishop. *var.* episcopicidal, *adj.*

epit. *abbrev.* Epitaph.

epitaph *n.* A memorial inscription on a grave marker; a brief written commemoration of a dead person. *var.* epitaphic, *adj.*

equalizer *n. slang. Mexican.* Death in personified form.

equivocal death *n. phr.* A death in which the means is known but the motive is unresolved.

ER or **E.R.** *abbrev. Med.* Emergency room of a hospital.

E.R. see **ER**

erase *tr. v. slang.* To murder. *var.* erased, erases, erasing, *v.*

erasure *n. slang.* Murder.

Erebus *n. Gk. myth.* A dark region of the underworld through which the dead must pass before reaching Hades; Hades.

Ereshkigal see **Ereskigal**

Ereskigal or **Ereshkigal** *n. Sumerian myth.* Goddess of the underworld.

eric *n. archaic.* Payment to the family of the victim by the murderer under ancient Irish law.

Erinyes *pl. n. Gk. myth.* Avenging goddesses of the underworld who pursue sinners, esp. those who have murdered members of their own families.

Erlik *n. Samoyed myth.* God of the netherworld.

Erra or **Irra** *n. Babylonian myth.* God of plague.

E.S.A. *abbrev.* Euthanasia Society of America.

escalated interpersonal altercation *n. phr. Sociol.* Murder.

escape *intr. v. slang.* To die. *var.* escaped, escapes, escaping, *v.*

eschat. *abbrev. Theol.* Eschatology.

eschatology *n. Theol.* The study of the four last things: death, judgment, heaven, and hell. *var.* eschatological, *adj.*, eschatologically, *adv.*, eschatologist, *n.*

escheat *n. Law.* The reversion of property to the state in the absence of legal heirs or claimants; property that has reverted to the state in the absence of legal heirs or claimants. *intr.* and *tr. v.* To revert or cause to revert by escheat. *var.* escheatable, *adj.*, escheated, escheating, escheats, *v.*

escheatage *n. Law.* The right to receive by escheat.

esprit *n. Haitian myth.* The spirits or soul of the dead.

established disease *n. phr.* A psychosocial stage of terminal illness lasting from response to the diagnosis through the reactions prior to the onset of the terminal period, including relapses, remissions, progress, and arrest.

estate *n. Law.* Everything in one's possession, esp. the property and debts of a dead person.

Etemmu *n. Babylonian myth.* The soul of an unburied body.

eternal *adj.* Of spiritual communion with God after death. *var.* eternally, *adv.*, eternality, eternalness, *n.*

eternal care unit *n. phr. slang.* The afterlife; death.

eternal rest *n. phr.* Death.

eternity *n.* The afterlife; immortality.

eternity-box *n. slang.* A casket.

eternize *tr. v.* To immortalize. *var.* eternized, eternizes, eternizing, *v.*

Eurynomous *n. Gk. myth.* A demon who eats the flesh of corpses.

euthanasia *n.* The killing of an individual for reasons considered to be merciful; pleasant death. *Law.* Painless inducement of death administered by a physician.

euthanize *tr. v.* To kill a person for reasons considered merciful. *var.* euthanized, euthanizes, euthanizing, *v.*

evaporate *intr. v. slang.* To die. *var.* evaporated, evaporates, evaporating, *v.*

everlasting life *n. phr.* The afterlife; immortality.

e viv. disc. *abbrev. Lat.* Departed from life.

EW or **ew** *abbrev. Mil.* Electronic warfare.

ew see **EW**

EWP *abbrev. Mil.* Emergency war plan.

ex. *abbrev.* Executed.

exactor mortis *n. phr. archaic. Lat.* The centurion who supervises crucifixion and is responsible for determining death.

exanimate *adj.* Lifeless; dead.

excusable homicide *n. phr.* The accidental killing of one person by another; intentional but justifiable killing of a person by accident or misfortune without gross negligence.

exec. *abbrev.* Execute; executed; execution. *Law.* executor.

execute *tr. v.* To murder; to carry out a legal death sentence. *Law.* To complete a will; to do what is required by a will. *var.* executable, *adj.*, executed, executes, executing, *v.*

executee *n.* A person under sentence of death.

execution *n.* The act of putting to death as a legal penalty.

execution block see **block**

execution box *n. phr.* A container in which an executioner stores equipment.

execution by injection *n. phr.* Sentence of death by injection of air or poison into a blood vessel.

execution chamber *n. phr.* The room in which a death sentence is carried out.

executioner *n.* One who puts another to death, esp. by carrying out a legal sentence.

execution ground *n. phr.* An area in which sentence of death is carried out, esp. by firing squad; the site of a mass murder.

execution in effigy *n. phr.* The symbolic execution of a person by burning or destroying a model of him or her; mock execution.

execution sermon *n. phr.* An oration by a minister before a death sentence is carried out.

execution shed *n. phr.* The area within a prison which contains the gallows.

execution squad *n. phr.* The people employed to carry out a legal death sentence, esp. by firing squad.

execution-style *adj.* Of a murder characterized by cruel efficiency, esp. by shooting in the back of the head.

executive action *n. phr.* The assassination of a foreign leader in a coup; capability to carry out assassinations [used by the CIA].

executor *n. Law.* A person appointed by a testator to execute his or her will. *var.* executorial, *adj.*, executorship, *n.*

executory bequest *n. phr. Law.* A bequest of personal property or money which takes effect after the occurrence of a possible or certain future event.

executory devise *n. phr. Law.* A situation in which no estate vests under the will until the occurrence of a future event.

executress *n. Law.* An executrix.

executrix *n. Law.* A woman appointed by a testator to execute his or her will.

exedra *n.* A porch or portico adjacent to a grave.

exequies *pl. n.* Funeral rites; funeral procession.

exequy *n.* Funeral ceremony or procession.

exheredate *tr. v.* To disinherit. *var.* exheredation, *n.*, exheredated, exheredates, exheredating, *v.*

exhume *tr. v.* To remove from a grave; disinter. *var.* exhumation, *n.*, exhumed, exhumes, exhuming, *v.*

exit *intr. v. slang.* To die. *var.* exited, exiting, exits, *v.*

exit plan *n. phr. slang.* Assassination plan; murder plan.

exophagy *n. Anthropol.* Cannibalism practiced upon enemies or people from outside the tribe.

exor. *abbrev. Law.* Executor.

expendable *adj. Mil.* Of a life or lives considered acceptable to sacrifice in war.

expire *intr. v.* To die. *var.* expired, expires, expiring, *v.*

expr. *abbrev.* Expire.

exr. *abbrev. Law.* Executor.

exrx. *abbrev. Law.* Executrix.

exsanguinate *intr. v.* To bleed to death. *tr. v.* To drain the blood from. *var.* exsanguination, *n.*, exsanguinated, exsanguinates, exsanguinating, *v.*

extended *adj. Archeol.* Of a skeleton found on its back with feet extended and arms at the sides.

extermish *tr. v. slang.* To exterminate; kill.

extinct *adj.* No longer existing and having no living successors; having no personal continuity after death, except through tangible evidence on earth. *var.* extinctive, *adj.*, extinction, *n.*

extinguish *tr. v.* To kill; destroy. *var.* extinguishable, *adj.*, extinguisher, extinguish-

ment, *n.*, extinguished, extinguishes, extinguishing, *v.*
extraordinary means *pl. n. phr. Med.* Technological procedures used to prolong life, esp. of an aged, brain-dead, or terminally ill person.
extreme penalty *idiom.* Death.
extreme unction *n. phr. obs. Rom. Cath.* The sacrament in which a priest annoints and prays for one in danger of death [replaced with **annointing of the sick**].
extrx. *abbrev. Law.* Executrix.
exx. *abbrev. Law.* Executrix.
eyebank *n. Med.* A facility in which human corneas are stored for later transplantation.

F

fadeout *n. slang.* Death.
fade out *v. phr. slang.* To die.
failure of issue *n. phr. Law.* A situation in which no children have been born to or no children survive a decedent; the condition of dying without issue.
fake *tr. v. slang.* To kill; murder. *var.* faked, fakes, faking, *v.*
family killing *n. phr.* A homicide in which the murderer and victim are related by blood or marriage.
family picnic basket *n. phr. slang.* The basket in front of a guillotine into which the head falls.
family plot *n. phr.* Adjacent burial spaces reserved for members of a particular family.
fan out *v. phr. slang.* To die.
fatal *n. slang.* A deadly accident. *adj.* Causing or capable of causing death. *var.* fatally, *adv.*
fatal accident *n. phr.* An unexpected occurrence which results in a death.
fatal casualties vulnerability number *n. phr. Mil.* The number of losses which would put an army at a disadvantage during war.
fatal illness *n. phr.* A sickness from which there is no expected recovery.
fatality *n.* A death that results from an unexpected occurrence; one who is killed as a result of an unexpected occurrence; the capability of causing death or disaster; the condition of being doomed.
fatality rate *n. phr.* Death rate.
fatiferous *adj.* Destructive; deadly.
Fatit or **Miren** *pl. n. Albanian myth.* Three female beings

who determine the fate of each newborn child.

favored beneficiary *n. phr. Law.* One who inherits property of greater value than others having equal claim to an estate.

fc *abbrev.* Foot candle.

FCAP *abbrev.* Fellow of the College of American Pathologists.

FCVN *abbrev.* Fatal casualties vulnerability number.

F.C.W. *abbrev.* Fellowship of Christian Widows.

F.D.E.C. *abbrev.* Forum for Death Education and Counseling.

fd50 *abbrev. Med.* Median fatal dose.

FDR *abbrev.* Fast death response.

Feast Day *n. phr.* A day to commemorate a saint or martyr, often the anniversary of his or her death.

featherman or **feather-page** *n. obs.* One who carried a tray of black plumes in a Victorian funeral procession.

feather-page see **featherman**

FEBA or **feba** *abbrev.* Forward edge of battle area.

feba see **FEBA**

Februus *n. Rom. myth.* God of purification who dwells in the underworld.

feed a fatal pill *idiom.* To shoot and kill.

feed the fishes *idiom.* To drown.

feeling no pain *v. phr. slang.* Dead.

fee simple *n. phr. Law.* An estate of almost infinite duration and of absolute inheritance free of any conditions imposed on heirs.

fee tail *n. phr. Law.* A transfer by will to a person and his or her heirs; a fixed line of inheritance.

fell *adj.* Capable of killing. *tr. v.* To kill. *var.* fellable, *adj.*, feller, fellness, *n.*

fell asleep *idiom.* Died.

felo-de-se or **felos-de-se** *pl.* **felones-de-se** *n. Law.* The act of suicide; one who commits suicide; one who dies as a result of committing an unlawful and malicious act [lit., felon of himself].

felonious homicide or **felonious murder** *n. phr.* The taking of life suddenly without intended malice; an unlawful killing committed in the act of committing or attempting to commit another crime.

felonious murder see **felonious homicide**

felony murder see **felonious homicide**

felos-de-se see **felo-de-se**

feme sole *n. phr. obs.* An unmarried or widowed woman.

femicide *n.* The killing of a woman; one who kills a woman; a female murder victim. *var.* femicidal, *adj.*

fenestrella *n.* A small opening in an altar for viewing the tomb within.

feral *adj.* Funereal.

feretory *n.* An ornate case for storing or transporting relics; a bier; a chapel for a bier.

fetal death *n. phr. Med.* The death of an unborn child.

fetch *n. Brit.* An apparition or double interpreted as an omen of death.

fetch-light *n.* A spectral glow said to appear before a death and travel to the grave; a corpse candle.

feticide or **foeticide** *n.* The intentional destruction of a fetus; an abortion. *var.* feticidal, *adj.*

F.F.D.A. *abbrev.* Federated Funeral Directors of America; Flying Funeral Directors of America.

F.H.P.S.G.I. *abbrev.* Funeral Home Public Service Group International.

Field of Asphodel *n. Gk. + Rom. myth.* The place where the souls of heroes and commoners await their fate.

Field of Offerings *n. phr. Gk. myth.* The afterlife; heaven.

Field of Reeds or **Field of Rushes** *n. phr. Egypt. myth.* The afterlife; heaven.

Field of Rushes see **Field of Reeds**

Fields of Punishment *pl. n. phr. Gk. myth.* The place where the guilty benefit from their crimes after death.

filicide *n.* The killing of one's son or daughter; the murder of a child older than one day by one or both of its parents; one who kills one's son or daughter. *var.* filicidal, *adj.*

filling for a casket *n. phr. slang.* A corpse.

final call *idiom.* Death.

final curtain *idiom. Theater.* Death.

final decline *n. phr.* The marked worsening in the condition of a terminally ill person just prior to death.

final disposition *n. phr.* The interment, entombment, or other treatment of human remains.

final kickoff *idiom.* Death.

final kiss-off *idiom.* Death.

final payoff *idiom.* Death.

final port of call *idiom.* The grave.

final pushoff *idiom.* Death.

final resting place *idiom.* The grave.

Final Solution *n. phr.* The extermination of all European Jews as attempted by Adolf Hitler during World War II.

final summons *idiom.* Death.

finestra *n.* An opening in the wall of a tomb, esp. for ventilation.

finger *tr. v.* To mark for assassination. *var.* fingered, fingering, fingers, *v.*

finis *n. slang.* Death, esp. as complete cessation.

finish *n.* The death of a person. *tr. v.* To kill; destroy. *var.* finisher, *n.*, finished, finishes, finishing, *v.*

finished *p.part. slang.* Dead; killed.

finish off *idiom.* To kill; murder.

fire one's last shot *idiom.* To die, esp. in combat.

firing squad *n. phr.* The group assigned to execute a condemned prisoner by shooting.

firing wall • forensic odontology 69

firing wall *n. phr.* The backdrop of an execution by firing squad.

first-class relic *n. phr. Rom. Cath.* A body part of a saint; an instrument used during Jesus Christ's crucifixion.

first-degree manslaughter *n. phr. Law.* A killing committed without express or implied malice.

first-degree murder see **murder in the first degree**

first devisee *n. phr. Law.* The first recipient of an estate devised by will.

first life cycle *n. phr. Cryonics.* The period of time between birth and deanimation.

first-order denial *n. phr.* The perception by a patient of the primary facts of his or her terminal illness.

first strike *n. phr. Mil.* An initial attack with nuclear weapons.

first use *n. phr. Mil.* The introduction of nuclear weapons into an armed conflict.

five-day case *n. phr. slang.* An unidentified body which remains unclaimed in the morgue.

fix *tr. v. slang.* To kill; murder. *var.* fixed, fixes, fixing, *v.*

fizz *v.* or **fizzle out** *v. phr. slang.* To die. *var.* fizzed, fizzes, fizzing, *v.*

Flatnosed *n. slang. Fr.* Death in personified form.

flattened *p.part.* or **flattened out** *idiom.* Dead.

flatten out *idiom.* To kill; die.

flexed *p.part. Archeol.* Of a skeleton found in a bent or twisted position.

flicker out *idiom.* To die.

F.L.M.P. *abbrev.* Forest Lawn Memorial Park.

floriut *n. Lat.* The dates of a person's birth and death, esp. appearing in brackets after his or her name.

flower car *n. phr.* An automobile or van used to transport flowers to the grave.

flummoxed *p.part. slang.* Dead.

flunk out *idiom.* To die.

flush marker *n. phr.* A rectangular plaque set into the ground to mark a grave.

flybait *n. slang.* A corpse.

fly off the handle *idiom.* To die.

foeticide see **feticide**

fold *n. slang.* Death. *intr. v.* To die. *var.* folding, folds, *v.*

folded *p.part.* or **folded up** *v. phr. slang.* Dead.

fold-up *n. slang.* Death.

food for worms *n. phr. slang.* A corpse.

foot candle *n. phr.* A candle placed at the foot of a grave or casket during a funeral or burial service.

footstone *n.* A stone marker placed at the foot of a grave.

fordo or **foredo** *tr. v. archaic.* To kill; murder.

foredo see **fordo**

forensic medicine *n. phr. Law.* The legal application of medical knowledge, esp. to determine cause of death.

forensic odontology *n. phr. Law.* The application of dentistry, esp. to identify a body.

forest cemetery *n. phr.* [A proposed term for] a type of cemetery characterized by trees, sculpture, and architecture.

forisfamiliate *tr. v.* To disinherit. *var.* forisfamiliated, forisfamiliates, forisfamiliating, *v.*

forlie *tr. v.* To smother to death by lying upon, esp. a mother on her child. *var.* forlied, forlies, forlying, *v.*

forma *n.* A grave beneath the floor of a catacomb.

Fortunate Fields *pl. n. phr. Gk. myth.* Elysian Fields.

fossarian *n. archaic.* A gravedigger; a clergyman who also digs graves.

fossor *n. archaic.* One employed to excavate galleries and graves in a catacomb; gravedigger.

foul play *n. phr. slang.* Murder.

foundation sacrifice *n. phr. Anthropol.* The practice of sealing a live human in the cornerstone of a building during its construction.

found in the bay *v. phr. slang.* Of a body discovered in the water, esp. the victim of a murder disguised as a drowning.

frag *tr. v. slang. Mil.* To assassinate an unpopular officer in Vietnam [shortening of fragmentation grenade].

fratricide *n.* The killing of one's brother or sister; one who kills his or her sibling. *var.* fratricidal, *adj.*

free *idiom.* Dead.

freestanding hospice *n. phr.* An independent hospice which employs its own staff and raises its own funds.

free ticket *idiom.* Murder.

freezee *n. slang.* Cryonics. A body in cryonic suspension.

French blade *n. phr. slang.* Guillotine.

frozen death *n. phr. slang.* Cryonic preservation [derogatory].

frugal one *n. phr. slang. Mexican.* Death in personified form.

fry *intr. v. slang.* To die in the electric chair; to be electrocuted. *tr. v. slang.* To execute by electrocution; to electrocute. *var.* fried, fries, frying, *v.*

F.S.C.A.P. *abbrev.* Funeral Service Consumer Arbitration Program.

F.S.I.D.S.P. *abbrev.* Federal SIDS Program.

F.T. *abbrev.* Foundation of Thanatology.

ft. c. *abbrev.* Foot candle.

FTS *abbrev.* Funeral Telegraph Service.

full couch *adj. phr.* With the casket lid raised completely; a body in a casket with the lid raised completely.

fun. *abbrev.* Funeral; funerary.

functional method see **itemization**

funeral *n.* The performance of rites, ceremonies, and customs associated with burial or cremation; an organized, purposeful, time-limited, group-

funeral achievement • funeral sermon 71

centered response to death [definition of the National Funeral Directors Association]; participants in a burial or memorial service. *slang.* Death; murder.

funeral achievement *n. phr. archaic.* A display of the family coat of arms on a house in which a death has occurred; hatchment.

funeral car *n. phr.* A hearse.

funeral coach *n. phr.* A hearse.

funeral customs *pl. n. phr.* Rites associated with death in a culture or religion.

funeral direction *n. phr.* Management of a funeral home.

funeral director *n. phr.* The owner or manager of a funeral home.

funeral establishment *n. phr.* A funeral home.

funeral etiquette *n. phr.* Customary behavior or rituals observed during a wake, funeral, or burial.

funeral expenses *pl. n. phr. Law.* The costs incurred from rites and ceremonies associated with burial.

funeral functionary *n. phr. archaic.* A funeral director's assistant.

funeral furnisher *n. phr. archaic.* A contractor of funeral services; an undertaker.

funeral furniture *n. phr.* see **funerary furniture**

funeral gloves *pl. n. phr. obs.* The customary gift presented as an announcement of a funeral in the 18th c.

funeral goods *pl. n. phr. Archeol.* Items buried with a corpse.

funeral home *n. phr.* An establishment in which bodies are prepared for burial or cremation and in which wakes and funerals are held.

funeral hymn *n. phr. Music.* A dirge.

funeral industry *n. phr.* The collective businesses involved in the disposal of the dead, esp. funeral homes, cemeteries, and crematories.

funeral in one's family *n. phr. slang.* Death; murder.

funeralization *n. Anthropol.* Activities, rites, and rituals associated with the final disposition of the dead in a culture.

funeral manager *n. phr.* A funeral director.

funeral music *n. phr. Music.* Dirges; hymns played during a funeral.

funeral oration *n. phr.* Funeral sermon.

funeral parlor *n. phr. archaic.* A funeral home.

funeral procession *n. phr.* A line of people or vehicles moving from a funeral to the place of burial.

funeral pyre *n. phr.* Materials gathered to burn a corpse as part of the funeral rite; incineration of a corpse.

funeral rite *n. phr.* The ceremony associated with the burial or cremation of the dead.

funeral sermon *n. phr.* A

speech by a minister at a funeral or memorial service.

funeral service *n. phr.* A rite held in the presence of the body, with open or closed casket; the profession of funeral directing.

funeral service education *n. phr.* Professional training in owning and operating a funeral home.

funeral service practitioner *n. phr.* A funeral director; embalmer.

funeral service room or **funeral service chapel** *n. phr.* A chamber in a funeral home in which funeral services are held.

funeral shelter *n. phr. obs.* A roofed structure under which the parson stands during burial services in the rain.

funeral tasks *pl. n. phr.* The duties associated with preparing a corpse for burial.

funeral train *n. phr. obs.* A rail system designed to carry caskets and mourners to cemeteries outside the city limits.

funeral trolley car *n. phr. obs.* A trolley car designed to transport the casket, undertaker, and bearers to the cemetery, with mourners following in conventional trolley cars.

funeral upholder see **upholder**

funeral vehicle *n. phr.* A hearse.

funerary *adj.* Associated with a funeral or burial.

funerary furniture or **funeral furniture** *n. phr.* Household goods buried with a corpse to provide comfort after death.

funerary offerings *pl. n. phr.* Gifts bestowed on the dead.

funereal *adj.* Associated with a funeral. *var.* funereally, *adv.*

funest *adj.* Causing death; fatal.

Furies or **Erinyes** *pl. n. Gk. myth.* Gods who punish by pursuing murderers until they are driven insane by remorse.

furnishing undertaker *n. phr. obs.* A colonial American undertaker who sold supplies to other undertakers in addition to offering funeral services to the public.

fusillade *tr. v.* To kill with a simultaneous or successive discharge from a number of firearms. *var.* fusilladed, fusillades, fusillading, *v.*

future home *n. phr. slang.* A cemetery; grave.

G

Gabriel *n. Judaism.* An angel of retribution and death.

Gaea or **Gaia** *n. Gk. myth.* Goddess of death and the afterlife.

G.A.F.D. *abbrev.* Guild of American Funeral Directors.

Gaia see **Gaea**

galgenmeister *n. Ger.* A hangman or executioner [lit., master of the gallows].

Galla or **Gallu** *n. Sumerian myth.* A demon of the underworld.

gallery 13 *n. phr. slang.* A prison graveyard.

gallows *n.* A structure consisting of two or more posts supporting a crossbeam from which a noose is suspended for execution by hanging; execution by hanging.

gallows bird *n. phr. slang.* One who deserves to be hanged.

gallows humor *n. phr.* Comic treatment of a frightening or serious situation.

gallows literature *n. phr.* Printed information about an execution or murder, esp. in the form of a broadsheet.

gallows man *n. phr. informal.* An executioner; an executioner's assistant.

gallowstree *n.* A gallows.

Gallu see **Galla**

gamble with death *idiom.* To attempt suicide.

ganch *n.* An apparatus used to impale. *tr. v.* To execute by impalement on stakes or hooks. *var.* ganched, ganches, ganching, *v.*

gang hit *n. phr. slang.* A gang murder.

garrote see **garrotte**

garrotte or **garrote** *n.* A method of execution in which the neck is broken by tightening an iron collar; a collar used for execution; strangulation. *tr. v.* To execute by garrotte; to strangle. *var.* garroter, *n.*

gas *tr. v.* To execute in a gas chamber. *var.* gassed, gasses, gassing, *v.*

gas chamber *n. phr.* A sealed chamber in which execution by poison gas is carried out.

gasphyxiation *n. slang.* Death resulting from exposure to poisonous gas. *var.* gasphyxiated, gasphyxiates, gasphyxiating, *v.*

gassing *pr.part.* Execution in the gas chamber.

gatekeeper *n. slang.* A person in an advantageous position to prevent suicide, esp. a health-care or social worker.

gavelkind *n. Law.* Equal inheritance.

Gehenna *n.* Hell; the place in which sinners are punished after death [from the Valley of Hinnom, south of Jerusalem].

G.E.I. *abbrev.* Grief Education Institute.

genocide *n.* The systematic extermination of a particular group of people; one who systematically kills members of a particular group. *var.* genocidal, *adj.*

geronticide *n.* The killing of people considered dependent or no longer productive, esp. the aged; one who kills people considered dependent or unproductive.

gest *abbrev. Ger.* Dead.

get *tr. v. slang.* To kill; murder, esp. in revenge. *var.* gets, getting, got, *v.*

get a free ticket or **get a one-way ticket** *v. phr. slang.* To be killed.

get a permanent or **have a permanent** *idiom.* To be executed by electrocution

getaway *n. slang.* Death.

get hers see **get his**

get his or **get hers** *idiom. Mil.* To receive a fatal wound in battle.

get it in the neck *v. phr. slang.* To be executed by hanging.

get it out *v. phr. slang.* To express one's grief.

get one's come-uppance *v. phr. slang.* To be killed, esp. in revenge.

get one's everlasting *idiom.* To be killed; to die.

get one's gruel *idiom.* To be killed.

get one's ticket punched *idiom.* To die; be killed.

get out from under *idiom.* To die.

get paid off *idiom.* To die.

get pooped *idiom.* To be killed.

get rid of *v. phr. slang.* To kill; murder.

get the ax *idiom.* To be killed.

get the business *idiom.* To be killed.

get the call *idiom.* To die.

get the skids *idiom.* To be killed.

get the works *idiom.* To be sentenced to death; to be killed.

get 30 *idiom.* To be killed.

G.G.P. *abbrev.* Good Grief Program [a bereavement organization].

ghastly *adj.* Associated with death or the spirits of the dead. *var.* ghastlier, *adj.*, ghastliness, *adj.*

ghettocide *n. slang.* A murder committed in the inner city.

ghost *n.* The spirit of a dead person, esp. as an apparition. *n. archaic.* The spiritual as opposed to the physical body. *var.* ghostly, *adj.*

ghost-soul *n. archaic.* The human spirit which inhabits the body and passes out of it at death.

ghoul *n.* A grave robber; one who delights in the morbid. *n. Islamic myth.* A demon who feeds on buried corpses. *var.* ghoulish, *adj.*, ghoulishly, *adv.*, ghoulishness, *n.*

ghuls *pl. n. Arab. myth.* Female cannibals who kill solitary desert travelers.

gibbet *n.* A gallows with a projecting arm from which the condemned is hanged. *tr. v.* To execute by hanging in chains or a cage until starved to death; to expose the tarred body of an executed criminal, esp. near the scene of the crime. *var.* gibbeted, gibbeting, gibbets, *v.*

giganticide *n.* The killing of a giant; one who kills a giant. *var.* giganticidal, *adj.*

gillette one's way out *v. phr. slang.* To commit suicide by slashing one's wrists with a razor blade [after the Gillette

Giltine • go into the shadows 75

Co., a manufacturer of shaving products].

Giltine *n. Lithuanian myth.* Goddess of death who strangles or suffocates the critically ill.

gimmaces *pl. n. archaic.* Chains used in gibbeting.

gisant *n.* A life-sized sculpture of a person on the lid of his or her tomb; a monument in which the body is depicted both as it looked in life and as it looks after decay.

give a permanent wave *idiom.* Electrocute.

give in *idiom.* To die.

give life the go-by or **give life the slip** *v. phr. slang.* To die.

give life the slip see **give life the go-by**

give one's everlasting *idiom.* To kill; murder.

give one the works *idiom.* To kill, esp. by shooting.

give short shrift to *idiom. archaic.* To allow a condemned criminal a brief time for confession before execution.

give the ax *idiom.* To kill; murder.

give the bump *idiom.* To kill; murder.

give the Grand Bounce *idiom.* To kill; murder.

give the last compliment *idiom.* To bury.

give the push or **give the push-off** *idiom.* To kill; murder.

give the rap *idiom.* To kill; murder.

give the shuffle *idiom.* To kill; murder.

give up *idiom.* To die.

give up the ghost *idiom.* To die; release one's soul.

give up the ship *idiom.* To die.

give up the struggle *idiom.* To die.

gloom *n.* A mournful atmosphere. *intr. v.* To be mournful. *tr. v. archaic.* To make mournful. *var.* gloomy, *adj.*, gloomily, *adv.*, gloominess, *n.*

go across or **go across the river** *idiom.* To die.

go across the river see **go across**

go belly up see **turn belly up**

go bung *idiom.* To die.

go cuckoo *idiom. slang.* To die.

go dead *v. phr. slang.* To die.

godly butchery *n. phr. obs.* The practice of drawing and quartering as a method of execution, thought by some to have justification in the Bible.

go down blazing *v. phr. slang.* To be killed, esp. shot to death.

God's acre *n. phr.* A cemetery, esp. a churchyard.

God's field *n. phr.* A cemetery.

go for the jugular *idiom.* To attack fatally [often used figuratively].

go home feet first *v. phr. slang. Mil.* To die in combat.

go home in a box *v. phr. slang. Mil.* To die in combat and have one's remains packaged and returned to the next of kin.

go into eclipse *idiom.* To die.

go into the shadows *idiom. Japanese.* To die [used of emperors].

golden room *n. phr.* The chamber in an ancient Egyptian tomb which contains the coffin and mummy.

gold star mother *n. phr. Mil.* A woman whose son has died in the armed forces.

go Lethewards *v. phr. poetic.* To die.

Golgotha *n.* The hill near Jerusalem where Jesus Christ was crucified [lit., place of the skull].

golgotha *n.* A place of burial or sacrifice.

gone *adj.* Dying; dead.

gone across the creek or **gone over the creek** *idiom.* Died of unnatural causes.

gone beyond *idiom. Fr.* The dead.

gone cold *adv. phr. slang.* Died.

gone for a Burton *idiom. Mil.* Drowned; died; presumed dead [after Burton Ale].

gone over the creek see **gone across the creek**

gone pffft or **gone phut** *idiom.* Dead.

gone phut see **gone pffft**

goner *n. slang.* A corpse; one marked for death.

gone the way of all flesh *v. phr. poetic.* Died.

gone to a better place or **gone to a better world** *v. phr.* Died.

gone to a better world see **gone to a better place**

gone to Davey Jones's locker *v. phr. slang. Nautical.* Died.

gone to glory *idiom.* Died.

gone to heaven *v. phr.* Died.

gone to one's maker *idiom.* Died.

gone to Riga *idiom. Ger.* Died.

gone under *idiom.* Died.

gone up salt river *idiom.* Died.

gone west *idiom.* Died.

good *adj. slang.* Dead.

go-off *n. slang.* Death.

go off the handle *idiom.* To die.

go out *idiom. Med.* To die.

go out in the country *idiom.* To be murdered, esp. by gangsters.

go over *idiom.* To die.

gore *n.* Blood; bloodshed.

gory *adj.* Associated with bloodshed and violence. *var.* gorier, goriest, *adj.*, gorily, *adv.*, goriness, *n.*

go the way of all flesh *v. phr. poetic.* To die.

go to grass *v. phr. Biblical.* To die; be buried.

go to kingdom come *v. phr. slang.* To die.

go to one's account *idiom.* To die.

go to one's just reward see **go to one's last reward**

go to one's ka *v. phr. Egypt.* To die.

go to one's last reward or **go to one's just reward** *idiom.* To die.

go to pot *idiom.* To be buried.

go to the last roundup *idiom.* To die.

go to the races *idiom.* To die.

go under *idiom. Med.* To die.

go up the flue *idiom.* To die.

go up the handle *idiom.* To die.

govi *n. Haitian myth.* A sacred

clay vessel used to house the spirit of the dead.
go west *idiom.* To die.
go without a passport *idiom.* To commit suicide.
G.P.G. *abbrev.* Grieving Process Group.
G.R. *abbrev.* Graves Registration.
gradual suicide *n. phr. Sociol.* Chronic self-destructive behavior.
Grand Bounce *idiom.* Murder.
Grandchildren's New Year *n. phr. Japanese.* A funeral.
grave *n.* An excavation for the burial of a corpse; a burial place; death.
grave-clothes *pl. n.* The garments in which a corpse is buried.
grave crimes *pl. n. phr. archaic.* Felonies including murder, manslaughter, and arson.
grave-dancer *n. slang.* One who profits from another's misfortune.
gravedigger *n.* One who excavates burial plots.
grave-finds *pl. n. Brit. Archeol.* Discoveries associated with tombs or burial places.
grave gifts *pl. n. phr.* Offerings buried with a corpse.
grave goods *pl. n. phr.* Items placed in a tomb for use by the deceased in the afterlife.
grave liner *n. phr.* A concrete or metal container in which a casket is buried to prevent the ground from settling.
grave one *n. phr. slang. Mexican.* Death in personified form.
grave orientation *n. phr. Archeol.* The direction in which a burial is aligned.
gravepost *n.* An upright wooden grave marker.
grave rails *pl. n. phr.* Wooden markers placed along the length of a grave with posts at head and foot and a board between.
grave recycling *n. phr.* The practice of reusing a grave by removing and storing the bones after the corpse decays.
grave robber *n. phr.* One who plunders tombs or graves for valuables; one who steals corpses, esp. for illicit dissection.
graveside service *n. phr.* A formal rite held at the cemetery in addition to or instead of a funeral service.
gravesite *n.* A burial plot.
Graves Registration Company or **Graves Registration** *n. phr. Mil.* Army units responsible for the burial of combat casualties overseas, the registering of army graves worldwide, and the return of personal effects to the next of kin.
gravestone *n.* A stone, often inscribed, which marks a burial site.
grave-watcher *n. Chinese.* A guard who protects the Imperial tomb.
grave wax *n.* A soapy substance which forms from the body under proper conditions of moisture and heat; adipocere.

graveyard *n.* A burial ground; cemetery.

the graveyard school *n. phr.* A group of Romantic poets, including Edward Young and Thomas Gray, who received their inspiration from churchyards.

grease the track *idiom.* To be run over and killed by a train.

Great Death *n. phr.* The Black Plague.

great divide *n. phr. slang.* The grave.

Great Leveller *n. phr.* Death in personified form.

Great Out *n. phr. slang.* Death.

Great Transfer *n. phr. Tibetan myth.* The complete translation of a body into the elements when the spirit is transferred.

Great Whipper *n. phr.* Death in personified form.

green funeral *n. phr. Indian.* An initial cremation ceremony followed by a memorial service a year later.

grief *n.* Deep mental anguish over the death of a loved one; sorrow.

grief counseling *n. phr.* Therapy after a death which addresses its physical, emotional, and social impact on survivors.

grief counselor *n. phr.* A therapist who assists the bereaved through the grieving process.

grief psychology *n. phr.* The study of individual human reaction to bereavement.

grief resolution *n. phr.* The final stage of bereavement in which the death is accepted.

grief work *n. phr.* The process of accepting and adjusting to the death of a loved one.

grieve *intr. v.* To mourn. *var.* grievingly, *adv.*, grieved, grieves, grieving, *v.*

grim *adj.* Ghastly; morbid. *var.* grimmer, grimmest, *adj.* grimly, *adv.*, grimness, *n.*

Grim Monarch *n. phr.* Death in personified form.

Grim Reaper *n. phr.* Death in personified form.

grisly *adj.* Gory. *var.* grislier, gristliest, *adj.*, grisliness, *n.*

gross estate *n. phr. Law.* Total value of a decedent's assets at his or her death.

ground burial *n. phr.* Interment in the earth.

grounded for good *v. phr. slang. Mil.* Of flyers who have died in combat; dead.

ground sweat *idiom.* Burial; grave.

group killers *pl. n. phr.* Mutual participants in a murder or series of murders.

grow stiff *v. phr. Old English.* To die.

GrReg or **grreg** *abbrev.* Graves Registration.

grreg see **GrReg**

GRS *abbrev.* Graves Registration Service.

Guan Di *n. Chinese myth.* A god of war.

Guede *n. Haitian myth.* The god of the dead.

guerilla see **guerrilla**

guerilla warfare see **guerrilla warfare**

guerrilla *n. Mil.* One who participates in irregular warfare, esp. as a member of an independent group.
guerrilla warfare or **guerilla warfare** *n. phr. Mil.* Irregular warfare by independent groups.
guillotine *n.* A machine equipped with a blade which falls between upright guides to behead a condemned person. *tr. v.* To behead with a guillotine [after Joseph I. Guillotin (1738–1814)]. *var.* guillotined, guillotines, guillotining, *v.*
Gula *n. Mesopotamian myth.* A goddess associated with the underworld.
Gun-Fon *n. African myth.* God of war.
gun-murder *n.* A homicide carried out with a firearm.
gw *abbrev. Mil.* Guerrilla warfare.
Gwydyon *n. Welsh myth.* God of war.
Gwynn *n. Celtic myth.* A god of the underworld.
gynaecide see **gynecide**
gynecide or **gynaecide** *n.* The killing of a woman; one who kills a woman. *var.* gynecidal, *adj.*

H

H *abbrev. Law.* Homicide.
h. *abbrev. Law.* Heir.
Ha *n. Egypt. myth.* God of the west associated with death.
Hachiman *n. Japanese myth.* God of war.
hadephobia *n. Psychol.* Fear of hell. *var.* hadephobic, *adj.* + *n.*
Hades *n. Gk. myth.* God of the underworld; abode of the dead.
hades *n.* Hell. *var.* hadean, *adj.*
had it *idiom.* Is weary and ready for death.
had one's name on it or **had one's number on it** *idiom.* Destined to cause one's death [used of a bullet or other missile].
had one's number on it see **had one's name on it**
haint *n. archaic.* A ghost, esp. when heard but not seen.
hair curler *n. phr. slang.* The electric chair.
half-couch *adj.* With the casket lid raised halfway; of a corpse in a casket with half the lid raised.
half-hanged *adj.* Having survived execution by hanging; having endured the punishment of half-hanging.
half-hanging *n.* A method of punishment or torture in which a person is slowly

lifted by a rope around the neck and lowered before death occurs.

halidom *n. archaic.* A holy relic.

Hall of Odin *n. phr. Norse myth.* Rocks from which the Berserkers jumped into the sea when they tired of living.

halter *n.* A hangman's noose.

hand down *v. phr. informal.* To arrange for the inheritance of after death.

hand in one's chips or **pass in one's chips** *idiom.* To die.

hand in one's dinner pail *idiom.* To die.

handle *n. slang.* To kill; murder. *var.* handled, handles, handling, *v.*

hand of glory *n. phr.* A hand cut off the body of an executed murderer, which is dried and used in magic spells; a charm made of the hand of an executed criminal.

hang *tr. v.* To execute by suspending by the neck, esp. by a rope noose. *var.* hanged, hanging, hangs, *v.*

hanged, drawn, and quartered *v. phr.* A method of execution in which the condemned is hanged and his or her body is dismembered and exposed.

hang in effigy *v. phr.* To symbolically execute a person by hanging a model of him or her; to conduct a mock execution.

hanging judge *n. phr. slang.* A judge who often sentences criminals to the death penalty.

hangman *n.* One employed to carry out sentence of death by hanging.

Hangman's Day *n. phr. obs.* Friday, the day of the week on which public executions were traditionally carried out in England.

hangman's meal *n. phr. archaic.* The last meal eaten by the condemned before execution.

hang up *idiom.* To die.

hang up one's harness or **hang up one's tackle** *idiom.* To die.

hang up one's hat *idiom.* To die.

hang up one's tackle see **hang up one's harness**

happy dispatch *n. phr. slang. Brit.* Hara-kiri.

Happy Hunting Ground *n. phr. Native American myth.* The afterlife [derogatory].

hara-kiri or **hari-kari** *n. Japanese.* Ritual suicide by disembowelment formerly practiced to avoid capture or dishonor or allowed as an alternative to execution.

Harendotes *n. Egypt. myth.* A protective goddess often depicted on sarcophagi.

hari-kari see **hara-kiri**

Haros *n. Gk. myth.* A huntsman on horseback who collects the souls of the dead.

hasn't come back for his or her cap *idiom.* Has been killed.

hatchet man *n. phr. slang.* A hired assassin.

hatchments *pl. n. archaic.* Announcements of death hung on a deceased person's house for a year or less and afterward displayed in the parish church; panel upon which a dead person's coat of arms is displayed during a funeral.

Hathor *n. Egypt. myth.* A goddess of slaughter and destruction who presides over funerals and consoles the dead.

haunt a grave *v. phr.* To visit a burial place often.

Haurvatat *n. Parsee myth.* A goddess associated with life after death.

have a funeral in one's family *v. phr. slang.* To be murdered, esp. by a hitman [used as a threat].

have a garden on the stomach *idiom.* To be buried.

have a permanent see **get a permanent**

have one's goose cooked *idiom.* To be killed.

have one's gruel *v. phr. slang.* To be killed.

having found rest see **at rest**

head-breaker *n. slang.* The part of a guillotine fastened over the head of the condemned to keep it steady.

head-chopping *pr.part. informal.* Beheading.

headcrusher *n. slang.* A hitman.

head for Cloud Nine *idiom. Med.* To die.

headhunter *n. Anthropol.* One who severs and preserves the heads of enemies as trophies. *slang.* A hired killer.

headhunting see **head-hunting**

head-hunting or **headhunting** *pr.part. Anthropol.* The practice of severing and preserving the heads of enemies as trophies.

headsman *n.* A public executioner who carries out sentences of death by beheading.

heads will roll *idiom.* Many will be guillotined [often used figuratively].

health alteration committee *n. phr. obs.* A special assassination unit of the CIA.

hearse *n.* A vehicle used to transport a casketed corpse to a church or cemetery. *obs.* A structure over a casket or tomb used to hold candles.

heart death *n. phr. Med.* The cessation of heartbeat and pulse; cardiac death.

hear the final call *idiom.* To die.

heaven *n.* The abode of souls granted eternal life. *var.* heavenly, *adj.*, heavenward, heavenwards, *adv.*

heavy fall *n. phr. slang. Fr.* Death.

hecatomb *n.* A mass slaughter; mass human sacrifice.

H.E.I. *abbrev.* Hospice Education Institute.

heir *n. Law.* One who inherits the estate of another, esp. under the terms of a will. *n.* A person who succeeds or will succeed to a hereditary position.

heir apparent *n. phr. Law.* One whose right to inherit is indefeasible by law provided he or she survives his or her ancestor.

heirdom *n. Law.* Hereditary succession; an inheritance.
heiress *n.* A female heir, esp. to great wealth.
heir presumptive *n. phr. Law.* One whose claim to inheritance or succession can be defeated by the birth of a closer relative prior to the death of the ancestor.
heirship *n. Law.* The condition of being an heir; the right to inherit.
Hekate *n. Gk. myth.* Goddess of the underworld and patron of necromancy.
Hel *n. Norse myth.* The abode of the dead; queen of the dead who rules all but slain warriors.
hell *n.* A place of punishment for condemned souls after death; the underworld. *var.* hellish, *adj.*
hell's half-acre *n. phr. slang.* A cemetery; churchyard.
hell-stone *n.* A large stone used to cover a grave.
hempen *adj. archaic.* Associated with a hangman's noose.
hempen cravat *n. phr. slang.* Noose.
hempen four-in-hand *n. phr. slang.* Hangman's noose.
hemp fever *n. phr. slang.* Death by hanging.
her. *abbrev. Law.* Heir.
herald *n. obs.* A 16th-c. occupation which included the duty of supervising funerals.
hereafter *n.* The afterlife.
heredipety *n.* Legacy hunting; attempting to beg an inheritance.

hereditable *adj. Law.* Capable of being inherited.
hereditament *n.* or **hereditaments** *pl. n. Law.* Property that can be inherited; everything that passes by right to the heir.
hereditary hangman *n. phr.* An executioner by hanging whose father was also an executioner.
hereditary succession *n. phr. Law.* Inheritance which applies in the absence of a valid will; intestate succession.
hereds *abbrev.* Heirs.
hereticide or **heretocide** *n.* Killing of a heretic; one who kills a heretic. *var.* hereticidal, *adj.*
heretocide see **hereticide**
heretrix or **heritrix** *n. Law.* An heiress.
hericide *n.* Killing of a lord or master; one who kills a lord or master. *var.* hericidal, *adj.*
heriot *n.* Payment or services rendered to a feudal lord on the death of a tenant.
heritable *adj.* Capable of inheriting or of being inherited.
heritage *n.* Property which is or can be inherited.
heritor *n. Law.* Inheritor.
heritress *n. Law.* An heiress.
heritrix see **heretrix**
Hermes *n. Gk. myth.* The god who leads the dead to Tartarus and revives those allowed to return.
hero *n.* One who has risked or sacrificed his or her life for a noble purpose. *var.* heroic, heroical, *adj.*, heroically,

Heros • holocaust

adv., heroicalness, heroics, heroine [fem.], heroism, *n.*
Heros *n. Thracian myth.* God of the dead.
heros *n. Gk.* Hero [used of the dead].
H.F.B.A. *abbrev.* Hebrew Free Burial Association.
Hibakusha *pl. n. Japanese.* Those people affected by an explosion [used of survivors of the atomic bomb dropped on Hiroshima by the U.S. during WWII].
hic jac *abbrev. Lat.* Here lies.
hic jacet *n. phr. slang. Lat.* Tombstone; epitaph [lit., here lies].
highbinder *n. archaic.* A professional killer; hired assassin.
high block *n. phr.* A headrest for execution by beheading which allowed the condemned to kneel and was usually reserved for royalty.
high-grief death *n. phr.* A death perceived by survivors as unjust or premature.
high-profile murder *n. phr.* A homicide with the potential to arouse widespread public interest or outrage.
Hine see **Hine-Nui-Te-Po**
Hine-nui-te-po or **Hine** *n. Maori myth.* Goddess of the underworld who originally caused death to enter the world.
hired gun *n. phr. slang.* A paid assassin.
hired mourner *n. phr.* One who is employed to grieve or wail at a funeral rite.

hit *n. slang.* An assassination. *tr. v. slang.* To kill; assassinate. *var.* hits, hitting, *v.*
hit home *idiom.* To inflict a mortal wound.
hit list *n. phr. slang.* A list of intended murder victims as drawn up by a crime syndicate.
hitman *n. slang.* Professional killer; hired assassin.
hit murder *n. phr. slang.* Killing by a hired assassin.
hit the rocks *idiom. Nautical.* To die.
H.J. *abbrev. Lat.* Here lies.
H.J.S. or **h.j.s.** *abbrev. Lat.* Here lies buried.
h.j.s. see **H.J.S.**
H.L.F. *abbrev.* Human Life Foundation.
HLS *abbrev. Law.* Holograph letter signed.
hobo short line *idiom.* Death caused by being struck by a train; suicide committed by allowing oneself to be struck by a train.
hogback *n. slang.* A Viking tombstone consisting of a large carved stone with a curved top.
hoist *tr. v. slang.* To hang. *var.* hoisted, hoisting, hoists, *v.*
hold up the Bermuda grass *idiom.* To be buried.
Holle *n.* Goddess of the underworld who receives the souls of the dead.
Holocaust *n.* The genocide of European Jews by the Nazis during World War II.
holocaust *n.* Great destruction,

84 holographic • house of vigor

esp. by fire. *var.* holocaustal, holocaustic, *adj.*
holographic or **olographic** *adj.* Of a handwritten will.
holographic will or **olographic will** *n. phr. Law.* A will written, signed, and dated entirely by the hand of the testator in the form of a letter.
holograph letter *n. phr.* A holographic will.
home *idiom.* Dead and with God in heaven.
homicidal mania *n. phr. Psychol.* A mental disorder manifesting itself as an urge to kill. *var.* homicidal maniac, *n.*
homicide *n. Law.* Killing of one person by another; one who kills another person. *var.* homicidal, *adj.*
Homicide City *n.* [Nickname given to] the city with the highest murder rate in a state or country.
homicide report *n. phr. Law.* The official written description of a murder.
homicidomania *n.* An insane compulsion to kill. *var.* homicidomaniac, *adj.* + *n.*
Homo necans *n. phr.* Human killer [species name proposed to replace *Homo sapiens*].
HomRep *abbrev. Law.* Homicide report.
honk out *idiom.* To die.
hop a twig *idiom.* To die.
hop off *idiom.* To die.
hop off the perch *idiom.* To die.
hop the last rattler *idiom.* To die [used of hobos].

Horae *pl. n. Gk. myth.* The three goddesses who guard the gates to heaven.
horizontal memorial *n. phr.* A slabstone or tablestone used to mark a grave.
hospice *n. Med.* A specialized health care program that serves patients with critical illnesses during the last days of their lives.
hospital autopsy rate *n. phr. Med.* The ratio of postmortem examinations performed in a hospital to the total number of deaths.
hospital-based hospice *n. phr. Med.* A hospice which provides for inpatient care within a hospital and offers home care through hospital staff or a local public health nursing agency.
hosticide *n.* The killing of one's enemy; one who kills one's enemy. *var.* hosticidal, *adj.*
Hotep *n. Egypt. myth.* A god personifying the Field of Reeds.
hot seat *n. phr. slang.* Electric chair.
hot shot *n. phr. slang.* A container of pure or poisoned heroin used to kill an informer.
hound of hell *n. phr. Gk. myth.* Cerberus.
house of eternity *n. phr. Egypt.* A tomb chapel.
house of the ka *n. phr. Egypt.* A tomb.
house of vigor or **house of vitality** *n. phr. Egypt.* An embalming workshop.

house of vitality see **house of vigor**

HRC *abbrev.* Human remains case.

HRIP *abbrev.* Here rests in peace.

H.R.I.P. *abbrev. Lat.* Here rests in peace.

H.S. *abbrev.* Hemlock Society [an organization in favor of active euthanasia]. *Lat.* Here is buried.

Hsi-Wang-Mu *n. Chinese myth.* God of plague and calamity who possesses the herb of immortality.

H.S.M.F. *abbrev.* Holocaust Survivors Memorial Foundation.

hud *n. obs.* A roofed structure in a churchyard used to shelter the parson during burial services in the rain.

huff *tr. v. slang.* To kill; murder. *var.* huffed, huffing, huffs, *v.*

Huitzilopochtli *n. Aztec myth.* God of war.

human cold storage *n. phr. slang.* Cryonic preservation [derogatory].

human dissection *n. phr. Med.* The autopsy of the human body, esp. for teaching purposes.

human fruit *n. phr. slang.* The victim of an execution by hanging; victim of a lynching.

human hyena *n. phr. slang.* A cannibal.

human remains case *n. phr.* A container used to transport a corpse, esp. by common carrier.

human sacrifice *n. phr.* Ritual killing of a person, esp. to propitiate a god; one who is ritually killed.

hummingbird *n. slang.* The electric chair.

Hunhau or **Ahpuch** *n. Mayan myth.* God of death and the underworld.

Hun-soul *n. Chinese myth.* An aspect of the spirit which survives death but does not survive cremation.

husband-killer *n.* A woman who murders her spouse. *var.* husband-killing, *pr.part.*

hydriotaphia *n. archaic.* Urn burial.

hypogeum *n.* A private or family sepulchre in a catacomb; an underground burial chamber.

hypoinjection *n.* The process of pumping embalming fluid directly into body tissues.

hypostasis *n. Med.* The settling of the blood in the body after death which causes discoloration.

hypoxemia *n. Med.* Lack of blood in the brain [the ultimate cause of every death].

hysterotomy *n. Med.* A caesarean delivery after which the baby is killed or allowed to die through neglect; a method of abortion in which the fetus and placenta are surgically removed through the abdomen.

I

I.A.C.M.E. *abbrev.* International Association of Coroners and Medical Examiners.

I.A.E.T.F. *abbrev.* International Anti-Euthanasia Task Force.

iafd *abbrev. Med.* Intentionally administered fatal dose.

I.A.N.D.S. *abbrev.* International Association for Near-Death Studies.

I.A.S.P. *abbrev.* International Association for Suicide Prevention.

I.A.W.P. *abbrev.* International Association for Widowed People.

ICam-srin see **Beg-tse**

I.C.A.R. *abbrev.* International Campaign for Abortion Rights.

ice *tr. v. slang.* To kill, esp. an informer. *var.* iced, ices, icing, *v.*

icebox see **ice box**

ice box or **icebox** *n. phr. slang.* A morgue, esp. in a prison.

ice coffin *n. phr. obs.* A coffin fitted with a cooling board to delay decomposition.

iceman *n. slang.* A killer; hitman.

I.C.F. *abbrev.* International Cremation Federation.

I.C.H.S.W.W. *abbrev.* International Committee for the History of the Second World War.

I.C.I.S. *abbrev.* International Council for Infant Survival.

I.C.S.A. *abbrev.* International Cemetery Supply Association.

ICU or **icu** *abbrev. Med.* Intensive care unit.

icu see **ICU**

identification *n.* The process of determining the identity of a corpse or corpses based on clothing, jewelry, fingerprints, teeth, tattoos, scars, and other physical evidence. *var.* identified, identifies, identify, identifying, *v.*

identity reconstruction *n. phr.* The adjustment of a surviving spouse to a new role in life without his or her partner.

ID racket see **id racket**

id racket *n. phr.* Illegal production of false documents, including death certificates.

I.F.A. *abbrev.* International Funeral Association.

Igau *n. Egypt. myth.* Anubis.

i.h. *abbrev. Lat.* Here lies.

I.I.S.D.I. *abbrev.* International Institute for the Study of Death and Immortality.

I.L.B. *abbrev.* Institute for Loss and Bereavement.

immolate *tr. v.* To kill sacrificially; to destroy. *var.* immolation, immolator, *n.*, immolated, immolates, immolating.

immortal *adj.* Having eternal

life or fame; associated with everlasting life. *n.* One who has eternal life or fame. *var.* immortality, *n.*, immortalize, immortalized, immortalized, immortalizing, *v.*
immortalism *n.* Perpetual survival of an incorporated soul.
immure *tr. v.* To entomb in a wall. *var.* immured, immures, immuring, *v.*
immurement *n.* Entombment, esp. of cremated ashes.
impale *tr. v.* To kill by piercing with a sharp object. *var.* impalement, impaler, *n.*, impaled, impales, impaling, *v.*
imperil *tr. v.* To put in a deadly situation. *var.* imperilment, *n.* imperiled, imperiling, imperils, *v.*
improper grief *n. phr.* Grief expressed by persons who are not expected to mourn and are therefore not the object of emotional and social support.
I.M.R. *abbrev.* Infant mortality rate; Institute for Mortuary Research.
Inanna see **Ishtar**
in articulo mortis *prep. phr. Lat.* At the point of death.
I.N.A.W.P. *abbrev.* InterNational Association for Widowed People.
inchoate dower *n. phr. Law.* A wife's share in her husband's lands prior to and contingent upon his death.
incineration *n.* Cremation.
incinerator *n.* Crematorium.
in cold blood *idiom.* Without compassion or mercy; deliberately and cruelly.

in cold storage *prep. phr. slang.* Dead and buried; cryonically preserved [derogatory].
incorruptible *n. Rom. Cath.* A saint whose body has resisted decay despite surrounding conditions, taken as proof of his or her sanctity.
indirect involuntary euthanasia *n. phr.* Euthanasia carried out by the doctor and family, with the patient's wishes unknown.
indirect voluntary euthanasia *n. phr.* Euthanasia requested by the patient.
in extremis *prep. phr. Lat.* At the point of death; in anticipation of death.
infanticide *n.* The killing of an infant; one who kills an infant. *var.* infanticidal, *adj.*
infant mortality rate *n. phr.* The number of deaths of children under one year of age per 1,000 live births.
inferiae *pl. n. phr. Lat.* Sacrifices made to the gods of the underworld.
inferno *n.* Hell.
inherit *tr. v.* To receive property by legal succession or will. *intr. v.* To claim a property bequeathed by will. *var.* inherited, inheriting, inherits, *v.*
inheritance *n. Law.* Property transferred to another by legal will; legal succession to a title.
inheritance powder *n. phr. slang.* Arsenic; poison.
inheritance tax *n. phr. Law.* A tax on property acquired upon a death.

inheritor *n.* One who inherits by succession or will.
inheritrix *n.* A woman who inherits by succession or will.
inhume *tr. v.* To bury a body in the earth. *var.* inhumation, inhumer, *n.*, inhumed, inhumes, inhuming, *v.*
in mem. *abbrev. Lat.* In memory of.
in memoriam *prep. phr. Lat.* In memory of.
inofficious *adj. Law.* Contrary to natural affection or moral responsibility [used of a will in which the testator disinherits a rightful heir without adequate reason].
in peril *prep. phr.* Of one whose death is likely and expected but not immediately.
inquest *n. Law.* A medical examiner's inquiry to determine the cause of a suspicious death; a jury called upon to decide the facts about a suspicious death.
insarcophagusment *n.* The deposit of a body in a sarcophagus.
inscription *n.* An epitaph carved or engraved on a gravestone.
installed in furnace No. 10 *idiom.* Dead; cremated.
instantaneous cadaveric spasm *n. phr.* An immediate rigor, usually in one part of the body upon sudden death involving violence or intense activity.
in storage *n. phr. slang.* Dead and buried.
intensive care *n. phr. Med.* Hospitalization which applies emergency medicine, new treatments, and life-prolonging technology.
intentional death *n. phr.* A killing in which the victim takes an active part in his or her death through deliberate or impulsive acts.
intentional natural mummification *n. phr. Anthropol.* Preservation of the body by purposely exploiting natural conditions of dryness, heat, cold, or absence of air.
inter *tr. v.* To bury in a grave or tomb. *var.* interred, interring, inters, *v.*
intermediate fetal death *n. phr. Med.* The death of a fetus occurring during the twenty-first to twenty-eighth week of gestation.
intermediate state *n. phr.* Purgatory.
interment *n.* Burial.
international disposal man *n. phr. slang.* A hired assassin, esp. working for a government espionage agency.
internecine *adj.* Fatal to both sides; associated with bloodshed or destruction.
internecion *n.* Mutual destruction.
in terrorem *prep. phr. Law.* Of a warning in a will which voids a legacy if it is disputed by the legatee.
interruption *n.* The period of time between clinical death and resuscitation. *Cryonics.* The period in which one is under cryonic suspension.

intestacy *n. Law.* The condition of dying without a valid will.
intestate *n. Law.* One who dies without executing a valid will. *adj. Law.* Without having executed a will.
intestate succession *n. phr. Law.* The disposition of property according to law when a person dies without leaving a valid will or without accounting for his or her entire estate.
in the dustbin *idiom.* Dead and buried.
in the hereafter *prep. phr. slang.* In heaven; in the afterworld.
intramural burial *n. phr.* Interment within city limits.
intumulate *tr. v.* To bury. *var.* intumulation, *n.*, intumulated, intumulates, intumulating, *v.*
inurnment *n.* The deposit of cremated ashes in an urn or other receptacle. *var.* inurned, inurning, inurns, *v.*
inventory *n. Law.* A detailed list of the property of a dead person.
Inviter to Funerals *n. phr. archaic.* A courier who delivered funeral notices and mourning cards.
involuntary euthanasia *n. phr.* Killing a person in what is believed to be his or her best interest, regardless of his or her own wishes.
involuntary manslaughter *n. phr. Law.* Unlawfully killing a person while committing a misdemeanor; commission of a legal act which produces death illegally or negligently.
I.O.G.R. *abbrev.* International Order of the Golden Rule [an organization of funeral directors].
iophobia *n. Psychol.* Fear of being poisoned. *var.* iophobic, *n.* + *adj.*
iron maiden *n. phr.* A medieval torture device consisting of an upright metal enclosure containing interior spikes on which the victim is impaled.
iron out *idiom.* To murder, esp. by shooting.
Irra see **Erra**
I.S. *abbrev.* Immortalist Society [a cryonics organization].
I.S.D.B. *abbrev.* Institute for Studies of Destructive Behaviors.
Isdes *n. Egypt. myth.* God and judge of the dead.
Ishtar *n. Sumerian myth.* A goddess of war and destruction.
Islands of the Blessed see **Isles of the Blessed**
Isle of the Blessed *n. phr. Gk. myth.* The place where those who are beloved of the gods dwell after death; heaven.
itemization or **functional method** or **multi-unit method** *n.* A method of pricing a funeral in which the cost of each item of service, facility, and transportation is listed separately.
ius gladii *n. phr. obs. Lat.* Authority to pronounce sentence of death.

I.W.G.C. *abbrev.* Imperial War Graves Commission.
I.W.P.S. *abbrev.* Institute of War/Peace Studies.
Ixtab *n. Mayan myth.* Goddess and guardian of suicides.
Izanami *n. Shintoism.* Goddess of the underworld.

J

Jack Ketch or **John Ketch, Esq.** *n. phr. archaic.* The nickname traditionally given to public executioners in England [after Richard Jacquet, infamous executioner at Tyburn in the 17th c].
janker *n. obs.* A large oblong stone or metal sheet used to cover a new grave to deter grave robbers.
Jarri *n. Hittite myth.* God of plague and pestilence.
J.C.M.E. *abbrev.* Joint Committee on Mortuary Education.
jeremiad *n.* A lamentation; a mournful story.
J.F.D.A. *abbrev.* Jewish Funeral Directors of America.
Jigoku *n. Japanese myth.* An underground inferno to which sinners are relegated after death.
John Ketch, Esq. see **Jack Ketch**
John R. Corpse *n. phr. slang.* A dead body, esp. one which is unidentified or unclaimed.
join the immortals or **be among the immortals** *idiom.* To die; to go to heaven.
join the majority *idiom.* To die.
jointure *n. Law.* Designation by a husband of property to be used to support his wife after his death; property set aside for the support of one's wife after one's death. *tr. v.* To will an estate to a woman to become effective on the death of her husband. *var.* jointress, *n.*
joint will *n. phr. Law.* A single will executed by two or more persons.
Jolly Roger *n. phr.* A black flag depicting a skull and crossbones and associated with pirates.
Judgment Day *n. phr. Judaism, Christianity, + Islam.* The day of God's final assessment of all human souls.
judicial hanging *n. phr.* Legal sentence of death by hanging.
judicial murder *n. phr.* Capital punishment.
juggernaut *n.* Something which elicits ruthless human sacrifice [after an idol of the Hindu deity Krishna under the

wheels of which worshippers are said to have sacrificed themselves during its annual procession].
jugulate *tr. v.* To cut the throat of; strangle. *var.* jugulated, jugulates, jugulating, *v.*
juice *idiom.* To electrocute. *var.* juiced, juices, juicing, *v.*
Jumala *n. Norse myth.* A god who determines length of life.
jump the last hurdle *idiom.* To die.
jungle warfare *n. phr. Mil.* Armed conflict carried out in a wooded area.
Jurojin *n. Japanese myth.* God of longevity.
justifiable homicide *n. phr. Law.* The legitimate killing of a person under the law, esp. by a police officer in the line of duty.
J.W.W *abbrev.* Jewish Widows and Widowers.

K

ka *n. Egypt. myth.* One's divine essence which remains in the world of eternity until death; spiritual life force.
Kaddish *n. Judaism.* A prayer recited by mourners after the death of a close relative.
Kami *pl. n. Japanese myth.* The deified spirits of dead ancestors [lit., superior ones].
kamikaze *n.* A Japanese pilot who carried out a suicide mission in World War II; an airplane to be flown in a suicide mission. *adj.* Suicidal.
kapout see **kaput**
Kapu mate see **Velu mate**
kaput or **kapout** *adj. slang.* Dead.
karao *n.* The custom of the marriage of a Hindu widow to her brother-in-law.
Karttikeya or **Skanda** or **Scanda** *n. Indian myth.* God of war.
kayoed for the long count *idiom.* Killed.
kba *abbrev.* Killed by air.
k.c. *abbrev. slang.* Kingdom come.
kd *abbrev.* Killed.
keelhauling *n. Nautical.* A punishment in which the victim was dragged beneath the vessel from side to side, often causing death from drowning or bleeding.
keel over *v. phr. slang.* To die.
keelraking *n. Nautical.* A punishment in which the victim was dragged beneath the vessel from stem to stern, often causing death from drowning or bleeding.
keen *n.* or **keening** *pr.part.* A ritualized wailing or lament for the dead, esp. praising his

or her virtues. *intr. v.* To lament loudly. *var.* keener, *n.*, keened, keening, keens, *v.*

keening see **keen**

keep body and soul together *idiom.* To remain alive; survive.

kelchyn *n. obs.* A payment exacted to compensate for a homicide.

Ke'lets *n. Siberian myth.* A demon of death who uses dogs to hunt down humans.

Kerberos see **Cerberus**

Keres *pl. n. Gk. myth.* Avenging goddesses of death; vengeful spirits of the dead.

kfo *abbrev. Law.* Killing federal officer.

kha *abbrev. Mil.* Killed by hostile action.

Khentimentiu *n. Egypt. myth.* A god who decides the fate of the dead.

khet *n. Egypt.* Corpse.

KIA or **kia** *abbrev. Mil.* Killed in action.

kia see **KIA**

kibosh *n. slang.* Death.

kiboshed *p.part.* Killed; murdered.

kick *intr. v. slang. Med.* To die. *var.* kicked, kicking, kicks, *v.*

kicked off *idiom.* Died.

kick into the beyond *idiom.* To kill; murder.

kick off *intr. v. phr.* To die.

kick-off *idiom.* Death.

kick the bucket *idiom.* To die.

kick the bucket from under *v. phr. slang.* To kill; murder.

kick up one's heels or **kick up one's toes** *idiom.* To die.

kick up one's toes see **kick up one's heels**

kifo *n. Swahili.* Death.

kill *tr. v.* To cause the death of; murder. *intr. v.* To cause death; commit murder. *n.* An act of killing. *var.* killed, kills, *v.*

killer *n.* One who causes the death of another. *adj.* deadly.

killer by persuasion *n. phr.* One who coerces another to commit murder.

killing *pr.part.* Murder; death. *adj.* Deadly. *var.* killingly, *adv.*

killing nurse *n. phr. obs.* A woman who takes in foster children for a flat fee and abuses them until they die.

killing power *n. phr.* The lethal potential of a bullet or weapon.

killing spree *n. phr.* A series of murders committed within a short span of time by one person.

kill off *v. phr.* To cause the death or extinction of.

kill zone *n. phr. Law.* The area of the human chest at which law enforcement officers are trained to aim when deadly force is necessary.

kilt *p.part. slang.* Killed; murdered.

kimona *n. slang.* Coffin.

kingdom come *n. phr. slang.* The afterlife.

kiss of death *idiom.* A direct cause of death or destruction [from the kiss by which Judas betrayed Jesus Christ].

kiss-off *n. slang.* Death.

kiss off *idiom.* To die.
Kiss of Peace *n.* A final gesture of affection given to a person after death. *obs.* A formal liturgical rite in which the deceased is kissed by survivors.
kiss one off *idiom.* To kill a person.
kiss oneself goodbye *idiom.* To commit suicide.
kiss the dust *idiom.* To die.
kitchen *n. slang. obs.* The area in Newgate Prison where executed corpses were roughly preserved with pitch for gibbeting.
kj *abbrev.* Killer judo.
kk *abbrev.* Killer karate.
klama *n. Gk.* Ritual weeping.
knell *intr. v.* To sound a funeral bell or toll. *tr. v.* To summon to a funeral by tolling. *n.* A toll; a distress signal. *var.* knelled, knelling, knells, *v.*
knock or **knock cold** *idiom.* To kill; murder. *var.* knocked, knocking, knocks, *v.*
knock cold see **knock**
knocked cold *idiom. Australian. Mil.* Killed.
knock off *idiom.* To kill; murder.
knock-off *idiom.* Death.
knock out *idiom.* To kill; murder.
knock over *idiom.* To kill; murder.
knock-over *idiom.* Murder.
knock the daylights out of *idiom.* To kill; murder.
knoll *tr.* + *intr. v. archaic.* To ring mournfully; knell.
k.o.'d *abbrev. slang.* Dead.
koimesis *n. Eastern Orthodox.* A feast day celebrating the death and assumption of the Virgin Mary.
konk-out *n. slang.* Death.
Kottavei *n. Indian myth.* Goddess of war.
kp *abbrev.* Kill probability.
Kuan-Ti *n. Chinese myth.* God of protection against the horrors of war.
Kuolema *n. Norse myth.* Death in personified form.
Kuthu *n. Sumerian myth.* The abode of the dead.
Kuzimo *n. Bantu myth.* An underground abode of the dead.
Kwei *pl. n. Chinese.* The spirits of the dead.
K.W.M. *abbrev.* Korean War Memorial.
K.W.V.M.A.B. *abbrev.* Korean War Veterans Memorial Advisory Board.

L

Lachesis *n. Gk. myth.* One of the three fates who determines the length of each human life.

lachrymatory *n. Archeol.* A small bottle found in ancient tombs and believed to have contained the tears of mourners.

Lady Guillotine *n. phr. archaic. Fr.* [A nickname for] the guillotine.

Lady of the West *n. phr. Egypt. myth.* [A nickname for] Hathor, goddess of destruction and the afterlife.

la fosse *n. phr. archaic. Fr.* Live burial, esp. as punishment.

L.A.F.S. *abbrev.* Los Angeles Funeral Society.

laid out *v. phr.* Arranged for display at a wake or funeral [used of a corpse]. *v. phr. slang.* Dead.

laid to rest *v. phr.* Dead and buried.

lament *n.* An expression of grief; elegy. *tr. v.* To grieve over; mourn for. *intr. v.* To wail. *var.* lamenter, *n.*, lamented, lamenting, laments, *v.*

lamia *n. Gk. myth.* A bloodsucking demon who abducts children; vampire.

land of Badb *n. phr. Ir. myth.* The battlefield.

Land of the Moon *n. phr. Eskimo myth.* The afterlife.

landowner *n. slang.* One who is dead and buried; corpse.

landscape cemetery *n. phr.* [A proposed term for] a type of future cemetery characterized by a landscaped, park-like setting.

lapidate *tr. v. archaic.* To stone to death. *var.* lapidation, lapidator, *n.*, lapidated, lapidates, lapidating, *v.*

lares *pl. n. Gk. + Rom. myth.* The souls of virtuous people.

larvae *pl. n. Gk. + Rom. myth.* The souls of wicked people.

last abode *idiom.* Cemetery; grave.

last anointing *n. phr. Rom. Cath.* A Holy Sacrament administered in anticipation of death [pref. **anointing the sick**].

last bow *idiom. Theater.* Death.

last breath *n. phr.* One's final aspiration before dying.

last call *idiom. Theater.* Death.

Last Confession *n. phr. Rom. Cath.* Making the sacrament of Holy Confession prior to execution.

last cue *idiom. Theater.* Death.

Last Day *n. phr. Judaism, Islam, + Christian.* The Day of Judgment.

last days *pl. n. phr.* The period preceding a person's death.

last debt *idiom.* Death.
last go-off *n. phr. slang.* Death.
last home *idiom.* Cemetery; grave.
Last Judgment *n. phr.* The final assessment of all souls by God.
last laugh *n. phr. slang.* The sound a person makes when a bullet penetrates the chest cavity.
last lodging *idiom.* Grave.
last meal *n. phr.* The final meal eaten by the condemned before execution.
last mile *n. phr. slang.* The walk the condemned makes from the prison cell to the place of execution.
last muster *idiom.* Death.
last oblivion *idiom.* Death.
last offices *pl. n. phr.* Tasks carried out to prepare a corpse for burial.
last rattler *idiom.* Death.
last respects *pl. n. phr.* A show of regard for the dead, esp. by attending his or her funeral.
last rites *n. phr. Rom. Cath.* The Holy Sacrament of Annointing the Sick.
last roll call *idiom.* Death.
last roundup *idiom.* Death.
last send-off *idiom.* Death.
last suit *idiom. obs.* The chains or cage in which an executed criminal's body was exposed.
last waltz *idiom.* The condemned prisoner's walk to the place of execution.
last will and testament see **will**
last wish *n. phr.* A final request granted to a condemned prisoner prior to execution.
last words *pl. n. phr.* The final communications of a person at the moment of expiration; words spoken on a death-bed.
late *adj.* Dead [used before the name of one who has recently died].
late fetal death *n. phr. Med.* Death of a fetus occurring after twenty-eight weeks of pregnancy.
laudation *n.* A eulogy.
launch into eternity *v. phr. slang. Nautical.* To die.
laundered man *n. phr. slang.* One who is smuggled into another country, taught its customs, and trained and used as an assassin.
lay down one's knife and fork see **lay down one's shovel and hoe**
lay down one's life *v. phr.* To die for one's country; to sacrifice one's life for a particular cause.
lay down one's shovel and hoe or **lay down one's knife and fork** *idiom.* To die.
lay down on the job *idiom.* To die.
lay 'em down *idiom.* To die.
layer out of the dead *n. phr. obs.* One who washes, dresses, and prepares a body for viewing; a funeral director.
laying-out *n. phr.* The preparation of a corpse for viewing or burial.
lay one's bones *v. phr. slang.* To be buried.
lay on the shelf *idiom.* To kill; murder.

lay out *v. phr.* To prepare a corpse for burial, esp. at home. *slang.* To kill; murder.
lay out cold *idiom.* To kill; murder.
laystall *n. obs.* A cemetery.
lay to rest *v. phr.* To bury or entomb.
lay up in lavender *v. phr. obs.* To lay out and embalm a body with herbs.
lay violent hands on oneself *v. phr.* To commit suicide.
LD *abbrev. Med.* Lethal dose.
ld *abbrev. Med.* Lethal dose.
ld50 *abbrev. Med.* Median lethal dose.
L.D.P. *abbrev.* Living/Dying Project.
lead apes in hell *idiom.* To die unmarried.
lead away *v. phr. Lat. + Gk.* To execute.
lead-poison *tr. v. slang.* To shoot and kill.
lead poisoning *n. phr. slang.* A shooting death.
leaping-board *n. archaic.* A wooden grave marker consisting of two posts and a board which extends lengthwise from head to foot.
least fatal dose *n. phr. Med.* The smallest quantity of a substance which may cause death.
leave feet foremost *v. phr.* To die, esp. in a prison or hospital.
leave one leaning *idiom.* To kill; murder.
ledger stone *n. phr.* A large flat stone, often inscribed, which covers a grave.

legacy *n.* Property bequeathed by will; something which perpetuates identity after death.
legal death *n. phr. Law.* The status of no longer living as recognized by the state.
legal intervention *n. phr. Law.* Death brought about by a law enforcement officer in the line of duty.
legatee *n. Law.* One who receives a legacy.
legator *n. Law.* One who makes a will; testator.
Lelwani *n. Hittite myth.* Deity of the underworld associated with charnel houses and mausolea.
lemures *pl. n. Gk. + Rom. myth.* The souls of the wicked who wander at night.
Lemuria *n. Rom. myth.* The semi-annual festival at which the ghosts of the dead were honored.
L.E.S. *abbrev.* Life Extension Society [a cryonics organization].
lethal *adj.* Deadly; associated with death. *var.* lethally, *adv.*, lethality, *n.*
lethal dosage or **lethal dose** *n. phr.* The amount of a drug which will cause death.
lethal dose see **lethal dosage**
lethal injection *n. phr.* A legal sentence of death by administering a fatal dose of poison by needle.
lethality *n.* Deadliness.
Lethe *n. Gk. myth.* The river of forgetfulness bordering Hades. *var.* lethean, *adj.*

lethiferous *adj.* Deadly; destructive.

letters of administration *pl. n. phr. Law.* A document in which a person is authorized to administer the estate of one who has died intestate or without appointing an executor.

letters testamentary *pl. n. Law.* A document which legally informs an executor of his or her appointment and authorizes the discharge of responsibilities under the will.

letters to the dead *pl. n. phr. Egypt.* Messages conveyed from the living to the dead on the surfaces of pottery bowls containing food offerings.

level four *n. phr. Med.* A lethal dose or injection of a drug which causes breathing to stop.

levirate *n.* The practice of the marriage of a man to his brother's widow under ancient law. *var.* leviratic, *adj.*, leviratical, *adj.*

levirate marriage *n. phr. Hebrew.* Sexual intercourse with the widow of one's brother to ensure a male heir.

LFD *abbrev. Med.* Least fatal dose.

lfd *abbrev. Med.* Least fatal dose.

libera *n. archaic. Rom. Cath.* The Rite of Absolution recited over the casket.

libido moriendi *n. phr. Psychiatry.* Death drive.

Libitina *n. Rom. myth.* Goddess of corpses, burials, and funeral arrangements. *n. poetic.* Death.

libitinarius *n. obs. Lat.* The funeral director in an ancient Roman funeral.

lich *n. archaic.* Corpse.

lich bell *n. phr. archaic.* A chime announcing a death; toll.

lich gate *n. phr. archaic.* The gate in a cemetery or churchyard through which the casket was carried; a roofed structure to protect pallbearers from the weather before the burial service.

lich rest *n. phr. archaic.* The grave.

lich stone *n. phr. archaic.* A stone on which the casket was placed before the burial service.

lich way *n. phr. archaic.* The path over which the casket was carried to the cemetery or churchyard.

licked *p.part. slang.* Dead.

lick the dust *idiom.* To be killed.

liebestol *n. Ger.* The belief that lovers reunite after death.

lie in state *v. phr.* To be put on public display after one's death, esp. temporarily.

lie like an epitaph *v. phr. informal.* To exaggerate.

life *n.* The period of time between one's birth and death.

life after death *n.* Afterlife; immortality.

lifeboat *n. slang.* The commutation of a death sentence.

life expectancy *n. phr.* The

average number of years of life which remain to one of a certain age under current conditions.
life expectancy at birth *n. phr.* The average number of years of life which one born at a certain time will live based on contemporary age-specific death rates.
life extension *n. phr.* Technological or other means of prolonging life.
life history *n. phr.* The pattern of changes experienced by an organism from conception to death.
life-in-death *n.* Afterlife.
life insurance *n. phr.* A purchased policy which guarantees a specific sum of money to a designated beneficiary upon the death of the insured.
lifeless *adj.* Dead. *var.* lifelessly, *adv.*, lifelessness, *n.*
life-or-death *adj.* Life-threatening; critical.
life-prolonging *adj.* Capable of postponing death.
life review *n. phr.* An experience of one near death in which scenes from life seem to flash before one's eyes; a stage of dying in which one relives important memories or replays of one's entire life history.
life signal *pl. n. phr.* An invention designed to indicate to the living whether a buried body retains life.
lifespan *n.* The period of time between birth and death.

life-support equipment see **life-support system**
life-support system or **life-support equipment** *n. phr. Med.* Hospital equipment used to save or sustain the life of one who may be unable to survive independently.
lifetime *n.* The period of time between birth and death.
lifted up *v. phr. archaic.* Crucified.
lights out *idiom.* Death; time to die.
like crows on a corpse *idiom.* Very quickly.
like death warmed over *idiom.* Corpselike.
limbo *n. Christian.* The abode of the unbaptized after death; abode of souls of people excluded from heaven for reasons other than sin.
line-of-duty death *n. phr. informal. Law.* The killing of a law enforcement officer while he or she is on duty.
lipsanotheca *n.* A container for holy relics.
liquidate *tr. v.* To murder; destroy. *var.* liquidation, liquidator, *n.*, liquidated, liquidates, liquidating, *v.*
liquidated *p.part. slang.* Dead.
literary executor *n. phr.* One entrusted with managing the papers and unpublished works of an author who has died.
litigation *n. Law.* A civil suit brought to contest a will.
little window *n. phr. slang. Fr.* The guillotine.
live *intr. v.* To survive; remain

liver death • loss of life 99

in human memory. *var.* lived, lives, living, *v.*

liver death *n. phr. Med.* Sudden death following surgery on the gallbladder and bile tracts.

living dead *n. phr. slang. Med.* One who is brain-dead. *pl. n.* Reanimated corpses which often attack the living.

living-dying interval *n. phr.* The period before death.

living will *n. phr.* A document used to state in advance one's wishes regarding use of life-sustaining procedures when dying; a will in which one requests that he or she be allowed to die rather than to prolong life with the support system, esp. in the case of terminal illness.

livor mortis *n. phr. Med.* The color of a corpse, esp. used to determine time of death.

L.L. *abbrev.* Let Live [an organization opposed to capital punishment].

Llorona *n. Sp. myth.* A female spirit who lures people to their deaths by drowning.

lockman *n. archaic. Scottish.* A hangman [from the practice of allowing the executioner a lock of meal from each sack in the city market].

loculus *n., pl.* **loculi** A grave cut in the wall of a catacomb.

loimic *adj.* Associated with plague.

loimology *n.* Study of plagues. *var.* loimologist, *n.*

longevity *n.* A long life; length of life. *var.* longevous, *adj.*

long good-bye *idiom.* Final leave-taking before death or execution.

long home *n. phr. slang.* The grave.

long knife *n. phr. slang.* An assassin; hitman.

long pig *n. phr.* Human flesh prepared as edible meat.

look through cottonwood leaves *idiom.* To be executed by hanging; to be lynched.

loom *n. archaic. slang. Scottish.* Property other than real estate which is inherited after the death of the owner.

loon-slatt *n. Scottish. obs.* The hangman's fee.

Lord High Executioner *n. phr. archaic.* [A title given to] a hangman in England.

Lord of the Cave Mouth *n. phr. Egypt. myth.* Anubis, god of the dead.

Lord of the Divine Hall *n. phr. Egypt. myth.* Anubis, god of the dead.

lose *tr. v.* To be deprived of by death. *slang.* To kill; murder. *var.* loses, losing, lost.

lose breath *v. phr. Borneo.* To die.

lose the decision *idiom.* To die.

lose the number of one's mess *idiom. Nautical.* To be killed.

L.O.S.S. *abbrev. obs.* Loving Outreach for Survivors of Sudden-Death.

loss *n.* One who has died, esp. leaving survivors; suffering caused by a death.

losses *pl. n.* Casualties.

loss of life *n. phr.* Death, esp. caused by disaster or accident.

lost *p.part. slang.* Dead; murdered.
louisette *archaic. Fr.* The guillotine.
louison *archaic. Fr.* The guillotine.
love-lorn *adj.* Deprived of one's lover by death.
low block *n. phr. archaic.* A headrest for execution by beheading which requires the condemned to lie prone.
lower world *n. phr.* The abode of the dead beneath the surface of the earth.
low grief death *n. phr.* A death with minimal impact, such as that of a newborn baby, aged person, or terminal patient.
LSE *abbrev. Med.* Life support equipment.
LSS *abbrev. Med.* Life support system; lifesaving service.
Lug *n. Celtic myth.* God of war.
lugubrious *adj.* Mournful, esp. exaggeratedly. *var.* lugubriously, *adv.*, lugubriousness, *n.*
Lugus see **Lug**
lunette *n.* The semi-circular depression which steadies the head of a person executed by guillotine.
lust killer *n. phr.* A serial murderer.
lust murder *n. phr.* A serial murder; a killing which sexually stimulates the murderer.
L.W.C.A.A. *abbrev.* Liberated Women's Coalition Against Abortion.
lych see **lich**
lychgate see **lichgate**
lychweake *n. archaic.* A deathwatch; wake.
lying in state see **lie in state**
lynch *tr. v.* To execute without legal process, esp. by hanging; to kill by mob action. *var.* lynched, lynches, lynching, *v.*
lynch-execution *n.* A lynching.
lynching *n.* A hanging done without legal legal process, esp. by a mob.
lynch law *n. phr.* The punishment of suspected criminals without due process of law.
lynch-murder *n.* A lynching.
lynch-victim *n.* One who has been lynched.
lypemania *n.* A condition of extreme mournfulness. *var.* lypemaniac, *adj.* + *n.*

M

m. *abbrev.* Martyr. *Lat.* Of death.
Maat *n. Egypt. myth.* God who weighs souls.
macabre *adj.* Suggestive of death and decay; representing or associated with death. *var.* macabrely, *adv.*

macrobian *adj.* Long-lived.
macrobiosis *n.* Longevity. *var.* macrobiotic, *adj.*, macrobiote, *n.*
mactation *n.* A sacrifice or slaughter.
MAD *abbrev. Mil.* Mutual assured destruction.
M.A.D. *abbrev. Mil.* Mutual assured destruction.
madonna della febre *n. phr. Ital.* A depiction of the dead body of Jesus Christ in the arms of his mother.
Mag Mel *n. Celtic myth.* A plain occupied by the souls of the dead and characterized by pleasure and feasting.
Mahasakti *n. Indian myth.* Goddess of war.
Mahuika *n. Polynesian myth.* Goddess of the edges of the underworld.
Maiden *n. archaic slang. Scottish.* The gibbet.
makarios *adj. Gk.* Blessed [used of the dead].
makarites *n. Gk.* Blessed person [used of the dead].
make a corpse of *v. phr. slang.* To kill; murder.
make a die or **make a die of it** *v. phr. slang.* To die.
make a die of it see **make a die**
make a hole in the water *idiom.* To drown oneself.
make bones *v. phr. slang.* To assassinate; murder.
make dead *v. phr. slang.* To kill; murder.
make meat of *v. phr. slang.* To kill; murder.
make mincemeat of *v. phr. slang.* To kill; murder.
Make my day! *Exclam.* Do something which would justify my fatally shooting you [said by Clint Eastwood in his role as "Dirty Harry" in films].
make one easy *idiom.* To kill; murder.
make one go cool *idiom.* To kill; murder.
make one's final exit *v. phr. slang.* To die.
make out of the way *v. phr. slang.* To kill; murder.
make short work of *idiom.* To kill.
malice aforethought *n. phr. Law.* A deliberate intent to kill.
Mamitu or **Mammitu** or **Mammetu** *n. Akkadian myth.* A judge in the underworld.
Mammetu see **Mamitu**
Mammitu see **Mamitu**
Manala or **Tuonela** *n. Norse myth.* The underworld inhabited by mortals awaiting rebirth.
man box *n. phr. slang.* A casket.
man-eater *n.* A cannibal.
Manes *pl. n. Rom.* The deified souls of the dead.
manes *pl. n. Gk.* + *Rom. myth.* The souls of the dead.
man. one *abbrev. Law.* First degree manslaughter.
manqueller *n. archaic.* Murderer.
manslaughter *n. Law.* The unintentional death of a person brought about through another's carelessness or neglect; the unlawful killing

of one person by another without premeditation.
manslayer *n.* A murderer; an animal that kills a human being.
man. two *abbrev. Law.* Second degree manslaughter.
manufactured lightning *n. phr. slang.* The electric chair.
marabout *n. Moslem.* The tomb of a holy man or a shrine to his memory.
marantology *n. Med.* [A proposed term for] a specialty field in which the aged and incurable would be cared for and allowed to die without the use of life-support systems. *var.* marantologist, *n.*
Marble City see **marble orchard**
marble orchard or **Marble City** *n. phr. slang.* A cemetery.
Marg *n. Persian myth.* Asto Vidatu.
marital homicide *n. phr. Law.* Killing one's spouse.
mariticide *n.* Killing of one's husband; one who kills one's husband.
mark *tr. v. slang.* To order the murder of. *var.* marked, marking, marks, *v.*
marker *n.* A gravestone.
Mars *n. Rom. myth.* God of war.
mart. *abbrev.* Martyr; martyrology.
martyr *n.* One who sacrifices his or her life rather than renounce religious convictions. *tr. v.* To make a martyr of. *var.* martyred, martyring, martyrs, *v.*

martyrdom *n.* The condition of being a martyr; the mortal suffering of a martyr.
martyrize *tr. v.* To martyr. *var.* martyrized, martyrizes, martyrizing.
martyrolatry *n.* Excessive veneration of martyrs.
martyrology *n.* A list or history of religious martyrs, the study of martyrs. *var.* martyrologist, *n.*
martyry *n.* A church constructed over the tomb of a martyr.
massacre *n.* The wanton killing of many people. *tr. v.* To kill indiscriminately; slaughter. *var.* massacrer, *n.*
massacree *n. slang.* A massacre.
mass-hanging *n.* The execution of three or more persons at one time on the gallows.
mass killing *n. phr.* A massacre.
mass murder *n. phr.* The killing of four or more victims in close proximity of time and place [often used mistakenly as a synonym of **serial murder**].
Mass of Christian Burial *n. phr. Rom. Cath.* The rites of interment.
mass suicide *n. phr.* A number of suicides committed simultaneously and identically, esp. for an altruistic purpose.
mastaba *n.* An ancient Egyptian tomb shaped like a truncated pyramid and containing an underground burial chamber.

master of high works *n. phr. slang.* Hangman.

masturbatory strangulation *n. phr.* Autoerotic strangulation.

Mater Dolorosa *n. phr. Ital.* The depiction of the Virgin Mary grieving the death of her son Jesus Christ, esp. at the foot of the cross [lit., sorrowing mother].

mati *n. Indonesian.* Death.

matricide *n.* The killing of one's mother; one who kills one's mother. *var.* matricidal, *adj.*

matriherital *adj.* Pertaining to inheritance in the female line of a family.

mausoleum *n.* A large tomb housing above-ground burial of an individual or family; a structure containing niches for above-ground burial of human remains [after King Mausolus (d. 353 B.C.) of Caria, whose tomb was one of the Seven Wonders of the World]. *var.* mausolean, *adj.*

Mayin *n. Siberian myth.* Supreme god who receives the souls of those who have led a good life.

mazzatello *n.* A method of execution in which the condemned was knocked unconscious and his or her throat then slit; the heavy mallet or poleaxe used to knock a condemned person unconscious before slitting his or her throat.

M.B.A. *abbrev.* Monument Builders of America.

M.B.N.A. *abbrev.* Monument Builders of North America.

mbt *abbrev.* Murder before treason.

M.C.A. *abbrev.* Memorial Craftsmen of America.

M.C.P.L. *abbrev.* Minnesota Center for Pregnancy Loss.

M.D.I. *abbrev.* Mortuary Designs International.

ME *abbrev.* Medical examiner.

M.E. *abbrev.* Medical examiner.

meanings of death *pl. n. phr. Sociol.* The ways in which dying is understood by a patient.

measure out *idiom.* To kill; murder.

meat *n. slang.* A corpse.

meat-axe *tr. v. slang.* To kill; murder. *var.* meat-axed, meat-axes, meat-axing, *v.*

meat wagon *n. phr. slang.* A van or other vehicle used to transport bodies to the morgue.

mechanic *n. slang.* An assassin.

mechanisms of death *pl. n. phr. Biol.* The physical processes of dying.

medical death *n. phr.* The cessation of all functions of human life.

medical examiner *n. phr.* A city or county official legally authorized and medically qualified to perform autopsies to determine causes of death.

medical-legal autopsy *n. phr. Law + Med.* Examination of a body, the findings of which may be required by a court of law.

medical vampirism *n. phr.* A

thirst for human blood satisfied by murder.
medicide *n.* Physician-assisted suicide; euthanasia. *var.* medicidal, *adj.*
meet *intr. v. Lat.* + *Gk.* To die.
meet one's allotted day *v. phr. Lat.* + *Gk.* To die.
megacorpses *pl. n. Mil.* One million corpses [used as a unit in reference to atomic warfare].
megadeath *n. Mil.* One million deaths [used as a unit in reference to nuclear warfare].
mem. *abbrev.* Memorial.
memento mori *n. phr.* A reminder or symbol of death or mortality, esp. a skull [lit., remember that you must die].
meml. *abbrev.* Memorial.
memorial *n.* A gravestone; monument erected over the tomb of a saint or martyr.
memorial cards *pl. n. phr. archaic.* Commemorative cards distributed as announcements of a funeral in the 19th c.
Memorial Day *n. phr.* A day designated to commemorate the dead, esp. of the armed services.
memorial music *n. phr.* Funeral music.
memorial park *n. phr.* A cemetery, esp. one which does not allow upright monuments.
memorial rite *n. phr.* A funeral or memorial service.
memorial service *n. phr.* A rite held in place of or in addition to a funeral service, at which the body is not present.
Memorial Services *pl. n. phr.* A department of the U.S. Army in charge of registering army graves throughout the world.
memorial society *n. phr.* A non-profit organization which makes advance arrangements to provide each member with a simple dignified funeral at a reasonable, fixed price; a group which provides information and advice on immediate post-death activities.
memorial tablet *n. phr.* A tombstone, esp. one which is horizontal.
memory picture *n. phr.* A positive and lasting mental image of a dead person, esp. a family member.
memory place *n. phr.* An area in a home in which a deceased family member is commemorated.
menology *n.* A calendar of the feast days of saints and martyrs.
Menthu see **Mentu**
Mentu or **Menthu** *n. Egypt. myth.* God of war.
merchant of death *n. phr.* [Nickname given to] a seller of alcohol, drugs, weapons, or other merchandise which may cause death.
mercy *n.* Commutation of a death sentence; sparing from execution.
mercy death *n. phr.* Mercy killing.
mercy killing *n. phr.* Unrequested taking of one's life by another to prevent further suffering; euthanasia.

Meresger *n. Egypt. myth.* Protective goddess of the Theban necropolis.

Meslamta'ea *n. Sumerian myth.* God of war.

metabolic death *n. phr.* A state of unconsciousness in which the organs and cells of the body can be kept alive by machines.

metamorphosis *n.* Belief in immediate rebirth after death without consciousness of previous existence.

metaphorical death *n. phr.* Symbolic or partial death.

metempsychosis *n., pl.* **metempsychoses** Passage of the soul from one body to another at death. *var.* metempsychose, metempsychosed, metempsychoses, metempsychosing, *v.*

metensomatosis *n.* Passage of the soul from one body into another before or after death.

MFD or **mfd** *abbrev.* Minimum fatal dose.

mfd see **MFD**

M.I. *abbrev.* Monumental inscription.

miasma *n.* A poisonous atmosphere formerly thought to arise from decaying matter in cemeteries. *var.* miasmal, miasmatic, miasmic, *adj.*

Mictlan *n. Aztec myth.* Hell; the abode of the dead.

Mictlantecutli *n. Aztec myth.* God of death and lord of the underworld.

military execution *n. phr. Mil.* Execution by a military firing squad.

military funeral *n. phr. Mil.* The funeral of a veteran or member of the armed forces, often including the traditional twenty-one gun salute.

mind day or **year day** *n. phr.* The anniversary of a death; the day on which a death is commemorated by a requiem service.

minimum fatal dose *n. phr. Med.* The smallest quantity of a poison which will cause death.

minister of consolation *n. phr.* A member of the clergy who offers emotional support to survivors at the time of death.

Minos *n. Gk. myth.* One of the three judges of the dead.

M.I.P.F. *abbrev.* Memorial Industry Promotion Fund.

mirabelle *n. slang. Fr.* The guillotine.

Miren see **Fatit**

miscarriage *n. Med.* The expulsion of the ovum or embryo from the uterus within the first six weeks of pregnancy; premature expulsion of a nonviolable fetus from the uterus.

misericord see **misericorde**

misericorde or **misericord** *n. obs.* A dagger used in Medieval times to dispatch a fatally wounded knight.

misopolemical *adj.* Hating war.

missing *pr.part. slang.* Dead.

Mister Mose *n. phr.* Death in personified form.

Mithra *n. Persian myth.* God of war and a judge of the dead.

mithridatize *tr. v. Med.* To render immune to poison by administering gradually increasing doses.

MLD or **mld** *abbrev. Med.* Median lethal dose; minimum lethal dose.

mld see **MLD**

mld50 *abbrev. Med.* Minimum lethal dose.

MM or **Mm** *abbrev.* Martyrs.

Mm see **MM**

M.M.P.N.C. *abbrev. Mil.* Medical Materiel Program for Nuclear Casualties.

moan *n.* A sound of grief; lamentation. *intr. v.* To wail or lament. *var.* moaned, moaning, moans, *v.*

moarte *n. Rumanian.* Death.

modernicide *n.* The killing of a person with modern views; one who kills a person with modern views.

moirologist *n.* A hired mourner.

mold *slang. Brit.* The earth of the grave.

molder or **moulder** *intr. v.* To become dust by decaying naturally [used of a corpse].

moloch *n.* A power gratified only by human sacrifice [from a god in the Old Testament who required worshippers to sacrifice children].

Moma *n. S. Amer. Indian myth.* Supreme deity responsible for death and the underworld.

mon. *abbrev.* Monument; monuments.

monody *n.* A personal lament or elegy. *var.* monodic, monodical, *adj.*, monodically, *adv.*, monodist, *n.*

Monsieur de Paris *n. phr. slang. Fr.* A guillotine operator; an executioner.

montjoy *n.* A pile of stones erected as a memorial.

monument *n.* A structure or sculpture erected as a memorial; an inscribed stone or other grave marker.

monumental inscription *n. phr.* An epitaph.

monument lot *n. phr.* A section of a cemetery in which upright markers are permitted.

monument poet *n. phr.* One who writes epitaphs.

mooncalf *n. archaic.* A deformed and aborted fetus.

mop up *idiom. Mil.* To kill; slaughter.

morbid *adj.* Preoccupied with death; gruesome. *var.* morbidly, *adv.*, morbidness, *n.*

morganize *tr. v.* To assassinate a person to prevent the release of information; kill secretly.

morgue *n.* A facility in which bodies of those who die unattended are autopsied, identified, or stored; a mortuary.

morgue-aged property *n. phr. slang.* A corpse.

moribund *adj.* Near death; soon to die. *n.* One who is near death. *var.* moribundly, *adv.*, moribundity, *n.*

morph injec *abbrev.* Death by administering morphine by needle.

Morrigan or **Morrigu** *n. Ir. myth.* Goddess of war and the underworld.

Morrigu see **Morrigan**

Mors *n. Rom. myth.* Death in personified form.

mort *n.* An iron coffin used in the 19th c. to discourage bodysnatchers. *Fr.* Death.

mort. *abbrev.* Mortal; mortality; mortician; mortuary.

mortal *n.* One who is subject to death. *adj.* Subject to eventual death; causing or associated with death.

mortal. *abbrev.* Mortality.

mortality *n.* The condition of being mortal; death rate. *n. archaic.* Death; deadliness.

mortality revolution *n. phr.* Decrease in death rate due to increased life expectancy, reduced infant mortality, and improved disease control.

mortal sin *n. phr. Theol.* The deliberate sin of murder or suicide that damns the soul.

mort bon Dieu *n. phr. Haitian.* Death as a call from God; a natural death.

mort cloth *n. phr. obs.* A pall.

morte *n. Ital.* + *Port.* Death.

mortician *n.* A funeral director; embalmer [pref. **funeral director**].

mortiferous *adj.* Fatal; deadly.

morto *n. Esperanto.* Death.

mortorio *n. Ital.* Sculpture depicting the crucified body of Jesus Christ.

mort-safe *n.* A burial vault or casket cover in which a casket was sealed in the 19th c. to deter grave robbers.

mortuary *n.* A funeral home or other facility in which dead bodies are temporarily stored or prepared for disposal. *Eccles.* A fee paid to a minister upon a parishioner's death.

mortuary behavior *n. phr. Anthropol.* Funeral customs.

mortuary cult *n. phr. Anthropol.* The regular provision of funerary offerings.

mortuary diener *n. phr.* One who assists a medical examiner or pathologist.

mortuary education *n. phr.* Professional funeral service training.

mortuary estate *n. phr. obs. Egypt.* Land set aside for the construction of a tomb.

mortuary fee *n. phr.* Dues collected from members of a funeral guild on the occasion of a death.

mortuary law *n. phr. Law.* Federal, state, or local statutes governing funeral service or burial.

mortuary practice *n. phr.* Funeral service.

mortuary priest *n. phr. Anthropol.* One who is appointed to bring daily funerary offerings to a tomb.

mortuary rites *pl. n. phr. Anthropol.* Religious or secular rites associated with the disposition of the dead.

mortuary science *n. phr.* The techniques used in embalming the dead.

mortuary statistics *pl. n. phr.* Burial statistics; death statistics.

mortuary temple *n. phr.* A chapel near a tomb where food offerings are made.

Mot *n. Phoenician myth.* God of death, drought, and the underworld.

motherless *adj.* Orphaned.

motif *n.* An individual symbol on a grave marker.

motiveless killer *n. phr.* A serial murderer.

motorcade *n.* A cortege.

mouillage *n. slang. Fr.* Disposal of a corpse, esp. that of a prisoner, by feeding it to sharks.

moulder see **molder**

mountain warfare *n. phr. Mil.* Armed conflict carried out in a mountainous region.

mourn *intr. v.* To experience grief; to express grief publicly. *tr. v.* To experience or express grief. *var.* mournful, *adj.*, mournfully, *adv.*, mourner, *n.*, mourned, mourning, mourns, *v.*

mourning *n.* The behavior of one who has suffered bereavement; conventional signs of grief for the dead, esp. wearing black clothes; the period during which a death is grieved. *var.* mourningly, *adv.*

mourning cart *n. phr. obs.* A wagon which carried the condemned to the place of execution.

mourning clothing *n. phr.* Apparel worn as an outward sign of bereavement, esp. black apparel.

mourning costume *n. phr.* Apparel worn as an outward sign of bereavement, esp. black apparel.

mourning etiquette *n. phr. Anthropol.* Customary behavior during the period of bereavement.

mourning picture *n. phr.* A memorial picture, embroidered or painted in the 19th c., which includes the dead person's name and dates of birth and death, and often a short verse and a cemetery image; a memorial lithograph mass-produced in the 19th c. with a space left for a name, dates of birth and death, and an inscription.

mourning process *n. phr.* Griefwork.

mourning wear *n. phr.* Apparel worn as an outward sign of grief, esp. black apparel.

mow down *v. phr.* To kill in great quantities, as in battle.

M.S.A.C. *abbrev.* Memorial Society Association of Canada.

m.s.p. *abbrev. Lat.* Died without issue.

M.T.C. *abbrev.* Make Today Count [a bereavement organization].

muerte *n. Sp.* Death.

mug *tr. v.* To assault with intent to kill the victim. *var.* mugged, mugging, mugs, *v.*

multicide *n.* A serial killing or mass murder; a serial killer or mass murderer. *var.* multicidal, *adj.*

multiple burials *pl. n. phr.* The use of a single grave for the interment of two or more people, esp. husband and wife.

multiple homicide *n. phr. Law.* A murder in which there are two or more victims.

multiple murder *n. phr.* A homicide in which there are two or more victims.

multiple wills *pl. n. phr. Law.* Copies of the same will, each executed as an original.

multi-unit method see **itemization**

mummified *p.part. slang.* Killed; murdered.

mummify *tr. v.* To preserve a corpse by embalming or drying. *var.* mummified, *adj.*, mummification, *n.*, mummified, mummifies, mummifying, *v.*

mummy *n.* A body preserved after death by natural or artificial means.

mummy-case *n. phr. archaic.* An outer casket or vault.

mummy coffin *n. phr. archaic.* An early American anthropoid casket.

mummy unrolling *n. phr. obs.* The public or private unwrapping of a mummy.

mundicide *n.* The destruction of the world; one who destroys the world. *var.* mundicidal, *adj.*

murder *n.* The unlawful premeditated killing of one person by another. *tr. v.* To kill unlawfully; to kill brutally or intentionally. *intr. v.* To commit a killing. *var.* murdered, murdering, murders, *v.*

murder capital see **Murder City**

Murder City or **murder capital** *n.* [A nickname applied to] the city with the greatest number of murders annually.

murderee *n.* Actual or intended victim of a murderer.

murderer *n.* A killer.

murderess *n.* A female killer.

murder for hire *n. phr.* Paid assassination.

murderholic *n. slang.* One who is addicted to killing; serial killer.

murder in the first degree *n. Law.* The deliberate, premeditated killing of one person by another.

murder in the second degree *n. Law.* The killing of one person by another, caused by reckless endangerment and characterized by lack of regard for human life; a killing committed in the heat of passion and without premeditation.

murder kit *n. phr.* A collection of tools and weapons carried by a killer.

murder merchandise *n. phr. slang.* Addictive drugs and lethal weapons.

murderologist *n.* One who studies or researches homicides.

murder one *n. phr. slang. Law.* Murder in the first degree.

murderous assault *n. phr. Law.* Attack with intention to kill.

murder sheet *n. phr. obs.* A broadside containing news about a contemporary murder or execution.

murder spree *n. phr.* A series of killings committed in a short span of time by one person.

murder-suicide *n.* A killing in which the murderer kills the victim or victims and then commits suicide.

murder trial *n. phr. Law.* A court proceeding in which the defendant is charged with intentionally killing another person.

murdrum *n. obs.* A homicide.

murther *n. obs.* A murder. *tr. v. obs.* To murder.

mute *n. obs.* An undertaker's assistant who formed part of a 19th c. funeral procession.

Mutu *n. Assyrian myth.* Personification of death and god of the underworld.

mutual and reciprocal wills *pl. n. phr. Law.* Instruments executed separately and containing reciprocal provision for the agreed upon disposition of individual property.

mutual assured destruction *n. phr. Mil.* A concept of reciprocal deterrence based on the ability of nuclear superpowers to inflict unacceptable damage on one another after surviving a nuclear first strike.

mutual pretense *n. phr. Med.* A situation in which the patient, family, and hospital staff are aware of impending death but tacitly agree to ignore it.

mutual suicide *n. phr.* A double-suicide; murder-suicide.

mutual will *n. phr. Law.* A will in which each testator makes a testamentary disposition in favor of the other.

myriologue *n. Gk.* A funeral song composed and sung by the girlfriend of the dead man.

N

N *abbrev.* Natural death.

N.A.A.F. *abbrev.* National Association of Abortion Facilities.

N.A.C. *abbrev.* National Abortion Council; National Association of Cemeteries; National Association of Coroners.

N.A.F. *abbrev.* National Abortion Federation.

nail in one's coffin *idiom.* Something which hastens death.

Nai Thombo Thombo *n. phr. Fiji myth.* The abode of the dead reached by an arduous journey.

N.A.M.E. *abbrev.* National Association of Medical Examiners.

Namtar *n. Sumerian* + *Baby-*

Ionian myth. God of the underworld and herald of death and disease.

N.A.M.W. *abbrev.* National Association of Military Widows.

N.A.M.W.M.W. *abbrev.* National Association of Minister's Wives and Minister's Widows.

N.A.P.N.W. *abbrev.* Nurses Alliance for the Prevention of Nuclear War.

napoo *tr. v. slang. Brit. Mil.* To cause the death of; kill. *adj.* Killed; dead.

N.A.R.A.L. National Abortion Rights Action League; National Association for the Repeal of Abortion Laws.

Nari *n. Slavic myth.* Demons who were originally the souls of children.

narrow home or **narrow house** *idiom.* The grave.

narrow house see **narrow home**

National Cemetery System *n. phr.* A federal system of over 100 cemeteries in the U.S. established by an act of Congress in 1862 for the burial of veterans and their dependents.

national razor *n. phr. slang. Fr.* The guillotine.

national shortener *n. phr. slang. Fr.* The guillotine.

natural death *n. phr. Med.* Death due to natural causes, esp. advanced age.

natural immortality *n. phr.* Continuity in nature through the decay and recycling of the body's ingredients.

natural life sentence *n. phr. Law.* The punishment of incarceration until the time of one's natural death.

natural mummification *n. phr. Archeol.* Preservation of the body as a result of dryness, heat, cold, absence of air, or a combination of these conditions.

Nav *pl. n. Slavic myth.* Spirits of those who die tragically or prematurely.

N.A.W.P. *abbrev.* National Association of Widowed People.

N.B.M.E. *abbrev.* National Board of Medical Examiners.

N.C.A. *abbrev.* National Cemetery Association.

N.C.A.D.P. *abbrev.* National Coalition Against the Death Penalty.

N.C.B.V.A. *abbrev.* National Concrete Burial Vault Association.

N.C.C.C. *abbrev.* National Catholic Cemetery Conference.

N.C.K.W.M. *abbrev.* National Committee for the Korean War Memorial.

N.C.R.F.Y.S. *abbrev.* National Conference on Risk Factors for Youth Suicide.

N.C.S. *abbrev.* National Cemetery System.

N.C.Y.S.P. *abbrev.* National Committee on Youth Suicide Prevention.

NDE *abbrev.* Near-death experience.

NDI *abbrev.* National Death Index.

Ndjambi *n. African myth.* A sky-god who raises aloft those who die a natural death.

Ndyambi-Karunga *n. Bantu myth.* God of the dead.

N.E.A.N. *abbrev.* National Execution Alert Network.

near and certain, but averted death *n. phr.* Near death from an illness, accident, or other threat which is narrowly escaped.

near and certain death *n. phr.* Death which may occur at any time, esp. that of the critically or terminally ill.

near and uncertain death *n. phr.* Death which is likely, but may not occur for some time, esp. that of a person with a dangerous occupation or serious medical condition.

near-death encounter *n. phr.* An event in which one narrowly escapes death; a near-death experience.

near-death experience *n. phr.* Conscious perception which occurs during clinical death and often suggests life after death.

neat oblong hole in the ground *n. phr. slang.* A grave.

Nebthet see **Nephthys**

necation *n.* Killing.

neck *tr. v. slang.* To strangle; decapitate. *var.* necker, *n.*, necked, necking, necks, *v.*

neck-cracking *n. slang.* Hanging.

necking verse *n. phr. slang.* The first verse of the 51st Psalm in the Bible [condemned people able to read or recite it were spared in the Middle Ages].

necktie *n. slang.* A hangman's noose.

necktie hanger *idiom.* Gallows.

necktie killing *n. phr.* A revenge murder in which the throat is slit and the tongue is pulled through the gash.

necktie party *idiom.* Execution by hanging; lynching or a lynch mob.

necr- see **necro-**

necro- or **necr-** *pref.* Corpse; death.

necrography *n.* Writing about death. *var.* necrographic, *adj.*, necrographer, *n.*

necrol. *abbrev.* Necrology.

necrolatry *n.* Worship of the dead or spirits of the dead, esp. excessive veneration.

necrologist *n.* One who writes obituaries.

necrologue *n.* Obituary.

necrology *n.* A list or register of those who have died, esp. recently; an obituary. *var.* necrologic, necrological, *adj.*, necrologist, *n.*

necromancy *n.* Communication with the spirits of the dead, esp. to predict the future. *var.* necromantic, *adj.*, necromancer, *n.*

necromania *n.* Morbid attraction to corpses. *var.* necromaniac, *adj.* + *n.*

necromimesis *n.* Feigned death; the delusion of being dead. *var.* necromimetic, *adj.*

necromorphous *adj.* Feigning death.

necrophage *n.* A cannibal, esp. of corpses. *var.* necrophagous, *adj.*
necrophagia *n.* Cannibalism, esp. of corpses.
necrophagy *n.* The consumption of corpses.
necrophile *n.* One who is physically or sexually attracted to corpses.
necrophilia or **necrophilism** *n.* A physical or sexual attraction to corpses in which one may have sex with, mutilate, exhume, or cannibalize a corpse. *var.* necrophiliac, necrophilic, necrophilous, *adj.*, necrophiliac, *n.*
necrophilism see **necrophilia**
necrophobia *n.* A fear of death or corpses. *var.* necrophobic, *adj.* + *n.*
necropolis *n.* A cemetery, esp. a large, ancient, or elaborate one. *var.* necropolitan, *adj.*
Necropolis of the South *n. phr. slang. archaic.* The city of New Orleans, Louisiana [because of frequent devastating epidemics].
necroponent *n.* Someone temporarily in charge of a household in which a death has occurred.
necropsy *n.* An autopsy. *tr. v.* To perform an autopsy. *var.* necropsied, necropsies, necropsying, *v.*
necroscience *n.* Study of the remains of the dead; paleopathology. *var.* necroscientific, *adj.*
necroscopy *n.* The observation of a corpse. *var.* necroscopic, *adj.*
necrotomy *n.* Dissection of the dead.
nectar *n. Gk. myth.* The drink of the gods which bestows immortality.
needless death *n. phr.* Preventable death.
negative euthanasia *n. phr.* The practice of allowing one to die of natural causes rather than attempting to prolong life artificially; death brought about indirectly by withholding treatment from a terminal patient.
negative patient-care outcome *n. phr. Med.* Death.
negligent manslaughter *n. phr. Law.* Causing death by recklessness or neglect.
Nehebkau *n. Egypt. myth.* A god representing the hope of the dead.
Neith *n. Gk. myth.* Goddess of war.
Nekker or **Nikker** *n. Ger. myth.* A water sprite who warns sailors who are in danger of drowning.
Nenokatatsu-kuni or **Neno-kuni** or **Yomotsu-kuni** *n. Japanese myth.* The abode of the dead reached by a winding path or by the sea.
Neno-kuni see **Nenokatatsu-kuni**
neomort *n. Med.* [Term proposed for] a brain-dead person whose body is kept alive for the harvest of organs, surgical practice and experimentation, and the testing of new drugs.

neonatal death *n. phr. Med.* Death within 28 days of birth; death of a newborn infant.

neonatal death rate *n. phr.* The number of infants who die in the first 28 days of life.

neonaticide *n.* The murder of an infant by one or both parents within 24 hours of birth; a parent who murders his or her infant within 24 hours of birth. *var.* neonaticidal, *adj.*

nepenthe *n. Gk. myth.* A drug used as a remedy for grief [lit., grief-banishing]. *var.* nepenthean, *adj.*

Nephthys or **Nebthet** *n. Egypt. myth.* Goddess of death and decay.

nepoticide *n.* Killing of a favored person; one who kills a favored person. *var.* nepoticidal, *adj.*

Nergal *n. Sumerian myth.* God of war, destruction, and pestilence and lord of the underworld.

net estate *n. phr. Law.* Property remaining after all debts, funeral costs, and other expenses are deducted from the estate of a decedent.

netherworld *n.* A world inhabited by the dead; the underworld. *var.* netherworldly, *adj.*

neural preservation *n. phr. Cryonics.* Preservation of the head or brain of a body for potential revival.

neutralize *tr. v.* To eliminate by assassination. *var.* neutralizer, *n.*, neutralized, neutralizes, neutralizing, *v.*

newborn euthanasia *n. phr.* The killing of a newly born child, esp. because of a physical or mental defect; infanticide.

next of kin *n. Law.* The closest relative of a dead person; one or more relatives entitled to the estate of a dead person under the statutes of distribution.

N.F.D.A. *abbrev.* National Funeral Directors Association.

N.F.D.A.P.A.C. National Funeral Directors Association Political Action Committee.

N.F.D.M.A. *abbrev.* National Funeral Directors and Morticians Association.

N.F.F.S. *abbrev.* National Foundation of Funeral Service.

Nga *n. Siberian myth.* God of death.

niche *n.* A recess or chamber in a columbarium which contains an urn of human ashes.

Nidhoggr *n. Norse myth.* Corpse-eating demon of the underworld.

Niflheim *n. Norse myth.* The realm of the dead in Norse mythology.

Nikker see **Nekker**

Ninazu *n. Sumerian myth.* God of the underworld.

Nine-Day *n. Jamaican.* The nine-day mourning period observed after a death.

Nine-Night *n. Jamaican.* A rite held after the period of mourning which lays to rest the ghost of the dead.

Nine Wells *n. phr. Chinese myth.* The realm of the dead; hell.

niobean *n.* An inconsolable bereaved woman; maternal grief in personified form [after Niobe, daughter of Phyrgian King Tantalus].

Nirrti *n. Indian myth.* Goddess of destruction of the living and the dead.

N.I.S.I.D. *abbrev.* National Institute for the Seriously Ill and Dying.

N.M.C.P. *abbrev.* National Memorial Cemetery of the Pacific.

N.N.F.D.M.A. *abbrev.* National Negro Funeral Directors and Morticians Association.

NNK or **nnk** *abbrev. Law + Med.* Notify next of kin.

nnk see **NNK**

no code *n. phr. Med.* An order given by a doctor to make no heroic efforts to resuscitate a dying patient.

noiseless assassin *n. phr. slang.* A lethal weapon which is silent.

nominal marriage *n. phr. Chinese.* A posthumous marriage arranged by the parents of the deceased.

no more chance than a rabbit *idiom.* Near death; dying.

nonage *n.* One ninth of a dead person's estate formerly collected by the church.

non-capital homicide *n. phr. Law.* A killing which does not carry the death penalty.

non-capital murder *n. phr. Law.* A killing which does not carry the death penalty.

noncupative see **nuncupative**

nondeath *n.* Survival of an incident in which one or more people are killed.

nonmurderer *n. Sociol.* One in the control group of a study who has never committed homicide.

non-negligent manslaughter *n. phr. Law.* Accidentally causing another's death without recklessness or neglect.

nonnuclear warfare *n. phr. Mil.* Armed conflict carried out with conventional weapons.

nonrecurrent cannibalism *n. phr. Anthropol.* Eating human flesh under conditions of starvation.

nonsexual homicide *n. phr. Law.* A murder without evidence of sexual activity.

nonsexual necrophilia *n. phr.* Experiencing pleasure by looking at or being near a corpse.

nonviable *adj.* Incapable of living independently [used of the human fetus].

non-voluntary euthanasia *n. phr.* Causing the death of a person who has no way to express his or her own wishes for reasons considered humane.

noose *n.* A loop formed in a rope by means of a slipknot used to cause death by hanging. *tr. v.* To hang; lynch. *var.* nooses, noosing, *v.*

noosed *p.part.* Hanged.

normal murderer *n. phr. Sociol.* A killer with no recognized mental disorder.

nosferatu *n. Transylvanian myth.* A vampire.

notification *n. Law + Med.* The task of informing the next of kin of a death. *var.* notified, notifies, notify, notifying, *v.*

now picking at the coverlet *idiom.* Dead.

noyade *n.* Execution of many people by drowning.

N.P.B.A. *abbrev.* National Perinatal Bereavement Association.

N.S.A.L.L. *abbrev. obs.* National Save-A-Life League.

N.S.I.D.S.C. *abbrev.* National Sudden Infant Death Syndrome Clearinghouse.

N.S.I.D.S.F. *abbrev.* National Sudden Infant Death Syndrome Foundation.

N.S.J.W.D. *abbrev.* National Shrine to Jewish War Dead.

N.S.M. *abbrev.* National Selected Morticians.

nubbing-cheat *n. archaic.* The gallows.

nuclear warfare *n. phr. Mil.* Armed conflict carried out with atomic weapons.

nucleomitaphobia *n. Psychol.* Fear of death by nuclear weapons.

nuke *tr. v. slang.* To kill or destroy using nuclear weapons. *var.* nuked, nukes, nuking, *v.*

nuncupative or **noncupative** *adj. Law.* Of a witnessed oral will; of a will communicated by word of mouth before death.

nursing home-based hospice *n. phr.* A hospice which provides for inpatient care or arranges for home care through a nursing home.

Nurundere see **Baiame**

N.W.E.P.A.P. *abbrev.* Nuclear War Effects Project Advisory Panel.

N.W.S.G. *abbrev.* Nuclear War Studies Group.

Nyia *n. Slavic myth.* God of the dead.

O

ob *abbrev. Lat.* He or she died.
ob. *abbrev. Lat.* He or she died.
obiit *n. Lat.* Died.
obiit sine prole *v. phr. Law.* Died without issue.
obit *n. inf.* An obituary; public announcement of a death or funeral.
obit. *abbrev.* Obituary.
obituarian or **obituarist** *n.* One who writes an obituary.
obituarist see **obituarian**
obituary *n.* Public notice of a

death, esp. including a brief biography. *var.* obituary, *adj.*
obliviated *p.part. slang.* Obliterated; killed.
obolus *n. Gk.* A coin placed in the mouth of the deceased to pay boat fare to Charon.
obsequies *pl. n.* Funeral rites or services.
obsequy *n.* A funeral ceremony.
obt. *abbrev. Lat.* He or she died.
occision *n.* Slaughter.
occupational mortality *n. phr.* Death rates of workers while on the job.
OD see **O.D.**
O.D. or **OD** *abbrev. Med.* Overdose. *n. slang.* An overdose of a drug; one who has taken an overdose of drugs. *intr. v. slang.* To intentionally or accidentally take a fatal dose of a drug.
Odin *n. Norse myth.* God of war and the dead.
off *tr. v. slang.* To kill; murder. *intr. v. slang.* To die. *var.* offed, offing, offs, *v.*
offering table *n. phr. Egypt.* A low slab on which food offerings are made to the dead.
Off the pigs! *Exclam.* Kill the police.
Ogun *African + Caribbean myth.* God of warriors.
Old Floorer *n. phr. slang.* Death in personified form.
Old Man Mose *n. phr. slang.* Death in personified form.
Old Mister Grim see **Old Mr. Grim**
Old Mr. Grim or **Old Mister Grim** *n. phr. slang.* Death in personified form.
Old Mr. Grim's House *n. phr. slang.* The morgue or mortuary.
old Newton got him or her *idiom. Mil.* He or she died in a military plane crash.
Old Smoky *n. phr. slang.* The electric chair.
Old Sparky *n. phr. slang.* The electric chair.
olographic see **holographic**
olographic will see **holographic will**
ol' sparky *n. phr. slang.* The electric chair.
omnicide *n.* Total nuclear destruction; one who causes total nuclear destruction. *var.* omnicidal, *adj.*
omophagic rites *pl. n. phr. Anthropol.* Cannibalism.
187 *abbrev. Law.* A homicide.
one foot in the grave *idiom.* Dying.
one foot in the grave and the other on a banana peel *idiom.* Dying quickly.
one's days are numbered *idiom.* One is soon to die.
one's hash is settled *idiom.* One is dead.
one's number is up *idiom.* One is destined for death; one is near death.
one's race is run *idiom.* One is dead.
one-way ride see **one-way ticket**
one-way ticket or **one-way ride** *idiom.* A ride to a secluded place for murder; death.
on ice *prep. phr. slang.* Dead; in the morgue.

on one's last leg *prep. phr.* Near death; about to expire.

on one's last pegs *prep. phr.* Near death; dying.

on the cooling board *prep. phr. slang.* Dead.

on the shelf *prep. phr. slang.* Dead.

on the spot *prep. phr. slang.* Near death; dying.

open awareness *n. phr.* A situation in which a terminally ill patient, his or her family, and the hospital staff all know and acknowledge that the patient will die.

operative death *n. phr. Med.* Death which occurs to a patient during surgery.

Orcus *n. Rom. myth.* The abode of the dead; lord of the underworld.

ordeal of the bier *n. phr. obs.* The practice of forcing a suspected murderer to approach the corpse of the victim to see if the wounds bleed to indicate guilt; cruentation.

organ death *n. phr. Biol.* The death at different rates of all the organs in the human body.

organic burial *n. phr.* Interment in which the body is wrapped in simple cloths and buried without a casket.

organismal death *n. phr. Biol.* The death of the components of a living body.

Oro *n. Tahitian myth.* God of war.

orphan *n.* One whose parents are dead, esp. a child. *adj.* The condition of being an orphan; associated with orphans. *tr. v.* To kill the parents of, esp. a child. *var.* orphanhood, *n.*, orphaned, orphaning, orphans, *v.*

orphanage *n.* A public facility for the care of orphans; the condition of being orphaned.

orphanotrophy *n.* Support of orphans; an orphanage.

orthothanasia *n.* Allowing a person to die.

O-sign *n. slang. Med.* The rounded, open mouth of a dead patient [derogatory].

Osiris *n. Egypt. myth.* God of the afterworld and judge of the dead.

o.s.p. *abbrev. Lat.* He or she died without issue.

ossature *n. Biol.* The human skeleton.

ossuary *n.* A charnel house; communal burial spot.

osteobiography *n.* Facts about a person's life and death as evidenced by skeletal remains.

ouranophobia or **uranophobia** *n. Psychol.* Fear of heaven. *var.* ouranophobic, *adj.* + *n.*

out *adj.* Dead. *tr. v. slang.* To kill; murder. *var.* outing, outs, *v.*

outed *p.part. slang.* Dead; killed.

out for blood *idiom.* Has murderous intentions.

out for the long count *idiom.* Dead.

out like a light *idiom.* Dead.

out of it *prep. phr. slang.* Dead.

out of one's misery *prep. phr.* Dead. *slang.* Killed.

out of one's pain *prep. phr.* Dead [often used by hospital staff].
out of the game *idiom.* Dead.
out of the picture *idiom.* Dead; killed.
out of the running *idiom.* Dead.
out of the way *idiom.* Dead; killed.
out of the woods *idiom.* No longer in danger of dying.
outside enclosure *n. phr.* A burial vault.
oven *n. slang.* One of a group of attached vaults stacked vertically and horizontally.
overboard *prep. slang.* Dead.
overburden *n. Archeol.* The surface soil covering a burial.
overdose *n. Med.* An amount of a drug which results in death; one who has taken a fatal amount of a drug. *intr. v.* To intentionally or accidentally take a fatal amount of a drug.
overjost *n. slang.* Overdose.
overkill *n. Mil.* Nuclear destructive capability in excess of that required to destroy an enemy; excessive killing or destruction. *tr. v.* To kill using excess force, esp. with nuclear weapons. *var.* overkilled, overkilling, overkills, *v.*
overlaying *n. archaic.* The accidental death of child caused by the mother smothering it when she rolls over in her sleep.
ovk *abbrev. Mil.* Overkill.

P

p *abbrev. obs.* Perished.
Pachacamac *n. Peruvian myth.* God of earthquakes.
pacification *n. Mil.* The killing of rebels or dissidents. *var.* pacified, pacifies, pacify, pacifying, *v.*
packed up *v. phr. slang.* Dead and buried.
pack up *idiom.* To die.
P.A.D.P. *abbrev.* People Abolishing the Death Penalty.
P.A.I.A.A. *abbrev.* Pre-Arrangement Interment Association of America.
pain principle *n. phr. Psychoanalysis.* The unconscious tendency to seek death or destruction.
Pakheth *n. Egypt. myth.* A goddess who guards the dead from evil spirits.
Pale Horse *n. phr.* Death in personified form.
pale horse *n. phr. slang.* Death.
paleopathology *n.* Forensic archeology.
palingenesis *n.* Reincarnation; the transmigration of souls.

pall *n.* A cover for a casket or tomb, esp. of velvet; a casket, esp. in a procession to the grave. *tr. v.* To cover with a pall. *var.* palled, palling, palls, *v.*
pallbearer *n.* One who carries a casket in a funeral procession.
Pancaraksa *n. Buddhism.* A group of five goddesses invoked to grant longevity and protection.
pandemonium *n.* The capital of Hell [from *Paradise Lost* by John Milton, 1667].
panegyric *n.* A formal eulogy. *var.* panegyrical, *adj.*, panegyrically, *adv.*
panegyrize *tr. v.* To eulogize. *var.* panegyrized, panegyrizes, panegyrizing, *v.*
pantocrator *n.* A depiction of Jesus Christ as he will appear at the Last Judgment.
paradise *n. Theol.* The abode where righteous souls await resurrection. *var.* paradisical, paradisiacal, *adj.*, paradisically, paradisiacally, *adv.*
parasuicide *n.* An attempt at suicide which remains incomplete; one who attempts but does not complete a suicide.
parcenary *n. Law.* Joint possession of an undivided inheritance by two or more heirs.
parcener *n.* A joint heir in an estate.
parentate *intr. v.* To perform funeral rites for a relative. *var.* parentated, parentates, parentating, *v.*
parentation *n. archaic.* Funeral rites for one's parents.
parenticide *n.* The killing of one or both of one's parents; one who kills one or both of his or her parents.
parent-killer *n.* One who kills one or both of his or her parents.
park cemetery *n. phr.* [A proposed term for] future cemeteries characterized by English-style gardens and luxurious vegetation.
parricide *n.* The killing of a parent, relative, or king; one who kills a parent, relative, or king. *var.* parricidal, *adj.*, parricidally, *adv.*
partial abortion *n. phr. Med.* To terminate one or more fetuses of a multiple pregnancy while allowing the remaining fetuses to be carried to term.
partial suicide *n. phr.* Engaging in life-shortening activities.
particular judgment *n. phr.* The belief that a righteous soul appears before God immediately after leaving the body.
pass away *v. phr.* To die.
passing-bell *n.* A toll announcing the death of a parishioner.
pass in one's chips see **hand in one's chips**
Passion *n. Christian.* The suffering and death of Jesus Christ; the suffering and death of a martyr.

passive euthanasia *n. phr.* Allowing a terminally ill person to die by witholding life-prolonging treatment.

pass on *idiom.* To transfer property by will; to die.

pass out *idiom.* To die.

pass out of the picture *idiom.* To die.

pass over *idiom.* To die; to enter the afterlife.

patent drop *n. phr. obs.* A method of execution by hanging designed to break the neck instantly to avoid slow strangulation.

patibulary *adj. archaic.* Associated with the gallows or hanging.

patibulate *tr. v.* To execute by hanging. *var.* patibulated, patibulates, patibulating, *v.*

patibulum *n.* The crossbeam of a Roman cross.

pat on the face with a spade *idiom.* To bury.

patricide *n.* The killing of one's father; one who kills one's father. *var.* patricidal, *adj.*

patrimony *n.* An inheritance from one's father or other ancestor. *var.* patrimonial, *adj.*, patrimonially, *adv.*

patriotic shortener *n. phr. slang. Fr.* The guillotine.

paunch *tr. v.* To kill a crocodile and examine its stomach contents for evidence that it has killed a person.

P.A.W.M. *abbrev.* People's Anti-War Mobilization.

payday *n. slang.* The day of one's death.

payoff *n. slang.* Death.

pay one's last debt or **pay the last debt** *idiom.* To die.

pay one's respects to *v. phr. slang.* To kill; murder.

pay St. Peter a visit *idiom.* To die.

pay the debt of nature *idiom.* To die.

pay the last debt see **pay one's last debt**

P.C.A.P.J.F.K. *abbrev.* President's Commision on the Assassination of President John F. Kennedy.

P.C.C.Y.D. *abbrev.* Presidential Commission on Child and Youth Deaths.

Pck *abbrev. Mil.* Conditional probability of kill.

pda *abbrev.* Personal death awareness.

peach-blossom cave *n. phr. Chinese.* A casket.

pecuniary legacy *n. phr. Law.* A gift of a sum of money by will.

pedocide *n.* The killing of a child; one who kills a child. *var.* pedocidal, *adj.*

peg *intr. v. slang. Australian.* To starve.

peg out *idiom.* To die.

pein forte et dure *n. phr. obs.* Execution by pressing to death under increasingly heavy weights.

people's avenger *n. phr. slang. Fr.* The guillotine.

per capita *n. phr. Law.* Equal distribution of an estate among the beneficiaries under a will.

perdition *n.* Eternal damnation of the soul; hell.

perfect murder *n. phr.* A murder which yields no clues and is therefore unsolvable.
performance suicide *n. phr.* Suicide in response to a sense of failure in meeting society's standards.
peril *n.* Danger of death; deadliness. *var.* perilous, *adj.*
perimortem *adj.* At the time of death.
perinatal death *n. phr. Med.* Death occurring shortly after birth.
perinatal mortality *n. phr.* Death rates of newborn infants.
perish *intr. v.* To die, esp. in an accident or a disaster. *var.* perished, perishes, perishing, *v.*
permanent rest camp *idiom.* A cemetery.
permanent vegetative state *n. phr. Med.* A condition in which higher functions of the brain have been lost but the brain stem remains alive.
pernicious *adj.* Often causing death; deadly. *var.* perniciously, *adv.*, perniciousness, *n.*
perpetual care *n. phr.* Prearranged tending of a grave indefinitely or for a stated period of time.
Persephone *n. Gk. myth.* Queen of the underworld.
personal death awareness *n. phr.* Sudden realization of one's mortality.
personal property *n. phr. Law.* Possessions other than land which are disposed of in a will.
personal representatives *pl. n. phr. Law.* Executors or administrators of the will of a dead person; next of kin.
per stirpes *adj. phr. Law.* Distribution of the estate of a dead person in which the share of a deceased heir shall pass on to his or her children; distribution of an estate which depends on the course of descent.
pessimism *n.* The principle that death should be administered when one's life becomes unbearable or useless.
pestilence *n.* A fatal contagious disease, esp. bubonic plague; an epidemic.
pestilent or **pestilential** *adj.* Causing death or disease.
pestilential see **pestilent**
Petbe *n. Egypt. myth.* God of retaliation and death.
petered out *idiom.* Dead.
petit treason see **petty treason**
petty treason or **petit treason** *n. phr. archaic.* The killing of one's superior; husband-killing.
Pey *n. Tamil myth.* Demonic beings associated with cannibalism of corpses.
P.F.D.I. *abbrev.* Preferred Funeral Directors International.
philosophicide *n.* The killing of a philosopher; one who kills a philosopher. *var.* philosophicidal, *adj.*
philotheoparoptesism *n.* Execution by roasting over a slow fire.

Phlegethon *n. Gk. myth.* A blazing river which borders Hades.
phonomania *n.* Insanity marked by homicidal tendencies. *var.* phonomaniac, *adj.* + *n.*
photographer *n. slang.* The assistant who positions a condemned person in the guillotine.
phthartic *adj.* Deadly; destructive.
phylactery *n.* A receptacle for the relics of a saint or martyr.
physical anthropology *n. phr. Anthropol.* The study of human skeletal remains.
pick off *idiom.* To shoot and kill.
Picullus *n. Prussian myth.* God of the underworld.
pietà *n. Ital.* A depiction of the Virgin Mary holding and grieving over the body of Jesus Christ.
pike *intr. v. slang.* To die. *var.* piked, pikes, piking, *v.*
pine *n. archaic.* Intense grief. *intr. v.* To suffer intense grief. *tr. v. archaic.* To grieve or mourn for. *var.* pined, pines, pining, *v.*
pine box *n. phr. slang.* Coffin; casket.
pine overcoat *n. phr. slang.* Casket.
pip *tr. v. slang. Mil.* To kill with a missile, esp. a bullet. *var.* pipped, pipping, pips, *v.*
pip out *idiom.* To die.
Pitaras *pl. n. Indian myth.* The venerable dead who were first to follow the path to heaven.
pit grave *n. phr. Archeol.* A simple hole in which a single body is deposited.
pizen *tr. v. slang.* To poison.
PK *abbrev. Mil.* Probability of kill.
placebo *n. Rom. Cath.* The rite of vespers for the dead [lit., I shall please, the first word of the first antiphon of the service].
placed on the stake *v. phr.* Executed by impalement.
placophobia *n. Psychol.* Fear of tombstones. *var.* placophobic, *adj.* + *n.*
plague *n.* A fatal epidemic, esp. of the bubonic plague.
plaintive *adj.* Expressing grief; mournful. *var.* plaintively, *adv.*, plaintiveness, *n.*
plangent *adj.* Mournful [used of a sound].
plangorous *adj.* Mournful.
planned termination *n. phr.* Suicide.
plant *tr. v. slang.* To bury; to kill. *var.* plants, *v.*
planted *p.part.* Dead and buried.
planting *pr.part. slang.* A funeral or burial.
planting crate *n. phr. slang.* A casket.
played one's last card *idiom.* Soon to die.
playing one's harp *idiom.* In heaven.
play one's last hand *idiom.* To die.
play opossum see **play possum**
play possum or **play opossum** *idiom.* To feign death.
play solitaire *idiom.* To commit suicide.

plot *n.* A piece of ground used for a burial, esp. in a cemetery.

plunder *intr. v.* To steal from a grave or tomb. *n.* Goods stolen from a grave or tomb. *var.* plunderable, plunderous, *adj.*, plunderer, plunderage, *n.*

Pluto *n. Rom. myth.* The god of the dead and ruler of the underworld.

PM or **pm** *abbrev.* Postmortem.

pm see **PM**

pnigerophobia *n. Psychol.* Fear of smothering. *var.* pnigerophobic, *adj.* + *n.*

pnigophobia *n. Psychol.* Fear of choking. *var.* pnigophobic, *adj.* + *n.*

POD or **pod** *abbrev.* Payable on death.

pod see **POD**

pogrom *n.* Systematic massacre of a minority group, esp. Jews. *tr. v.* To massacre minorities, esp. Jews. *var.* pogromed, pogroming, pogroms, *v.*

poi *abbrev. Med.* Poison; poisonous.

pois *abbrev. Med.* Poison.

poison *n.* A chemical which is capable of causing death; something deadly or destructive. *tr. v.* To kill using poison. *var.* poisonous, *adj.*, poisoner, *n.*, poisoned, poisoning, poisons, *v.*

poleax *tr. v.* To kill with a poleax. *var.* poleaxed, poleaxes, poleaxing, *v.*

police murder *n. phr.* The killing of a law enforcement officer; killing by a police officer in the line of duty.

polish off *idiom.* To kill; murder.

pollice verso *idiom. obs. Lat.* Condemned to death [lit., with the thumb turned down].

pollinctores *pl. n. obs. Lat.* Slaves or assistants of a Roman funeral director.

P.O.M.C. *abbrev.* Parents of Murdered Children.

poor hole *n. phr. obs.* A common or mass grave.

pop off *idiom.* To die.

pop off the hook *idiom.* To die.

population *n.* The decision of a terminal patient to die alone or in the company of other terminal patients.

populicide *n.* The killing of people, esp. in great numbers; one who kills many people. *var.* populicidal, *adj.*

pork *n. slang.* A corpse.

POS *abbrev.* Probability of survival.

P.O.S. *abbrev.* Parents of Suicides.

position *tr. v.* To arrange a corpse for display at a wake or funeral. *var.* positioned, positioning, positions, *v.*

positive euthanasia *n. phr.* The practice of painlessly administering death to the incurably ill.

Po-soul *n. Chinese.* The spirit which remains at the grave and takes revenge if funeral arrangements go awry.

post *n. slang. Med.* An autopsy [a shortening of **post-mortem**].

post-conceptive contraception *n. phr.* Abortion.

post-conceptive fertility control *n. phr.* Abortion.

post-death *adj.* Following death.

posth. *abbrev.* Posthumous.

posthuma *pl. n.* Posthumous writings.

posthumous *adj.* Occurring or continuing after death; published after the author's death. *var.* posthumously, *adv.*

posthumous exoneration *n. phr.* Pardon after death.

posthumous pardon *n. phr. Law.* Reversal of the legal conviction of a person who has since died.

post-mort *abbrev.* Post-mortem.

postmortal *adj.* After death.

post-mortem *adj.* Taking place after death; associated with an autopsy. *n.* An autopsy.

post-mortem changes *pl. n. phr.* Differences in coloring, temperature, and other characteristics of the body after death.

post-mortem examination *n. phr.* An autopsy.

postneonatal death rate *n. phr.* The number of infants who die annually at between 28 days and one year of age.

post-obit *adj.* Occurring or taking effect after a person's death; post-mortem. *n.* A post-obit bond.

post-obit bond *n.* A bond in which the borrower promises to repay the debt after the death of one from whose estate he or she expects to inherit.

postremogeniture *n. Law.* The right of the last-born son to inherit or succeed.

postsuspension counseling *n. phr. Cyronics.* Consultation with survivors of cryonic suspension.

postvention *n.* Activities which reduce the impact of a death or disaster in the lives of the survivors.

potted *p.part. slang.* Dead and buried.

potter's field *n. phr.* A plot of land used for the burial of the indigent or unidentified [from the potter's field mentioned in the Holy Bible].

praeco *n. obs. Lat.* One who summons the participants to a public funeral in Rome.

preagony *n.* The period immediately preceding death. *var.* preagonal, *adj.*

predeath *adj.* Prior to death.

predeath vision *n. phr.* A hallucination experienced by one who is dying.

predecease *tr. v.* To die before one. *var.* predeceased, predeceases, predeceasing, *v.*

pre-execution chamber *n. phr.* The cell to which a condemned prisoner is taken, esp. on the morning of the scheduled execution.

pregnancy reduction *n. phr. Med.* The termination of one or more fetuses of a multiple pregnancy while allowing the remaining fetuses to be carried to term.

premature burial *n. phr.* Intentional or accidental interment of a living person.

premature death *n. phr.* Death before one's time of productivity has ended.

premeditated murder *n. Law.* A killing in which the murderer has shown deliberate intent.

premonition *n.* A personal conviction that death is imminent.

prenatal euthanasia *n. phr.* Abortion.

preneed arrangements *pl. n. phr.* Planning and payment of a funeral made in advance of death, esp. through a funeral home.

preneed memorial estate *n. phr.* A burial plot purchased in advance of need.

prenticecide *n.* An apprentice murderer.

preparation room *n. phr.* The room in a funeral home in which bodies are embalmed; morgue.

present at the last muster *idiom.* Killed in combat.

present at the last roll call *idiom.* Killed in combat.

preserve *tr. v.* To prevent a corpse from decaying; to embalm. *var.* preserver, preservation, *n.* preserved, preserves, preserving, *v.*

pressing *n.* Execution by crushing the condemned under iron weights.

presuicidal *adj.* In a condition of mental or emotional disturbance prior to a suicide attempt.

presumptive death *n. phr.* Death which is legally assumed after an unaccounted absence of several years.

Preta *pl. n. Hinduism + Buddhism.* Spirits of the damned.

preterition *n. Law.* Neglecting to mention a legal heir in one's will.

prey on or **prey upon** *v. phr.* To kill consistently or exclusively.

prey upon see **prey on**

primary recognition *n. phr.* The period of time between the first awareness of a medical problem to the definitive diagnosis of a terminal illness.

primogeniture *n. Law.* The right of the oldest son or daughter to inherit the entire estate of one or both of his or her parents. *var.* primogenitary, primogenital, primogenial, *adj.*

prison cemetery *n. phr.* A plot of land in which prison inmates are buried.

prison coffin *n. phr.* A plain wooden box used to bury prison inmates, esp. a box perforated with many large holes to facilitate disintegration after burial.

prison homicide *n. phr. Law.* The murder of a guard, inmate, or visitor in a correctional facility.

private grief *n. phr.* Bereavement which is not seen or shared in by the public.

prob. *abbrev. Law.* Probate.

probate *n. Law.* The procedure of proving in court that a will is valid.

profectitious *adj.* Associated with inherited property.

professional mourner *n. phr.* One who is employed to wail or grieve during a funeral rite.

professional murder *n. phr.* A killing carried out by a hired assassin.

prolicide *n.* The killing of one's child or children; one who kills one's child or children. *var.* prolicidal, *adj.*

promoted to glory *idiom. Mil.* Killed during military service.

pronounce *tr. v. slang. Med.* To legally pronounce a patient to be dead [used by hospital staff]. *var.* pronounced, pronounces, pronouncing, *v.*

propaganda by deed *n. phr. archaic.* Assassinations and other violent acts carried out for political reasons.

proper death *n. phr. slang.* Death after cleansing one's soul and meeting all social obligations.

Proserpina or **Proserpine** *n. Rom. myth.* Goddess of the underworld.

Proserpine see **Proserpina**

prothesis *n. archaic. Gk.* Laying out the body of the dead.

protomartyr *n.* The first martyr in a cause, esp. the first Christian martyr, St. Stephen.

Prydain or **Prydein** *n. Celtic myth.* The abode of the dead.

pseudautochiria *n.* Murder disguised as suicide.

pseudo-death *n.* Symbolic death. *Psychol.* A period of withdrawal, incubation, fasting, or isolation.

pseudophonia *n.* Suicide disguised as murder. *var.* pseudophonic, *adj.*

psychiatric abortion *n. phr. Med.* + *Psychol.* Abortion performed due to the endangered sanity of the mother.

psychic death *n. phr.* Destruction of brain cells which produces a permanent vegetative state.

psychogenic death *n. phr.* A death caused psychosomatically.

psychological autopsy *n. phr. Sociol.* An investigation to determine whether a suicide was intentional or unintentional; reconstruction of the recent activities of a person to understand the psychosocial components of his or her death.

psychological death *n.* A state of unconsciousness; unawareness of oneself or one's surroundings.

psychological warfare *n. phr. Mil.* Armed conflict using tactics based on the emotional and behavioral characteristics of the enemy.

psychomancy *n.* Divination by communicating with the spirits of the dead.

psychopannychism *n.* The belief that souls sleep for the period of time from death to bodily resurrection.
psychopathic murderer *n. phr. Psychol.* A killer with no appreciation of laws or moral codes.
psychopomp *n.* A guide to the underworld; one who conducts souls to the abode of the dead.
Psychopompos *n. Gk. myth.* Hermes in his role as conductor of souls to Hades.
psychorrhagy *n.* The separation of the soul from the body. *var.* psychorrhagic, *adj.*
psychosomatic death *n. phr.* Death which is subconsciously self-willed.
psychosophy *n.* Doctrine about the human soul. *var.* psychosophic, psychosophical, *adj.*
psychostasia *n.* The weighing of souls after death.
psychothanatic *adj.* Associated with a person's psychological concept of death.
psycho-weaponry *n.* Fear of death implanted in the minds of victims by terrorists.
psywar *abbrev. Mil.* Psychological warfare.
public grave *n. phr.* A common or mass grave; potter's field.
public grief *n. phr.* Bereavement seen and shared in by the public.
public murder *n. phr.* Execution.
pull a Frankie and Johnny *idiom.* To kill one's husband in revenge.
pull a score *idiom.* To strangle someone.
pull in at the last terminal *idiom.* To die.
pull the plug *v. phr. slang.* To disconnect from life-support machines; to euthanize.
pulmonary resuscitation see **cardiopulmonary resuscitation**
pump off *idiom.* To shoot and kill.
puppet death *n. phr. slang.* The passive role played by the corpse in elaborate funeral ceremonies.
purgatory *n. Rom. Cath.* A state in which righteous souls expiate their sins. *var.* purgatorial, *adj.*
Pusan see **Pushan**
Pushan *n. Hinduism.* Conductor of the souls of the dead.
pushing the clouds around *idiom.* Dead; in heaven.
push off *idiom.* To kill; murder.
push-off *n. slang.* Death.
push up daisies see **count daisies**
P.U.S.J.D. *abbrev.* Pious Union of St. Joseph for the Dying.
P.U.S.J.D.S. *abbrev.* Pious Union of St. Joseph for Dying Sinners.
put a lily in one's hand *idiom.* To kill; murder.
put away *idiom.* To kill; murder.
put down *idiom.* To kill; murder.
put easy *idiom.* To kill; murder.

put in one's grave *v. phr.* To cause one's death.
put it to *idiom.* To kill; murder.
put on a marble slab or **put on a slab** *idiom.* To kill; murder.
put on a slab see **put on a marble slab**
put one easy see **put easy**
put one out of one's misery see **put out of one's misery**
put one out of the way see **put out of the way**
put one's checks back in the rack *idiom.* To die.
put one to bed with a shovel *idiom.* To bury; to kill and bury.
put on the extinguisher *idiom.* To kill; murder.
put on the spot *idiom.* To mark for death.
put out *idiom.* To kill; murder.
put out a contract *v. phr. slang.* To hire an assassin to kill someone.
put out of one's misery *v. phr.* To euthanize. *slang.* To kill; murder.
put out of the way *idiom.* To kill; murder.
put out one's light *idiom.* To kill.
put out one's nightlight *idiom. Fr.* To die.
put over *idiom.* To kill; murder.
put the brakes to *idiom.* To kill; murder.
put the chill on *idiom.* To kill.
put the cross on *idiom.* To mark for murder.
put the finger on *idiom.* To mark for murder.
put the finisher on *idiom.* To kill; murder.
put the rollers under *idiom.* To kill; murder.
put the settler on *idiom.* To kill; murder.
put the skids under *idiom.* To kill; murder.
put to bed see **put to sleep**
put to bed with a shovel see **put one to bed with a shovel**
put to sleep or **put to bed** *idiom.* To kill; murder.
put under *v. phr. slang.* To bury.
put under glass *idiom.* To bury.
put under hatches *idiom.* To bury.
PVS *abbrev. Med.* Permanent vegetative state.
PW *abbrev. Mil.* Psychological warfare.
Pwyll *n. Welsh myth.* God of the underworld.
pyramid *n.* An ancient Egyptian tomb or tomb complex.
pyramidology *n.* The study of pyramids, esp. Egyptian tombs.
pyre *n.* Materials gathered to burn a corpse as part of a funeral rite; a fire intended to incinerate a corpse.
pyx *n. Rom. Cath.* A container in which a priest transports a Holy Communion wafer to the house of a dying person.

Q

QIP *abbrev. Lat.* Rest in peace.
Q-sign *n. slang. Med.* The rounded, open mouth of a dead person whose tongue is protruding [derogatory].
quackle *tr. v. slang.* To choke; suffocate. *var.* quackled, quackles, quackling, *v.*
quaff the cup *idiom.* To commit suicide.
quarantine *n. archaic.* The forty-day period during which a widow is allowed to remain in the chief mansion house after her husband's death.
quarterage *n. obs.* The regular dues paid by members of a medieval burial guild.
quaternio *n. obs. Lat.* The squad of four men assigned to carry out a Roman crucifixion.
queer *tr. v.* To kill; murder. *var.* queered, queering, queers, *v.*
quemadero *n. Sp.* A site for execution by burning.
querken *tr. v.* To choke; smother. *var.* querkened, querkening, querkens, *v.*
quick *adj. archaic.* Alive. *n.* The living. *var.* quickness, *n.*
quietus *n.* A fatal blow; death.
Quirinus *n. Rom. myth.* God of war.
quit *intr. v. slang.* To die. quitted, quitting, quits, *v.*
quitter *n. slang.* A suicide.

R

radiological warfare *n. phr. Mil.* Armed conflict using weapons based on principles of radiology.
radwar *abbrev. Mil.* Radiological warfare.
rage and anger *n. phr.* A stage in terminal illness in which the patient psychologically and emotionally resents the fact that others remain healthy while she or he must die.
Ragnarok *n. Ger. myth.* The day on which the world will be annihilated; doomsday.
rainbow body *n. phr. Chinese myth.* A phenomenon in which all but the hair and nails of a corpse decays within seven days of death.
Rajna see **Rashnu**
Ran *n. Ger. myth.* Wife of the god of the sea who sinks

ships and ministers to drowned sailors.

ransom *n.* Sparing one's life in return for a demanded price; the payment demanded in return for sparing a life. *tr. v.* To obtain the live release of a person by paying a demanded price; to release alive after payment of a demanded price. *var.* ransomer, *n.*, ransomed, ransoming, ransoms, *v.*

ran the good race *idiom.* Dead.

rape-murder *n.* A killing in connection with which the victim was sexually assaulted.

rape-slaying *n.* A rape-murder.

Rashnu or **Rasnu** *n. Persian myth.* Judge of the dead and guardian of the bridge to the netherworld.

Rasnu see **Rashnu**

ra-stau *pl. n. Egypt. myth.* Passages in a tomb which are said to lead to the otherworld.

R.C.A.R. *abbrev.* Religious Coalition for Abortion Rights.

real property *n. phr. Law.* Land and buildings disposed of by will.

reanimation *n.* Resuscitation of a dead body. *var.* reanimator, *n.*, reanimated, reanimates, reanimating, *v.*

reaper man *n. phr. slang.* Death in personified form.

reburial *n.* The reinterment of a corpse after exhumation.

reciprocal ritual weeping *n. phr.* A formalized display of grief which affirms a social bond between two or more people.

reckless disregard *n. phr. Law.* Lack of concern for the endangerment of human life.

recreational killer *n. phr.* A serial murderer.

redivivus *adj.* Resuscitated.

red-light *tr. v. slang.* To kill; murder. *var.* red-lighted, red-lighting, red-lights, *v.*

refrigerium *n.* Refreshment of the soul in paradise; Abraham's bosom.

regicide *n.* The killing of a king or head of state; one who kills a king or head of state. *var.* regicidal, *adj.*

register book *n.* A memory book signed by those who attend a wake or funeral service.

registers of death *pl. n. phr.* Official records of vital statistics including date and place of death.

regret *n.* An expression of grief. *tr. v.* To grieve or mourn over.

rehabilitation *n. phr.* The second stage of postvention which consists of consultations with family members.

Reign of Terror *n.* The French Revolution in the late 18th c. during which thousands of persons were executed.

reign of terror *n. phr.* A period in which violence results in widespread terror.

reincarnation *n.* The transmigration of a soul from one body to another at death.

rejoin one's ka *v. phr. Egypt. myth.* To die.

rel. *abbrev.* Relics.

relic *n.* An object of religious veneration associated with the body or life of a saint or martyr, esp. a preserved body part.
relics *pl. n. archaic.* Human remains.
relict *n.* A widow; survivor. *adj.* Widowed.
religious immortality *n. phr.* Afterlife; reincarnation.
reliquary *n.* A receptacle for the storage or display of relics.
reliquiae *pl. n. Lat.* Human remains. *var.* reliquian, *adj.*
reliquism *n.* Worship of relics.
remains *pl. n.* A corpse; unpublished writings of a deceased author.
remnants *pl. n. slang.* A corpse.
removal *n.* The period of time between a death and the visitation period during which the body is separated from survivors.
removal cot *n. phr. Med.* A disguised stretcher in which bodies are transported to a hospital morgue.
remove *tr. v.* To transport a body from the place of death to a funeral home or mortuary. *slang.* To assassinate. *var.* removed, removes, removing, *v.*
renewal *n.* The third stage of postvention during which the mourning process begins to taper off.
rental casket *n. phr.* A casket in which a body is temporarily displayed but not permanently interred.

repose *n.* Presentation of a corpse for viewing.
repository *n.* A burial vault; tomb.
representation *n. archaic.* A wooden or wax effigy used for display in the Middle Ages in place of a corpse which had become unsuitable for viewing.
reprieve *n. Law.* Temporary suspension of a death sentence *var.* reprieved, reprieves, reprieving, *v.*
requiem *n. Rom. Cath.* A mass said for the soul of a dead person; a hymn or other composition performed at a funeral mass.
requiem service *n. phr.* A commemorative mass or rite, esp. on the anniversary of a death.
requiescat *n.* A prayer said for the repose of souls.
requiescat in pace *v. phr. Lat.* May he or she rest in peace.
Reshef *n. Egypt. myth.* God of war.
residuary bequest *n. phr. Law.* A bequest of the remaining estate after the payment of debts, administrative expenses, and gifts.
residuary clause *n. phr. Law.* The article in a will by which a testator disposes of property which remains after payment of debts, administrative expenses, and gifts.
residuary estate *n. phr. Law.* Property remaining in an estate after debts, adminis-

trative expenses, and gifts have been paid.

residuary legacy *n. phr. Law.* Residuary clause.

residuary legatee *n. phr. Law.* One who inherits the residue of an estate after payment of debts, administrative expenses, and gifts.

resistance *n.* An early stage of dying characterized by recognition of danger, fear of death, and the struggle to survive.

responsible conduct *n. phr.* The extent to which a terminally ill patient remains competent and capable of directed action.

rest *n.* Death.

rest camp *n. phr. slang.* A cemetery.

rest in Abraham's bosom or **be in Abraham's bosom** *idiom.* To be dead and with God in heaven.

resting *pr.part.* Dead.

resting easy *idiom.* Dead.

rest in peace *v. phr.* To repose without disturbance [used of a corpse or a soul].

rest in pieces *idiom.* To be killed by an exploding shell; to be dismembered at or after death.

restoration *n.* Life after death which includes the recollection of a former existence.

resume *tr. v. Austral.* To exhume a body. *var.* resumed, resumes, resuming, *v.*

resurrect *tr. v.* To restore to life; to raise from the dead. *intr. v.* To return to life; to rise from the dead. *var.* resurrected, resurrecting, resurrects, *v.*

Resurrection *n. Christian.* The rising of Jesus Christ three days after his Crucifixion; the rising of the dead at the Last Judgment. *var.* Resurrectional, *adj.*

resurrection *n.* The act of reviving or rising from the dead; the condition of one who has revived or risen from the dead.

resurrection days *pl. n. phr.* The era during which teachers of anatomy were compelled to obtain cadavers from grave robbers.

resurrectionist *n. archaic.* One who steals bodies from the grave to sell for dissection; body snatcher.

resurrection men *pl. n. phr.* Resurrectionists; body-snatchers.

resurrection syndrome *n. phr.* The state of conflicting emotions caused by the recovery of a patient who is considered terminal and whose imminent death has been adjusted to.

resuscitate *tr. v.* To restore to life. *intr. v.* To revive. *var.* resuscitatable, resuscitative, *adj.*, resuscitator, *n.*, resuscitated, resuscitates, resuscitating, *v.*

resuscitation *n.* The first stage of postvention in which the survivor is helped through the initial shock of grief.

resuscitee *n. Cryonics.* One who has been revived after cryonic suspension.

retainer sacrifice *n. phr. Anthropol.* The practice of following one's lord or leader into death as an act of supreme loyalty.

return home *n. phr.* Return of a family to an informal gathering of neighbors and relatives in their home after a funeral.

revenant *n.* A ghost; one who returns after supposed death.

reward *n. slang.* Murder; death.

Rhadamanthus or **Rhadamanthys** *n. Gk. myth.* One of the three judges of the dead and ruler of the Isles of the Blessed.

Rhadamanthys see **Rhadamanthus**

ride one out *v. phr. slang. Med.* To keep a hospital patient's body functioning until the shift change.

ride the lightning *idiom.* To be executed in the electric chair.

right to die *n. phr.* The disputed right to limit the lifesaving techniques used to resuscitate one; euthanasia.

right to life *n. phr.* The disputed right of an unborn embryo or fetus to be born or carried until viable.

rigor mortis *n. phr. Med.* A generalized stiffening of the muscles usually occurring within twelve hours after death and lasting twelve to twenty-four hours [lit., stiffness of death].

ring down the curtain *idiom.* To die.

ringed cross *n. phr. Hungary.* A cruciform grave marker with a rounded roof.

ring off *idiom.* To die.

ring out *idiom.* To die.

R.I.P. or **RIP** *abbrev. Lat.* May he or she rest in peace; may they rest in peace [used of the dead].

RIP see **R.I.P.**

rip off *idiom.* To assault and kill.

Ripperologist *n.* One who studies or investigates the murders committed by the anonymous Jack the Ripper in the 19th c.

rite of passage *n. phr.* A ceremony centering around the transition from life to death; funeral.

ritual death *n. phr.* A symbolic rite involving death and rebirth.

ritual murder *n. phr.* A killing carried out as part of a religious or cult rite.

ritual service *n. phr.* A formal funeral rite in a church or in the chapel of a funeral home.

roast *n. slang.* A burned corpse.

roast meat for worms *n. phr. slang.* A corpse.

rock-cut tomb *n. phr.* A burial chamber excavated from solid rock, esp. an ancient Egyptian one.

rod out *idiom.* To shoot and kill.

rolfincked *p.part.* To have had one's body snatched for dissection after death [after Werner Rolfinck (1599–1673), Professor of Anatomy at the University of Jena].

rood *n.* A crucifix, esp. in a medieval church.
rope *n.* A noose.
roue *n. obs. Fr.* One who deserves to be broken on the wheel.
rubbish *n.* The deceased [used by some Australian tribes to avoid using the names of the dead].
rub out *v. phr. slang.* To assassinate; kill.
Rugevit *n. Slavic myth.* The God of war.
run down *idiom.* To die.
run out *idiom.* To die.
rural cemetery *n. phr.* A cemetery located outside city limits.
Rusalka *n. Slavonic myth.* The spirits of drowned women who bewitch and drown passing men.
Russian roulette *n.* A deadly game of chance played by loading a revolver with a single shot, spinning the cylinder, pointing it to one's own head, and firing.
ruth *n.* Sympathy. *var.* ruthful, *adj.*
Ruti *n. Egypt. myth.* A pair of lions responsible for nourishing the dead.
RW or **rw** *abbrev. Mil.* Radiological warfare.
rw see **RW**

S

S *abbrev.* Suicidal death.
s. *abbrev. Lat.* Buried.
sacellum *n.* A chapel or burial vault built over the tomb of a saint or martyr.
Sachmet *n. Egypt. myth.* Goddess of war.
sack-'em-up men *pl. n. obs.* Grave robbers who procured corpses for medical dissection; resurrectionists.
sacred land *n. phr. Egypt.* The necropolis.
saddled cross *n. phr. Hungary.* A cruciform grave marker with a peaked roof.
sadistic murder *n. phr.* A killing involving torture.
safely gathered in *idiom.* Dead and in heaven.
saint *n. Theol.* A person officially recognized by the church after death as entitled to public veneration and capable of interceding for the living; one who has died and gone to heaven. *slang. Fr.* The guillotine. *var.* saintly, *adj.*, saintdom, sainthood, *n.*
Saint Guillotine *n. phr. slang. Fr.* The guillotine.
Saint Michael *n. Christian.* Guardian and judge of the souls of the dead.

saint's day *n. phr.* A day in a liturgical calendar that is observed in honor of a saint, esp. his or her death day.
saline abortion *n. phr. Med.* Salt poisoning of a fetus.
salt away *idiom.* To bury.
salt down *idiom.* To bury.
salt poisoning *n. phr.* A method of abortion used after the sixteenth week of pregnancy in which salt is injected into the amniotic sac to poison the baby which is later delivered stillborn.
samsara *n. Hinduism + Buddhism.* The eternal cycle of birth, suffering, death, and rebirth.
sanguinary or **sanguineous** *adj.* Accompanied by or associated with bloodshed.
sanguineous see **sanguinary**
sanitary embalmer *n. phr.* One who disinfects a corpse.
S.A.N.S. *abbrev.* Students Against Nuclear Suicide.
Saosyant or **Sosans** *n. Iranian myth.* God who resurrects the dead and offers a draught of immortality.
sapon. *abbrev.* Saponification.
saponification *n.* The natural preservation of a body through the formation of adipocere.
sarcophagus *n.* A stone burial receptacle. *var.* sarcophagic *adj.*
saulie *n.* A hired mourner.
save *n.* An emergency situation in which a person is rescued from danger or restored to health. *tr. v.* To rescue from danger or restore to health. *var.* saves, saving, *v.*
saved *p.part.* Having narrowly averted death from an illness, accident, or other threat.
Savitri *n.* Creator of immortality.
saw off *idiom.* To shoot and kill.
say goodbye to this world *idiom.* To die.
S.B.M.E. *abbrev.* State Board of Medical Examiners.
S.C.A. *abbrev.* Southern Cemetery Association.
scaffold burial *n. phr.* Interment of the body of the condemned at the place of execution.
Scanda see **Skanda**
scaphism *n.* A method of execution in which the condemned is covered with honey and left exposed to the sun and insects.
scarab *n. Egypt. myth.* Sacred beetle of immortality.
S.C.F. *abbrev.* Society of Compassionate Friends [a bereavement organization].
sciomancy *n.* Divination by communicating with the ghosts of the dead. *var.* sciomantic, *adj.*
scion *n.* A descendant or heir.
S.C.M. *abbrev.* Society of Connoisseurs in Murder.
scourge *n.* A cause of widespread and severe affliction, esp. a plague or war.
SCR *abbrev. Mil.* Standardized casualty rate.
scrag or **skrag** *tr. v. slang.* To kill, esp. by strangling.

scragsman *n. Brit.* Hangman.
scribe *n. Egypt.* The priest who marked the abdominal incision during the preparation of a mummy.
scuppered *adj. slang. Nautical.* Killed; dead in battle.
S.D.M.S. *abbrev.* San Diego Memorial Society.
sds *abbrev.* Sudden death syndrome.
sealer casket *n. phr.* A burial receptacle equipped with a gasket and locking mechanism.
secondary burial *n. phr.* Reinterment of bones after exhumation, esp. for cleaning.
secondary disposal see **compound disposal**
secondary treatment *n. phr. Anthropol.* The transfer of relics or human remains from a temporary to a permanent location.
second burial *n. phr. Chinese.* The exhumation, cleaning, and inurnment of the skeleton two years after the burial of a body.
second-class relic *n. phr. Rom. Cath.* Something sanctified by contact with the body of a saint or martyr, esp. an item used in life or an instrument of torture.
second death *n. phr.* Awareness of the limited fulfillment one can achieve in a lifetime; extinction of a person in human memory.
second-degree murder see **murder in the second degree**
second-order denial *n. phr.* The inferences which a patient draws or fails to draw about the implications of a terminal illness.
secundogeniture *n.* Inheritance by the second son; property inherited by the second son.
Segomo *n. Gaulic.* God of war.
Seker *n. Egypt. myth.* A god of the dead and the necropolis.
Sekhet-Aaru *n. Egypt. myth.* The island abode of souls.
Sekhmet *n. Egypt. myth.* Goddess of war.
selection room *n. phr.* A showroom for caskets in a funeral home.
selective reduction or **selective termination** *n. phr.* The abortion of one or more fetuses of a multiple pregnancy while allowing remaining fetuses to be carried to term.
selective termination see **selective reduction**
selfcide *n.* Suicide; one who commits suicide. *var.* selfcidal, *adj.*
self-defense *n. Law.* Prevention of the commission of a felony against one's person or property by means which may include homicide.
self-deliverance *n.* Suicide.
self-deliveration *n.* Euthanasia.
self-destruction *n.* The act of destroying oneself; suicide.
self-destructive behavior *n.* Engaging in activities which threaten or shorten life.
self-execution *n.* Suicide.
self-homicide *n.* Suicide.

self-immolation *n.* Deliberate sacrifice of oneself; suicide by fire.

self-imposed death *n. phr.* Suicide.

self-inflicted death *n. phr.* Suicide.

self-mummification *n. Japan.* The medieval practice of placing the body of a priest in an urn for later exhumation and enshrinement.

self-poisoning *n.* Suicide by poison; overdose.

self-starvation *n.* Suicide by refusing to eat.

self-termination *n.* Suicide.

Selket *n. Egypt. myth.* Goddess of the dead.

Selkis *n. Egypt. myth.* Guardian of coffins.

sell out *idiom.* To suffer death rather than surrender; to die.

sem or **sem-priest** *n. Egypt.* Funeral priest; supervisor of burial rites.

sem-priest see **sem**

send across *idiom.* To kill; murder.

send across the river *idiom.* To kill; murder.

send home *idiom.* To kill; murder.

send home in a box *idiom.* To bury.

send home via the red route *idiom.* To shoot and kill.

send-off *n. slang.* Death.

send to glory *idiom.* To kill; to officiate at the burial services of.

send to Jericho or **send to Jesus** *idiom.* To kill; murder.

send to Jesus see **send to Jericho**

send to kingdom come *idiom.* To kill; murder.

send to one's future home *idiom.* To bury.

send up Salt River *idiom.* To kill; murder.

send west *idiom.* To kill; murder.

seneucia *n.* Widowhood.

senicide *n.* The killing of the aged, esp. as a tribal custom; one who kills the aged.

separation anxiety *n. phr.* A symptom of grief in which one yearns for the dead to return.

seppuku *n. Japanese.* Ritual suicide by disembowelment; hara-kiri.

septic abortion *n. phr. Med.* Termination of an embryo or fetus performed to prevent sepsis in the mother.

sepulcher also **sepulchre** *n.* A burial vault; a reliquary, esp. in an altar. *tr. v.* To entomb; inter.

sepulchral *adj.* Associated with a burial vault or grave.

sepulchre see **sepulcher**

sepulture *n. archaic.* Burial; a grave or tomb. *tr. v.* To bury or entomb. *var.* sepultured, sepultures, sepulturing, *v.*

serdah *n. Egypt.* A tomb chamber which contains a statue of the dead.

serial murder *n. phr.* The killing of several victims at different times by a single killer; one such killing.

serial murderer *n. phr.* One who has killed several victims at different times.

sermon in stone *idiom.* An epitaph.
Serquet *n. Egypt. myth.* Goddess of the dead.
service car *n. phr.* A hearse; a vehicle used to transport bodies.
Sesemu see **Sesmu**
Sesmu or **Sesemu** or **Sezemu** *n. Egypt. myth.* A god who sustains the dead with wine and sends heads of sinners through a wine press.
set as the sun *idiom. Japanese.* To die [used of emperors].
set easy *idiom.* To kill; murder.
settle one's account *idiom.* To die.
settle one's hash *idiom.* To kill, esp. to silence.
sewed up *idiom.* Dead.
sex killer *n. phr.* A murderer who sexually assaults his or her victims.
sex murder *n. phr.* A killing in which the victim is sexually assaulted.
sexton *n.* One who is responsible for custodial duties of a churchyard, esp. the digging of graves.
sexual homicide *n. phr. Law.* Killing in which the victim is sexually assaulted.
sexual necrophilia *n. phr.* Sexual intercourse with a corpse.
Sezemu see **Sesmu**
S.F.B.C.S. *abbrev.* St. Francis Burial and Counseling Society.
S.H.A. *abbrev.* Society for Humane Abortion.
shade *n.* Hades; a ghost.
shadow grief *n. phr.* Lingering sorrow after a death of great importance.
shaft grave *n. phr. Archeol.* A vertical hole terminating in a small burial chamber.
shaky one *n. phr. slang. Mexican.* Death in personified form.
Shango *n. African myth.* God of war.
shawabti *n. Egypt.* A small statue entombed with a mummy to serve him or her in the afterlife.
SHC *abbrev.* Spontaneous human combustion.
sheep-board *n. obs.* A wooden grave marker consisting of two posts and a board which extends lengthwise from head to foot.
shellshock *n.* Any of various psychological and emotional effects of trauma suffered under fire in war; combat fatigue. *var.* shell-shocked, *adj.*
Sheol *n.* Hell; the underworld in which the spirits of the dead wander; the grave. *var.* Sheolic, *adj.*
shibah see **shiva**
shillibeer *n. obs.* A horse-drawn hearse equipped with seats for mourners [after London coachman George Shillibeer].
shingled cross *n. phr. Hungarian.* A cruciform grave marker with a rounded roof.
shinju *n. Japan.* A suicide pact, esp. between lovers.
ship *tr. v. slang.* To kill; murder. *var.* shipped, shipping, ships, *v.*

ship burial *n. phr. Norse.* A method of disposal in which the body is put out to sea in a ship which is set afire; burial or entombment in a ship.
shiva or **shibah** *n. Orthodox Judaism.* The rites observed for seven days after a burial.
shock *n.* One of the first stages of grief in which survivors may be numbed by and unable to react to a death. *tr. v. slang.* To execute by electrocution.
shocked to death *v. phr. slang.* Electrocuted.
shoot *tr. v.* To kill with a missile, esp. fired from a gun. *var.* shooter, *n.*, shooting, shoots, shot, *v.*
shoot-'em-up *n. slang.* A film or television show which includes excessive physical violence, esp. shooting and killing.
shoot-out *n. slang.* A gun fight.
short shrift *n.* The time granted to a condemned prisoner to make a confession before execution; a short respite from death.
Shou Lao *n. Chinese myth.* God of longevity.
shove across *idiom.* To kill; murder.
shove-off *n. slang.* Death.
shrine *n.* A reliquary; tomb of a saint or martyr.
shroud *n.* A cloth in which a body is wrapped for burial; winding sheet. *tr. v.* To wrap a body for burial. *var.* shrouded, shrouding, shrouds, *v.*

shuffled out of the deck *idiom.* Dead.
shuffle-off *n. slang.* Death.
shuggie-shue *n. slang.* The gallows.
shut up shop *idiom.* To die.
sicarian *n.* An assassin; murderer. *adj.* Murderous.
Sicilian Vespers *pl. n. phr. slang.* A massacre; mass murder [derogatory].
Sic transit gloria mundi *idiom. Lat.* So passes away earthly glory.
SID or **sid** *abbrev. Med.* Sudden infant death.
sid see **SID**
SIDS or **S.I.D.S.** *abbrev. Med.* Sudden infant death syndrome.
S.I.D.S. see **SIDS**
S.I.E.C. *abbrev.* Suicide Information and Education Centre.
Signal 7 *abbrev. Law.* A corpse.
significant survival *n. phr.* Having done something for which one may be remembered after death.
sign off *idiom.* To die.
silence *tr. v. slang.* To kill; murder. *var.* silenced, silences, silencing, *v.*
silencer *n. slang.* Murderer; assassin.
silent land *n. phr. Egypt.* The abode of the dead.
silent passenger *n. phr.* A corpse transported by rail.
simple disposal *n. phr. Anthropol.* Disposal of the dead by a single procedure at one time.

sindon *n.* Shroud; winding-sheet.
sindonology *n.* The study of shrouds, esp. the Shroud of Turin. *var.* sindonologist, *n.*
sin-eater *n. archaic.* A social outcast willing to assume the sins of the dead for a fee.
siren *n. Gk. myth.* Deity who lures sailors to death by singing.
sit in the hotseat *v. phr. slang.* To be executed in the electric chair.
six feet under *idiom.* Dead and buried.
six-foot bungalow *idiom.* A casket.
sizzle *intr. v. slang.* To be executed in the electric chair. *var.* sizzled, sizzles, sizzling, *v.*
sizzle seat *n. phr. slang.* The electric chair.
Skanda or **Scanda** *n. Indian myth.* God of war.
skel *abbrev.* Skeletal; skeleton.
skeletalize *intr. v.* To be reduced to bones by decay. *tr. v.* To reduce a body to bones.
skeletochronology *n. Biol.* The determination of age from growth rings in bones.
skeleton *n.* The bones of the human body or a representation of them [often symbolic of mortality]. *var.* skeletal, *adj.*
skeletonization *n.* The process of being reduced to bones, esp. by decay.
Skeleton Park *n. phr. slang.* Cemetery.
skinny *n. slang. Mexican.* Death in personified form.
skrag see **scrag**
skull *n.* The bones of the human head or a representation of them [often symbolic of mortality].
skull and crossbones *n. phr.* A representation of a human skull with two crossed long bones, esp. as a symbol of death [associated with pirate ships and poison].
skullbox *n. obs.* An enclosure in which the head of a corpse was placed to facilitate its later separation from the bones.
sky burial *n. phr. Tibetan.* A method of disposal in which the corpse is cut in small pieces and fed to vultures.
slab *n. slang.* An examination table or storage tray on which a body lies in a morgue; autopsy table.
slabstone *n.* A grave marker which is flush with the ground.
slam off *idiom.* To die.
slant marker *n. phr.* A gravestone with an angled surface several inches above the ground.
slasher film or **slasher flick** *n. phr.* A movie which depicts many murders or excessive violence.
slasher flick see **slasher film**
slat *n. slang.* Tombstone.
slated for a fancy epitaph *idiom.* Near death; dying.
slaughter *n.* A mass killing; massacre. *tr. v.* To kill

violently or in large numbers. *var.* slaughterous, *adj.*, slaughterer, *n.*, slaughtered, slaughtering, slaughters, *v.*
slaughterhouse *n.* The scene of bloodshed.
slay *tr. v.* To kill brutally or deliberately. *var.* slayer, *n.*, slain, slaying, slays, slew, *v.*
slay ride *idiom.* Murder.
sleep *n. slang.* Death. *intr. v.* To die.
slicer *n. Egypt.* One who makes the abdominal incision during the preparation of a mummy.
slide into the last oblivion *idiom.* To die.
slip off *v. phr. slang. Nautical.* To die.
slip one's breath *idiom.* To die.
slip one's cable *v. phr. slang. Nautical.* To die.
slip one's wind *idiom.* To die.
slip-string *n.* One who deserves to be hanged.
slip the bump *idiom.* To kill; murder.
slip the works *idiom.* To kill; murder.
slough *intr. v. slang.* To kill; murder.
slumber robe *n. phr.* Shroud; burial garment.
slumber room *n. phr.* The room in a funeral home in which the body is displayed.
smabbled *p.part. slang. Mil.* Killed in battle.
smogged *p.part. slang.* Executed in the gas chamber.
smokehouse *n. slang.* The gas chamber.
smoke out *v. phr. slang.* To shoot and kill.
smother *tr. v.* To cause the suffocation of. *intr. v.* To suffocate. *var.* smothered, smothering, smothering, *v.*
smotheration *n. slang.* Suffocation.
smr *abbrev.* Standard mortality rate.
smrt *n. Czech.* + *Serbo-Croatian.* Death.
S.M.W. *abbrev.* Society of Military Widows.
snabbled *p.part. slang. Mil.* Killed in battle.
snipe *intr. v.* To shoot and kill from a concealed location. *var.* sniper, *n.*, sniped, snipes, sniping, *v.*
snub out *idiom.* To kill.
snuff *tr. v. slang.* To kill, esp. quickly. *adj.* Associated with death or murder. *var.* snuffed, snuffing, snuffs, *v.*
snuffer *n. slang.* A sex killer; producer of a snuff film; hit man.
snuff film or **snuff movie** *n. phr.* A visual recording of an actual murder; a film which realistically depicts murder.
snuff it *v. phr. slang.* To die.
snuff movie see **snuff film**
snuffocation *n. slang.* Suffocation.
snuff out *v. phr. slang.* To die.
social death *n. phr.* Withdrawal or exclusion from society prior to death during a prolonged process of dying; progressive loss of one's role in society.
social disengagement see **disengagement**

social heir *n. phr.* One who inherits special or helpful knowledge from an associate, friend, or parent.

social immortality *n. phr.* Leaving an impact on society which continues after death.

social killing *n. phr.* The death penalty. *slang.* The electric chair.

social suppression *n. phr.* The punishment of execution.

social thanatology *n. phr.* The study of dying, death, and bereavement.

societal cannibalism *n. phr. Anthropol.* Cannibalism as an established social custom.

sociopathic murderer *n. phr. Psychol.* A killer with no appreciation of laws or moral codes.

soil silhouette *n. phr. Archeol.* A dark stain in the ground which marks the former presence of a body.

Sokar *n. Egypt. myth.* Lord of the necropolis.

solace or **solacement** *n.* Comfort in grief; consolation. *var.* consoler, *n.*, consoled, consoles, consoling, *v.*

solacement see **solace**

solemnities *pl. n.* Funeral rites.

solitaire *n. slang.* Suicide.

Solon's Happiness *n. phr. slang.* Death [after Solon's maxim "Count no man happy till he is dead"].

solve rate *n. phr. Law.* The percentage of homicides in which the killer is arrested.

somatic death *n. phr.* Cessation of all vital functions followed by molecular or cellular death; extinction of the personality.

soon-to-terminate *adv. phr.* Moribund.

sororicide *n.* The killing of one's sister; one who kills one's sister. *var.* sororicidal, *adj.*

sorrow *n.* Grief. *intr. v.* To grieve. *var.* sorrowful, *adj.*, sorrowfully, *adv.*, sorrower, sorrowfulness, *n.*, sorrowed, sorrowing, sorrows, *v.*

Sosans see **Saosyant**

sough *intr. v.* To breathe one's last; to die. *var.* soughed, soughing, soughs, *v.*

soul *n. Theol.* The vital and immortal human spirit which separates from the body at death.

soul aloft *idiom.* Dead.

soul rescue *n. phr.* The process by which a spirit is made to understand that it is no longer embodied or earthbound.

soul shot *n. phr. slang. obs.* The dues collected upon the death of a member of a medieval funeral guild.

sound off *idiom.* To die.

space *n.* The decision by a terminal patient of how much energy to devote to the role of dying.

space warfare *n. phr.* Armed conflict carried out beyond the earth's atmosphere.

Spandarament *n. Armenian myth.* Goddess of the dead; hell.

Sparticide *n. Ger.* The killing

of a member of the Spartacus party; one who kills a member of the Spartacus party.
SPC *abbrev.* Suicide prevention center; suicide prevention clinic.
specific bequest *n. phr. Law.* A gift by will of a specific item of property in an estate.
specific legacy *n. phr. Law.* A gift by will of a specific item of property in an estate.
specimen of humanity *n. phr. slang.* A corpse.
spifflicate or **spiflicate** *tr. v. slang.* To silence by killing; murder.
spiflicate see **spifflicate**
spill *tr. v. archaic.* To kill. *var.* spiller, spillage, *n.*, spilled, spilling, spills, spilt, *v.*
spirit *n.* The soul; ghost. *var.* spiritual, *adj.*, spiritually, *adv.*, spiritualness, *n.*
spiritual bouquet *n. phr. Rom. Cath.* The undertaking of certain rites or devotions in memory of a dead person.
spiritual death *n. phr.* A diminished mental state brought about by a lack of intellectual and emotional activity.
spiritualism *n.* The belief in communication between the living and the dead, esp. through a medium; communication with the dead. *var.* spiritualistic, *adj.*, spiritualist, *n.*
splicing the rope *v. phr. slang. Scottish.* An informal meeting, esp. in a tavern, to make final arrangements before an execution.
spoil *tr. v.* To plunder a grave. *slang.* To kill; murder. *n. archaic.* The act of plundering a grave. *var.* spoiler, *n.*, spoiled, spoiling, spoils, spoilt, *v.*
sponsoring *n.* The act of passing on special and helpful knowledge to an associate, friend, or child.
spontaneous abortion *n. phr. Med.* A miscarriage.
spontaneous human combustion *n. phr.* An unexplained phenomenon in which one burns to death suddenly and apparently internally.
spot *tr. v. slang.* To mark for death. *var.* spotted, spotting, spots, *v.*
spouse murder *n. phr.* The killing of one's husband or wife.
spouse-murderer *n.* One who kills one's husband or wife.
spree killer *n. phr.* A serial murderer.
sprout wings *idiom.* To die and enter heaven.
squat *intr. v.* To be executed by electrocution. *var.* squatted, squatting, squats, *v.*
Sraosha *n. Persian myth.* Bearer of the souls of the dead to paradise.
S.R.D. *abbrev.* Society for the Right to Die.
S.R.F. *abbrev.* Survival Research Foundation.
Sri *pl. n. Tibetan myth.* Vampires.
Sridevi *n. Tibetan myth.* Judge of the dead.

S.S.A.N.W. *abbrev.* Social Scientists Against Nuclear War.

S.S.B. *abbrev.* Seasons: Suicide Bereavement.

SSKP *abbrev. Mil.* Single-shot kill capability.

stacking *pr.part.* The use of a single grave for the interment of two or more bodies, esp. husband and wife.

staffman *n. archaic.* A hangman.

stall *intr. v. slang.* To die. *var.* stalled, stalling, stalls, *v.*

stall one's engine *idiom.* To kill; murder.

stance *n.* The personal philosophy expressed by a person who is dying.

starve *intr. v.* To die due to lack of food. *v. archaic.* To die from exposure to cold temperatures. *tr. v.* To cause to die from lack of food. *var.* starvation, starveling, *n.*, starved, starves, starving, *v.*

state chemist *n. phr.* One employed to legally execute convicts in a gas chamber.

state electrician *n. phr.* One employed to legally execute convicts in the electric chair.

state funeral *n. phr.* Formal rites upon the death of a president or other important official, esp. including the lying in state of the body.

Stations of the Cross *pl. n. phr. Eccles.* Commemoration or depiction of the fourteen events in the Passion of Jesus Christ.

statute of wills *n. phr. Law.* The laws of a jurisdiction which govern the validity of testamentary disposition.

staurolatry *n.* Worship of the cross or crucifix.

staurophobia *n. Psychol.* Fear of crosses or crucifixes. *var.* staurophobic, *adj.* + *n.*

stay see **stay of execution**

stay of execution *n. phr. Law.* Postponement of carrying out a legal death sentence.

stele *n., pl.* **stela** An inscribed memorial to the dead.

step into one's last bus *idiom.* To die.

step off the carpet *idiom.* To die.

step off the curb *idiom.* To die.

step out *idiom.* To die.

step out of the picture *idiom.* To die.

sterile arms *pl. n. phr.* Deadly weapons or devices whose origin cannot be traced.

stiff *n. slang.* A corpse. *adj.* Dead.

stiff hunter *n. phr. slang.* One employed by a medical school to procure corpses for dissection and anatomical study.

stiff racket *idiom.* Death.

stiffville *n. slang.* The cemetery.

stifle *tr. v.* To smother; suffocate. *intr. v.* To die of suffocation. *var.* stiflingly, *adv.*, stifler, *n.*, stifled, stifles, stifling, *v.*

stigmata *pl. n. Christian.* Marks or wounds corresponding to those suffered by Jesus Christ during his crucifixion, esp. on the bodies of saints and mystics during religious ecstasy.

stillbirth *n. Med.* The birth of a dead child or fetus; a child or fetus which is born dead.

stillborn *adj. Med.* Dead at birth.

stipes crucis *n. phr. Lat.* The upright beam of a Roman cross, esp. when permanently anchored in the ground.

St. Michael see **Saint Michael**

stone *n.* A grave marker. *tr. v.* To kill by pelting with rocks.

stone dead *adj. phr. slang.* Unquestionably dead; long dead.

stone pillow *n. phr.* The grave; gravestone.

stoning *n. obs.* The punishment of being pelted with stones until dead, esp. after surviving being pushed from a cliff.

stonkered *p.part. slang.* Killed.

stop *tr. v. slang.* To shoot and kill. *var.* stopped, stopping, stops, *v.*

stop a packet see **cop a packet**

stop in one's tracks *idiom.* To kill; murder.

S.T.O.P.N.W. *abbrev.* Student/Teacher Organization to Prevent Nuclear War.

stop one's clock *idiom.* To kill; murder.

stranger murder *n. phr.* Homicide in which the killer and victim were unknown to each other.

strangle *tr. v.* To suffocate or choke to death by squeezing the throat; to smother. *intr. v.* To suffocate; choke. *var.* strangler, *n.*, strangled, strangles, strangling, *v.*

strangulate *tr. v.* To strangle. *var.* strangulation, *n.*, strangulated, strangulates, strangulating, *v.*

strapped *adj.* Fastened into the electric chair.

streeking *n. obs.* The preparation of a body for burial.

stretch *intr. v. slang.* To hang; to execute by hanging. *var.* stretched, stretches, stretching, *v.*

stretch a neck *v. phr. slang.* To execute by hanging.

stretcher *n.* A litter used to transport the dead.

stretch hemp *idiom.* To execute by hanging.

stretch out the hands *idiom. obs.* To be executed by crucifixion.

strike out *idiom.* To die.

string up *v. phr. slang.* To execute by hanging; lynch.

strych injec *abbrev. Med.* Death by the injection of strychnine.

STTL *abbrev. Lat.* May the earth lie light upon you [used of the dead].

stuffocation *n. slang.* Suffocation.

stupa *n. Buddhism.* A domed shrine containing a relic of Buddha.

Stygian *adj. Gk. myth.* Associated with the river Styx; associated with hell.

stygian see **Stygian**

stygiophobia *n. Psychol.* Fear of hell. *var.* stygiophobic, *adj.* + *n.*

styrgia *n.* A vampire.

Styx *n. Gk. myth.* The river

across which the souls of the dead are ferried to Hades.

subintentional death *n. phr.* An accident or murder in which the victim plays an unconscious or partial role in his or her own death.

submarine warfare *n. phr. Mil.* Armed conflict using underwater vessels.

successful suicide *n. phr.* A suicide which ends in death [pref. **completed suicide**].

succession *n. Law.* The sequence in which one succeeds to a station or estate upon the death of another; one's right to succeed to a station or estate; the process of becoming legally entitled to inherited property. *var.* successional, *adj.*, successionally, *adv.*, successor, *n.*

suction *n. Med.* A method of abortion in which a tube is inserted through the cervix to remove the embryo and placenta.

sudden death *n. phr.* A natural death which is unexpected and instantaneous.

sudden infant death *n. phr. Med.* The sudden, unexplained death of a healthy infant, esp. during the first year of life.

sudden infant death syndrome *n. Med.* A phenomenon which causes the sudden, unexplained death of healthy infants, esp. occurring during sleep in the first year of life.

suffoc. *abbrev.* Suffocating.

suffocate *tr. v.* To cause death by preventing access to oxygen; to choke or asphyxiate. *intr. v.* To suffocate or smother. *var.* suffocative, *adj.*, suffocation, *n.*, suffocated, suffocates, suffocating, *v.*

suggillation *n.* Bruising which develops after death.

suicidal *adj.* Associated with killing oneself. *var.* suicidally, *adv.*

suicidal behavior *n. phr.* Self-destructive activity.

suicidal ideation *n. phr.* Serious contemplation of killing oneself.

suicidal impulse *n. phr.* An urge to kill oneself.

suicidal tendencies *pl. n. phr.* A predisposition toward suicide, esp. evidenced by a previous suicide attempt.

suicide *n.* An act of active or passive self-destruction; one who kills oneself.

suicide airplane *n. phr.* An aircraft flown by a kamikaze pilot.

suicide by proxy *n. phr. slang.* Euthanasia.

suicide cluster *n. phr. Sociol.* Groups of three of more completed suicides which are closely related in time and space.

suicide epidemic *n. phr. Sociol.* A series of suicides which spread through a community or country; a wave of suicides.

suicide gesture *n. phr. Sociol.* A life-threatening action that is taken to gain attention or to seek help from others.

suicide mission *n. phr. Mil.* A directive which the participants are not expected to survive.

suicide note *n. phr.* A message left for survivors by a person who has killed himself or herself.

suicide pact *n. phr.* An agreement between two or more people to commit suicide together.

suicide prevention *n. phr.* The averting of potential suicides, esp. through counseling.

suicide prevention center *n. phr.* A social agency established to allow potential suicides a sanctuary until a self-destructive impulse has passed.

suicide season *n. phr. slang.* The time of the Christmas and New Year holidays, during which suicide rates increase.

suicide shrine *n. phr.* Any place used frequently to commit suicide.

suicidogenic *adj.* Causing or capable of causing suicide.

suicidology *n. Sociol.* The study of suicide, suicidal behavior, and suicide prevention. *var.* suicidologist, *n.*

suid *abbrev.* Sudden unexplained infant death.

suikaput see **suiterm**

suirep *abbrev. Law.* Suicide report.

suiterm or **suikaput** *n.* [A proposed term for] suicide as a permanent end to life.

Sulmanu *n. Assyrian myth.* God of war and the underworld.

summary execution *n. phr.* Sentence of death carried out without due process of law; lynching.

Supay *n. Peruvian myth.* The god of death.

supercollate *tr. v.* To hang by the neck. *var.* supercollated, supercollates, supercollating, *v.*

suppedanem *n.* A shelf attached to the upright of a cross to support the feet of those crucified.

supreme penalty *n. phr. slang.* Death; execution.

surgical death *n. phr. Med.* Death occuring during or as a result of a surgical procedure.

surv. *abbrev.* Surviving.

survive *intr. v.* To continue to live. *tr. v.* To outlive; to live through. *var.* survivable, *adj.*, survivance, survivability, survival, survivorship, *n.*, survived, survives, surviving, *v.*

survivor *n.* One who has lost a relative or friend through death; one who lives on.

survivorship *n. Law.* The right to inherit property due to having survived another with a claim to it.

suspected awareness or **suspicion awareness** *n. phr.* A condition in which a terminally ill patient suspects he or she is dying but receives no verification from hospital staff.

suspected murder *n. phr. Law.* A death which appears but has not yet proven to be homicide.

suspended animation *n. phr.* A dormant condition characterized by reversible cessation of the vital functions.

suspensus per collum *n. phr. Lat.* Hung by the neck; hanged.

sus. per coll. *abbrev. Lat.* Hung by the neck; hanged.

suspicion awareness see **suspected awareness**

suttee *n. Hinduism.* The practice in which a widow is voluntarily cremated on her husband's funeral pyre; one who is cremated on her husband's funeral pyre.

Svantevit or **Svetovid** *n. Slavonic myth.* God of war.

Svetovid see **Svantevit**

swaddling clothes *pl. n. phr.* A winding-sheet; shroud.

swallow one's birth certificate *idiom. Fr.* To die.

swan song *idiom.* One's last creation before death, supposed to be one's finest work [from the belief that the swan sings for the only time when it feels the approach of death].

swing *intr. v.* To be executed by hanging. *var.* swinging, swings, swung, *v.*

swing oneself *v. phr.* To commit suicide by hanging.

sword of justice *n. phr. slang. Fr.* The guillotine.

symbolic death *n. phr.* The ostracizing of one who does something socially unacceptable, esp. leaving his or her country or marrying outside the faith.

symbolic immortality *n. phr.* Living on after death through one's memory or works; afterlife.

sympathy *n.* The experience or expression of pity or sorrow for the bereavement of another. *var.* sympathetic, *adj.*, sympathize, sympathized, sympathizes, sympathizing, *v.*

T

tabernacle *n.* A niche or receptacle in which a relic is enshrined. *var.* tabernacular, *adj.*

tablestone or **table stone** *n.* A grave marker consisting of a horizontal stone elevated on supporting pillars.

table stone see **tablestone**

table tomb *n. phr.* A tomb in a catacomb which is closed with a slab of stone.

Ta-Djesart *n. Egypt. myth.* The underworld.

taisch *n. Scottish.* An apparition of a living person which is considered an omen of his or her death.

T'ai Shan *n. Chinese.* God of death.

take a dirt nap *idiom.* To be buried.

take a life *v. phr.* To kill; cause the death of.

take a long walk off a short pier *idiom.* To be killed [used as a threat].

take a powder *idiom.* To commit suicide.

take a rope *idiom.* To commit suicide by hanging.

take care of *v. phr. slang.* To kill; murder.

take down the pike *v. phr. slang.* To kill; murder.

take for a ride *idiom.* To drive to a secluded spot and kill [used as a threat].

take hemlock *idiom.* To commit suicide.

taken *p.part. slang.* Dead.

take off *idiom.* To kill someone; murder.

take off for eternity *idiom.* To die.

take oneself away *v. phr. Japanese.* To die.

take one's gruel *idiom.* To be killed.

take one's last drink *idiom.* To drown.

take one's own life *v. phr.* To commit suicide.

take out *idiom.* To kill or destroy, esp. the enemy during war.

take the checkers *idiom.* To be killed.

take the count *idiom.* To die.

take the coward's way out *idiom.* To commit suicide.

take the easy way out *idiom.* To die.

take the final count *idiom.* To die.

take the gas pipe see **take the pipe**

take the juice *idiom.* To be executed by electrocution.

take the jump *idiom.* To die.

take the last cue from life's stage *idiom.* To die.

take the last jump *idiom.* To die.

take the long count *idiom.* To die.

take the pipe or **take the gas pipe** *idiom.* To commit suicide.

take the rope cure *idiom.* To commit suicide by hanging.

taking the fruit *idiom.* Practicing cannibalism.

talamaur *n. Melanesian myth.* A vampire soul which lives off the last spark of strength in the dying or newly dead.

tamashiro *n. Japanese.* A receptacle in which the soul is carried during a funeral rite.

taphephobia or **taphophobia** *n. Psychol.* Fear of being buried alive; fear of graves or cemeteries. *var.* taphephobic, *adj.* + *n.*

taphonomy *n.* The processes which occur within a corpse from death to complete dissolution.

taphophilia *n.* Love of funerals.

taphophobia • testamentary disposition

var. taphophiliac, *adj.* + *n.*
taphophobia see **taphephobia**
tapped *p.part. slang.* Killed; murdered.
taps *pl. n. Mil.* A bugle call or other signal sounded at funerals and memorial services. *pl. n. slang.* Death.
target *n.* The object of a planned assassination.
tartarology *n.* Doctrine about hell.
Tartarus *n. Gk. myth.* A region below Hades where the worst sinners are punished; hell. *var.* Tartarean, *adj.*
tax of the dead *n. phr. slang. Hungarian.* Brandy made from the fruit of trees grown in a cemetery.
technological death *n. phr.* An impersonal death monitored by machines; death in a modern hospital [derogatory].
teenicide *n. slang.* The death of a teenager in an automobile accident. *var.* teenicidal, *adj.*
teknophagy *n. Anthropol.* Cannibalism practiced on children.
tell the bad news *idiom.* To kill; murder.
telos *n. Gk.* Death as a fulfillment of destiny.
temporary death *n. phr.* Clinical death with the assumption of potential revival, esp. after cryonic suspension.
tenant *n.* The occupant of a grave.
tenant by the curtesy *n. phr. Law.* The right of a husband to his dead wife's estate for his lifetime if the couple has born one or more heirs.
10-18 *abbrev. Law.* Dead at the scene.
terminal *adj.* Occurring at death; causing death. *var.* terminally, *adv.*
terminal care *n. phr.* Hospitalization to provide physical, psychological, and practical assistance to the dying.
terminal expression *n. phr.* A facial expression which suggests imminent death.
terminate with extreme prejudice *v. phr. obs.* To assassinate; kill.
termination *n.* Cessation of the vital physiological processes, including heartbeat and respiration; biological death.
term life insurance *n. phr.* A policy which pays a benefit if the insured dies within a specified number of years or before a specified age.
testacy *n. Law.* The condition of having executed a will before death.
testament *n. Law.* A written document by which one disposes of one's personal property after death; a will.
testamentary *adj. Law.* Associated with a will or testament.
testamentary causes *pl. n. phr. Law.* Matters associated with wills, including probate, granting administrations, and suing for legacies.
testamentary disposition *n. phr. Law.* A gift of property which takes effect at one's death.

testate *adj. Law.* Having made a legally valid will before death.

testator *n. Law.* One who has made a legally valid will before death.

testatrix *n. phr. Law.* A woman who has made a legally valid will before death.

Teutates *n. Gaulic myth.* God of war.

Texas cakewalk *idiom.* Death by hanging.

T.F. *abbrev.* Theos Foundation [an organization of widows].

T.F.Y.S. *abbrev.* Task Force on Youth Suicide.

thanat. *abbrev.* Thanatology.

thanatism *n.* The belief in enjoying life with no expectation of an afterlife.

thanatize *tr. v.* To process in a lethal manner. *var.* thanatized, thanatizes, thanatizing, *v.*

thanatognomonic *adj.* Indicating death.

thanatography *n.* The description of a person's death. *var.* thanatographic, *adj.*

thanatoid *adj.* Deathlike; deadly.

thanatology *n.* The interdisciplinary study of death-related behavior including actions and emotions concerned with dying, death, and bereavement; the study of the nature and causes of death. *var.* thanatologic, thanatological, *adj.*, thanatologically, *adv.*

thanatomania *n.* Suicidal mania; homicidal mania; death by auto-suggestion; abnormal interest in death. *var.* thanatomaniac, *adj.* + *n.*

thanatomimesis *n.* Feigned death; imitation of the dead.

thanatophile *n.* One who loves death or subjects associated with death.

thanatophilia *n.* Love of death. *var.* thanatophiliac, *adj.* + *n.*

thanatophobia *n. Psychol.* Fear of death or dying. *var.* thanatophobic, *adj.* + *n.*

thanatopsis *n.* A meditation upon death.

Thanatos *n. Gk.* God of death and the underworld; death as a philosophical idea.

thanatos *n.* A death wish; instinctual drive toward death. *var.* thanatotic, *adj.*

thanatosis *n.* A state which imitates death.

thanatosophy *n.* The philosophy of death. *var.* thanatosophic, thanatosophical, *adj.*, thanatosophically, *adv.*

thanatousia *pl. n.* Funeral rites.

thanatropism *n.* A drive toward death.

that one *n. phr. Austral.* The deceased [used by some tribes to avoid speaking the name of the dead].

theater of terror *n. slang.* A public execution.

theoktony *n.* Death of a god. *var.* theoktonic, *adj.*

theological death *n. phr.* The moment at which the soul leaves a dying body.

theological immortality *n. phr.* Afterlife; reincarnation.

therapeutic abortion *n. phr. Med.* Termination of an embryo or fetus due to the physical or mental condition of the mother.

there *n. Gk.* Hades; hell.

third-class relic *n. phr. Rom. Cath.* An object or cloth which has come in contact with a first-class or second-class relic.

third-order denial *n.* The image of death and extinction held by the terminally ill.

30 *abbrev. Telegraphy.* Death.

This is it! *interj. Mil.* Possible or probable imminent death [used of an approaching missile].

3-Ds *abbrev.* Discouragement, disillusionment, and disappointment [a mnemonic device for the causes of suicide].

three-sides cross *n. phr.* A cross from which the victim was hanged by one leg and one arm.

threnetic *adj.* Mournful. *var.* threnetical, *adj.*

threnody *n.* A lament for the dead; elegy. *var.* threnodial, threnodic, *adj.*, threnodist, *n.*

thrill murder *n. phr.* Sadistic killing, esp. without sexual assault.

throat trouble *idiom.* Death by hanging.

thropple *tr. v. slang.* To throttle. *var.* throppler, *n.*, throppled, thropples, throppling, *v.*

throttle *tr. v.* To strangle or choke, esp. with the hands. *var.* throttler, *n.*, throttled, throttles, throttling, *v.*

throw from the cart *v. phr. archaic.* To hang.

throw in the dustbin *idiom.* To bury.

thrown for a loss *idiom.* Dead.

throw sixes *idiom.* To die.

throw up the cards *idiom.* To die.

throw up the sponge *idiom.* To die.

thud *interj. slang. Mil.* Died in an aircraft accident.

thug *n.* A cutthroat; killer. *Hinduism.* A member of the thuggee sect who worship Kali by strangling as many victims as possible. *var.* thuggish, *adj.*, thuggery, *n.*

thunderbolt *n. slang.* The electric chair.

Thyestean banquet *n. phr.* A feast at which human flesh is eaten.

Tien *n. Chinese myth.* Heaven.

time of death *n. phr.* The hour, day, or season in which a person dies.

tip off *idiom.* To die.

tissue death *n. phr. Med.* Fetal death; stillbirth.

Tiu *n. Ger. myth.* God of war.

Tlaloc *n. Aztec myth.* A rain god to whom children were sacrificed annually by drowning.

Tod *n. Ger.* Death.

todestrieb *n. Ger.* Death drive.

Todote *n. Siberian myth.* God of death.
toes up *idiom.* Dead.
tola *n. Ecuadorean + Peruvian.* A burial mound.
toll *n.* The number of deaths caused by a disaster; the sound of a bell to mark a death. *tr. v.* To sound a bell mournfully. *intr. v.* To sound mournfully [used of a bell]. *var.* toller, *n.*, tolled, tolling, tolls, *v.*
tomb *n.* A chamber in which the dead are buried; a monument to the dead.
tomb-dimensions *n. Archeol.* The spatial orientation of a grave or burial chamber.
tomb-location *n. Archeol.* The geographical and contextual orientation of a grave or burial chamber.
tombstone *n.* A gravestone.
Tonatiuh *n. Aztec myth.* A god who offered immortality to those who died in battle or in childbirth.
tonic immobility *n. phr. Biol.* Instinctual feigning of death.
tontine *n.* A group of beneficiaries who will property to each other until the last survivor gets the lot.
top *tr. v. slang.* To kill; murder. *var.* topped, topping, tops, *v.*
Tophet *n.* Hell [after a place of human sacrifice near Gehenna].
torch out *idiom.* To shoot and kill.
torpedo *n. slang.* Professional murderer; hitman.
toss in one's marbles *idiom. Austral.* To die.
total funeral *n. phr. inf.* A rite which includes a religious service and display of the embalmed corpse.
totentanz *n. Ger.* Dance of death.
touch home *idiom.* To inflict a mortal wound.
touching the flesh *v. phr. slang.* Practicing cannibalism.
tox *abbrev. Med.* Toxic; toxicology.
toxic *adj.* Deadly; poisonous. *var.* toxically, *adj.*
toxicant *n. Med.* A poison or deadly chemical. *adj.* Poisonous.
toxicophobia *n. Psychol.* Fear of being poisoned. *var.* toxicophobic, *adj.* + *n.*
toxiphobia or **toxophobia** *n. Psychol.* Fear of being poisoned. *var.* toxiphobic, *adj.* + *n.*
toxophobia see **toxiphobia**
trade embalmer *n. phr.* A freelance embalmer.
trag. *abbrev.* Tragedy; tragic.
tragedy *n.* A disaster or accident, esp. involving loss of life.
transcendence *n.* The final stage of dying in which mystical or religious states of consciousness are experienced.
transfer one's rifle to the left side *idiom. Fr. Mil.* To die.
transi *n. archaic.* A cadaver; image of a decaying corpse as a reminder of death [lit., the perished one].
translation *n.* The transfer of

relics from the original place of burial to a new location. *var.* translate, translated, translates, translating, *v.*

translation to heaven *n. phr. Theol.* Acceptance of a soul into heaven.

transmigration *n.* Transfer of the human soul from one body into another at death. *var.* transmigratory, *adj.*, transmigrate, transmigrated, transmigrates, transmigrating, *v.*

trauma death *n. phr.* A death involving sudden, violent physical injury.

traveling bag *n. phr. slang. Fr.* The weight attached to the blade of a guillotine.

tree burial *n. phr. Anthropol.* A method of disposal in which the body is entombed in a treehouse.

tremore et reverentia *idiom. Lat.* With fear of death and respect for the dead.

trental *n. Rom. Cath.* A series of thirty daily masses for the dead.

triangle murder *n. phr.* The killing of one's spouse and the spouse's lover in a jealous rage.

trigger *intr. v. slang.* To plan a murder. *var.* triggered, triggering, triggers, *v.*

trigger-happy *adj.* Liable to shoot and kill with little provocation.

triggerman *n. slang.* Assassin; killer.

triple tree *n. phr. obs.* A triangular gallows at Tyburn, England which was used for multiple executions.

tristisonous *adj.* Mournful [used of a sound].

tri-unit method *n. phr.* A method of pricing a funeral which includes separate charges for professional services, use of facilities, and casket.

trocar *n.* A long, hollow needle used to inject embalming fluid into a corpse.

trophy *n.* The tomb of a martyr; a monument marking the site of one's martyrdom.

trucidation *n.* Bloodshed.

trumped *p.part.* Dead.

trunk murder *n. phr.* A killing in which the body is dismembered, placed in a suitcase, and abandoned, esp. in a train station.

T.S. *abbrev.* Telophase Society [a cryonics organization].

tsantsa *n.* A shrunken and preserved human head, esp. prepared by a Jivaro Indian.

Tu *n. Polynesian myth.* God of war.

t.u. *abbrev.* Toes up.

Tuat *n. Egypt. myth.* The abode of the dead.

tube *intr. v. slang. Med.* To die. *var.* tubed, tubes, tubing, *v.*

tumbrel or **tumbril** *n. archaic.* A wagon used to transport condemned prisoners to the execution site.

tumbril see **tumbrel**

tumbrilitis *n. slang.* The transport of the condemned to the place of execution, esp. in a humiliating way.

tumulate *tr. v.* To entomb. *var.* tumulated, tumulates, tumulating, *v.*

tumulus *n. pl.* **tumuli** An ancient grave mound.

Tuonela *n. Finno-Ugrian myth.* The abode of the dead in which giants and mortals await rebirth.

Turms *n. Etruscan myth.* Guide of souls to the underworld.

turn belly up or **go belly up** *idiom.* To die.

turn into the wind *idiom. Chinese.* To revenge by leaving the slain bodies of enemies unburied.

turn it in *idiom.* To die.

turn off *idiom.* To kill; murder.

turn one's toes *idiom.* To die.

turn one's toes to daisies *idiom.* To die and be buried.

turn one's toes up or **turn up one's toes** *idiom.* To die.

turn out the lights *idiom.* To commit suicide.

turn up one's toes see **turn one's toes up**

twist in the wind or **twist slowly in the wind** *idiom.* To be executed by hanging [often used figuratively].

twist slowly in the wind see **twist in the wind**

two-legged mutton *n. phr. archaic. Chinese.* Human meat sold for consumption.

typewriter party *idiom.* Killing with a machine-gun.

Typhoid Mary *n. phr.* One who spreads a deadly disease [after Mary Mallon (?–1938), a carrier of typhoid].

Tyr *n. Ger. myth.* God of war who assists in choosing entrants to Valhalla.

tyrannicide *n.* The killing or killer of a tyrant; the doctrine which the killing of a tyrant justified.

tzompantlis *pl. n. Aztec.* Stone structures on which the skulls of human sacrifice victims were displayed.

U

U.A.G.A. *abbrev.* The Uniform Anatomical Gift Act.

U.C.P.N.W. *abbrev.* United Campuses to Prevent Nuclear War.

UDS *abbrev. Law.* Under death sentence.

ultimate crime *n. phr. slang.* Murder.

ultimate high *n. phr. slang.* Lethal injection as a method of legal execution.

ultimate penalty *n. phr. slang.* Death.

ultimate sacrifice *n. phr.* Death in service to one's country during war.

ultimogeniture *n. Law.* The right to inherit or succeed held by the youngest child.

ululate *intr. v.* To wail or lament, esp. loudly. *var.* ululation, *n.*, ululated, ululates, ululating, *v.*

uncoffined *p.part.* Not in a casket [used of a corpse].

unconscious person *n. phr.* A dead body [used euphemistically by police].

unconscious suicide *n. phr. Sociol.* Chronic self-destructive behavior.

unconventional warfare *n. phr. Mil.* Nuclear warfare.

undead *pl. n.* Corpses which revive, esp. to attack the living.

under a cottonwood limb *idiom.* Hanged.

under-bearers *pl. n. archaic.* Men employed to bear the actual weight of the bier for the pall bearers during the procession.

undercroft *n.* A vaulted burial chamber under a church.

under daisies *idiom.* Dead and buried.

underground jungle *idiom.* A cemetery.

under sailing orders *idiom. Nautical.* Dying.

undertaker *n.* One who arranges for the burial or cremation of the dead and assists at funeral rites in a professional capacity [pref. **funeral director**].

undertaking *n.* The profession or duties of a funeral director.

underworld *n. Gk. + Rom. myth.* The abode of the dead beneath the world of the living; Hades.

undo nature's work *idiom.* To commit suicide.

undtkr. *abbrev.* Undertaker.

unintended death *n. phr.* Death in which a person plays an active role in his or her demise.

unit method *n. phr.* A method of pricing a funeral in which all the costs for goods and services are included in a single charge.

unknelled *p.part.* Unmourned.

unmourned *p.part.* Not grieved for.

unseen one *n. phr. Gk. myth.* Hades.

untimely death *n. phr.* Premature death; death occurring at an inappropriate time.

unwept *adj.* Not grieved for.

upasian *adj.* Deadly; poisonous [after the upas tree, a source of arrow poison].

upholder *n. archaic.* A contractor of funeral services; undertaker.

upright monument *n. phr.* A grave marker consisting of a vertical slab mounted on a base.

up the flue *idiom.* Dead.

uranophobia see **ouranophobia**

urn *n.* A container in which the ashes of the dead are stored after cremation.

Ursanabi *n.* The ferryman of the underworld stream [from the Gilgamesh epic].

158 U.S.C.A.N.W. • vaticide

U.S.C.A.N.W. *abbrev.* United States Committee Against Nuclear War.
used up *idiom.* Dead; murdered.
U.S.G.R.S. *abbrev.* United States Graves Registration Service.
ushabti *n. Egypt.* A small statue entombed with a mummy to serve him or her in the afterlife.
USLA *abbrev. Mil.* Upper specification limit for averages of acceptable loss.
USW or **usw** *abbrev. Mil.* Underwater submarine warfare.
usw see **USW**
UW *abbrev. Mil.* Unconventional warfare.
uxoricide *n.* The killing of one's wife; one who kills one's wife. *var.* uxoricidal, *adj.*

V

v.a. *abbrev. Lat.* The number of years he or she lived.
Vahran see **Verethraghna**
Vaitarani *n. Hindu myth.* The river of death which flows between the lands of the living and the dead.
vakatoga *n. obs. Fijian.* The practice of severing a person's limbs and baking and eating them while he or she is still alive.
valet *n. archaic.* An executioner's assistant.
Valhalla *n. Norse myth.* The abode of the souls of slain warriors.
Valkyries *pl. n. Norse myth.* Female demons who choose the heroes to be slain and conduct their souls to Valhalla.
Valley of Jehoshaphat *n. phr.* The site of the Last Judgment [according to Biblical prophecy].
vamp *abbrev.* Vampire; vampirism.
vampire *n. Slavonic myth.* An evil spirit or revived corpse which sustains itself by sucking the blood of humans. *var.* vampiric, *adj.*
vampirism *n.* Depletion of another's blood or vitality.
v. and m. *abbrev.* Virgin and martyr.
vanities *pl. n. archaic.* Genre paintings in which reminders of death are depicted to signify vanity and mortality.
Vanth *n. Etruscan myth.* A messenger of death.
vaticide *n.* The killing of a prophet or poet; one who kills a prophet or poet. *var.* vaticidal, *adj.*

vault *n.* An underground burial chamber; a metal or concrete receptacle into which a casket or an urn is buried to prevent settling of the ground.
Vayu *n. Persian.* A god who assists the dead in their journey.
ve *abbrev. Fr.* Widow.
ved *abbrev. Ital.* Widow.
vegesimation *n.* The killing of every twentieth person.
vegetative death *n. phr. Med.* Brain death.
vehic manslgtr *abbrev. Law.* Vehicular manslaughter.
vehicular manslaughter *n. phr. Law.* Death caused by the negligent operation of a motor vehicle.
Veles *n. Slavonic myth.* God of the underworld.
Velu mate or **Kapu mate** *n. Latvian myth.* Queen of the dead who welcomes them to the cemetery.
venenation *n.* Poisoning.
Verethraghna or **Vahran** *n. Persian myth.* God of war.
vertical burial *n. phr.* The interment of a corpse in an upright position, esp. to save space.
vertical cemetery *n. phr. slang.* A high-rise mausoleum.
V.E.S. *abbrev.* Voluntary Euthanasia Society.
vetalas *pl. n. Vedic myth.* Evil spirits who inhabit corpses.
Via Dolorosa *n. phr. Lat.* The route in Jerusalem which Jesus Christ was forced to follow to the place of crucifixion [lit., road of sorrow].
via the rod route *adv. phr. slang.* By means of a fatal shooting.
viaticum *n. Eccles.* The sacrament of Holy Eucharist given to a dying or endangered person.
victim-precipitated homicide *n. phr. Sociol.* A murder in which the victim contributes to the events leading to his or her death.
vid. *abbrev. Lat.* Widow.
viduage *n.* Widowhood; a group of widows.
viduity *n.* Widowhood.
viduous *adj.* Widowed; bereaved.
viewing see **viewing the remains**
viewing the remains *v. phr.* or **viewing** *v.* Observing a corpse, esp. after arrangement in a casket; attending a wake.
village of the dead *n. phr. slang.* Cemetery.
Vily *pl. n. Slavonic myth.* The souls of young women in the form of wind and storm who lead men to death.
violent crime *n. phr. Law.* A crime of physical brutality, including murder.
violent death *n. phr.* A physically brutal death, esp. a murder.
viricide *n.* The killing of a man, esp. one's husband; one who kills a man. *var.* viricidal, *adj.*
virulent *adj. Med.* Poisonous. *var.* virulently, *adj.*, virulence, *n.*

visitation period *n. phr.* A social gathering before a funeral which may take on a religious function; a wake.

visitation room *n. phr.* The room in a funeral home in which the body is displayed.

vis major *n. phr. Law.* An act of God.

vital events *pl. n. phr.* Significant events in human life, including deaths.

vitalism *n.* The principle of maintaining life at any cost.

vital statistics *pl. n. phr.* Records of significant events and dates in human life, including deaths.

vivisepulture *n.* Burial of one who is alive; premature burial.

vk *abbrev.* Volume kill.

V&M *abbrev.* Virgin and martyr.

Vodnik *n. Slavonic myth.* The demon soul of a drowned unbaptized child.

volume of death *n. phr.* The numbers and proportion of death in a society within a given period.

voluntary euthanasia *n. phr.* Euthanasia carried out at the request of the one whose life is being taken.

voluntary manslaughter *n. phr. Law.* Manslaughter committed intentionally with reasonable provocation

voodoo *n. Haitian.* A cult or religion once involving human sacrifice and cannibalism which originated with African Ashanti cults and is still practiced in some places.

voodoo death *n. phr.* A death caused by sorcery.

V-P homicide *abbrev. Sociol.* Victim-precipitated homicide.

vrykolakas *n. Gk.* A vampire.

vulture *n. slang.* One who profits from the dead.

Vve *abbrev. Fr.* Widow.

W

w *abbrev.* War; widow.

waesuck *interj. Scottish.* [An expression of] sorrow or sympathy.

waghalter *n. archaic.* One who is likely to be hanged.

wail *n.* An audible expression of grief, esp. a ritualized cry. *intr. v.* To express grief audibly. *tr. v. archaic.* To grieve over. *var.* wailed, wailing, wails, *v.*

wailful *adj.* Mournful.

wake *n.* A watch kept over a body before burial; the display of an embalmed body for viewing.

walk onto a spot *idiom.* To

step into a deathtrap.
walk the plank *v. phr. Nautical.* A method of execution associated with pirates in which the victim was forced to walk blindfolded along a plank laid over the side of a vessel until he or she fell into the sea and drowned.
wall *n.* The backdrop of an execution by firing squad.
W.A.P.S.I.D. *abbrev.* Washington Association for Preventing Sudden Infant Death.
war *n.* A state or period of armed conflict; the techniques of armed conflict. *intr. v.* To take part in armed conflict.
war crime *n. phr.* A crime against humanity committed during a war in violation of established customs of warfare.
warfare *n.* Armed conflict.
war memorial *n.* A public monument commemorating military personnel killed in an armed conflict.
wartime *n.* A period of armed conflict.
wash away *idiom.* To kill; murder.
washed up *idiom.* Dead; dying.
washout *n. slang.* Death.
wash out *idiom.* To kill; murder.
wash up *idiom.* To kill; murder.
wash-up *n. slang.* Death.
waste *tr. v. slang.* To kill; murder. *var.* wastes, wasting, *v.*
wasted *p.part.* Dead; killed.
way of all flesh *idiom.* Death; the dying process.
W.C.C. *abbrev.* Widows Consultation Center.
W.E.A. *abbrev.* Women Exploited by Abortion.
wear cement shoes *v. phr.* To be killed, esp. by drowning [used as a threat].
Wed *abbrev.* Widow.
weed *n. archaic.* An unadorned black mourning garment.
weep *intr. v.* To mourn or grieve. *var.* weeping, weeps, wept, *v.*
weepers *pl. n.* A black or white band worn on the sleeve by men in mourning; hired mourners.
well-holed *adj.* Riddled with bullets [used of a corpse].
wergeld see **wergild**
wergild or **wergeld** *n. Ger.* A price paid to the relatives or lord of a slain man to compensate for the death and free the killer from further liability.
Werther effect *n. phr.* A suicide epidemic [after Goethe's *The Sufferings of Young Werther,* 1774].
west *adj. slang.* Dead.
westerners *pl. n. Egypt.* The collective dead.
whack out *idiom.* To murder.
whiro *n. Maori myth.* God of darkness and death.
white death *n. phr. slang.* The great white shark.
whole life insurance *n. phr.* A policy purchased with level premiums over life or for a specified period which guarantees a specific sum of money to a designated beneficiary upon the death of the insured.

wi *n. Egypt.* An embalmed and wrapped mummy.
wid *abbrev.* Widow; widower.
wid. *abbrev.* Widow; widower.
widdy *n.* A rope used for hanging. *adj.* Deserving to be hanged.
widow *n.* One whose husband has died and who has not remarried. *n. slang. Fr.* The guillotine. *tr. v.* To make a widow of. *tr. v. obs.* To be widowed by. *var.* widowed, widowing, widows, *v.*
widower *n.* One whose wife has died and who has not remarried.
widowerhood *n.* The state or period of being a widower.
widowhood *n.* The state or period of being a widow.
widow-maker *n. slang.* The left anterior descending artery of the heart; a dangerous horse; something which is life-threatening.
widow's election *n. phr. Law.* The right of a widow to choose to abide by the terms of her husband's will or reject the will and demand what is provided for a widow by law.
widow's weeds *pl n. phr.* Black clothing worn by women in mourning.
wife-killer *n.* The killing of a woman by her husband; a man who kills his wife.
wiitiko psychosis *n. Cree + Ojibwa.* A mental disorder characterized by an obsessive desire for human flesh which leads to homicidal cannibalism.
will *n. Law.* A legal document or declaration in which one disposes of his or her estate to take effect after death.
willful homicide *n. phr.* Deliberate killing.
William Boilman *n. phr. archaic.* [The nickname for] a public executioner.
willow coffin *n. phr. archaic.* A burial receptacle made of basketry or wicker to facilitate decay.
Windigo *n. Native Amer. myth.* A race of giants who practice cannibalism in winter when food is scarce.
winding-sheet *n.* A cloth used to wrap a corpse; shroud.
windup *n. slang.* Death.
wink out *idiom.* Die.
win one's glorious palm *idiom.* To be martyred.
winter *n. poetic.* A time of death.
winter body *n. phr.* A corpse stored during the winter until the ground thaws and a grave can be dug.
winterkill *n.* Death from exposure to cold weather.
wipe *slang. n.* A killing *tr. v.* To kill; murder. *var.* wiped, wipes, wiping, *v.*
wipe off the map *idiom.* To kill; destroy completely.
wipe oneself out *idiom.* To commit suicide.
wipe out *v. phr. slang.* Assassinate; kill; destroy completely.
wired *p.part.* Electrocuted.
wirra *interj. Ir.* [An expression of] sorrow or sympathy.

with a garden on the stomach *idiom.* Dead and buried.

with God *idiom.* Dead and in heaven.

within an inch of one's life *idiom.* Until one is almost dead.

W.N.A.A.C. *abbrev.* Women's National Abortion Act Coalition.

woe *interj.* [An expression of] sorrow. *n.* Deep grief or misfortune.

woebegone *adj.* Appearing mournful [lit., beset with woe].

woeful also **woful** *adj.* Causing or experiencing woe.

woful see **woeful**

wooden jacket *idiom.* A casket.

wooden kimono *idiom.* A casket.

wooden overcoat *idiom.* A casket.

wooden suit *idiom.* A casket.

work off *idiom.* To kill; murder.

works *pl. n. slang.* The electric chair.

the works *pl. n. phr. slang.* Killing; murder.

worm-food *n. slang.* A corpse.

W.P.S. *abbrev.* Widowed Persons Service.

wr *abbrev. Mil.* War risk.

wraith *n.* The apparition of a living person interpreted as an omen of death; ghost.

wreath *n.* A circular arrangement of flowers offered as a memorial.

wring one's neck *v. phr. inf.* To strangle [often used figuratively].

written off *idiom. Mil.* Killed, esp. carelessly.

wrongful death *n. phr. Law.* A death in which negligence was a contributing cause.

wrongful death statute *n. phr. Law.* A law which allows the death of an individual to be a cause of action in a civil suit.

wry-neck day *n. phr. archaic.* The day of a public hanging.

WT *abbrev. Mil.* War time.

WW *abbrev. Mil.* World war.

WWI *abbrev.* The first World War [1914-1918].

WWII *abbrev.* The second World War [1939-1945].

w.w.a. *abbrev. Law.* With the will annexed.

Wwe *abbrev. Ger.* Widow.

W.W.W.C. *abbrev.* World Without War Council; Women's War on War Conference.

W.W.W.I. *abbrev.* Widows of World War I.

X

X-17 *n. slang.* A mortality table.

xat *n. Native American.* A carved pole erected as a memorial to the dead.

X'd *p.part.* Executed.

X'd out *v. phr. slang.* Killed.

Xipe totec *n. Mexican myth.* A god of spring who wears the skin of a flayed captive who has been sacrificed to him.

Xi-wang-mu *n. Chinese.* Goddess of death who has the power to bestow immortality.

Xocotl *n. Aztec myth.* A god of fire and stars associated with dead warriors.

Xolotl *n. Aztec myth.* A dog-headed god who helps the dead cross the river and enter the underworld.

X out *idiom.* To kill.

Y

Yaaru *n. Egypt. myth.* The fields in the netherworld which are tilled to provide the dead with food; the Field of Reeds.

Yalaing *Oceanian myth.* The afterlife, reached by an arduous journey.

Yama *n. Hinduism.* The kingdom of the dead; a god and judge of the dead and the prince of hell.

Yamadutas *pl. n. Hinduism.* Guides of souls to Yama.

Yan-lo or **Yan Wang** *n. Chinese myth.* God of the dead.

Yan Wang see **Yan-lo**

yardarm *n. Nautical.* The place on a vessel which serves as a gallows.

Year Day *n. phr. archaic.* The anniversary of a death; the day on which a death is commemorated by a requiem service.

Yen-lo-wang or **Yen-Wang** *n. Chinese.* Yama, the Hindu god of the dead.

Yen-Wang see **Yen-lo-Wang**

Yin-cao *n. Chinese.* Judge of hell.

yod *abbrev.* Year of death.

yomer *adj.* Mournful.

Yomi *n. Japanese myth.* The netherworld.

Yomotsu-kuni see **Nenokatatsu-kuni**

you-know-where *n. slang.* Hell.

yowl *n.* A loud, mournful cry; wail. *intr. v.* To sound a mournful cry; wail. *var.* yowled, yowling, yowls, *v.*

Y.S.N.C. *abbrev.* Youth Suicide National Center.

Z

Zaba *n. Hurrite myth.* God of war.
Zagreus *Gk. myth.* God of rebirth and immortality.
zap *tr. v. slang.* To kill, esp. quickly; murder. *var.* zapped, zapping, zaps, *v.*
Zemes mate *n. Baltic myth.* Ruler of the dead.
Zhong-li Quan *n.* A god who revives the dead with a fan.
zombi see **zombie**
zombi astral *n. phr. Haitian.* An aspect of the soul which may be enslaved; a zombie of the spirit.
zombi cadavre *n. phr. Haitian.* A reanimated and enslaved corpse; a zombie of the flesh.
zombie also **zombi** *n. Haitian.* A reanimated corpse, esp. one which is enslaved and without will.
zombi savane *n. phr. Haitian.* One who has returned to life after being a zombie.
zonk oneself *v. phr. slang.* To commit suicide.
zotz *tr. v. slang.* To kill; murder. *var.* zotzed, zotzes, zotzing, *v.*
z-table *n. slang.* Mortality table.

THESAURUS

ABORTION
SYN. ab, ab., aborticide, amblosis, carve up, child destruction, child-murder, empty the uterus, feticide, foeticide, mooncalf, post-conceptive contraception, post-contraceptive fertility control, prenatal euthanasia, tissue death
Associations: A.A., A.A.A., A.A.I., a.a.a.l., A.A.S., A.H.A., A.I.D.B., A.L.R.A., A.R.A., A.R.M., A.S.A., C.C.S.A., C.R.A., C.S.A.C., I.C.A.R., L.W.C.A.A., N.A.A.F., N.A.C., N.A.F., N.A.R.A.L., R.C.A.R., right to life, S.H.A., W.E.A., W.N.A.A.C.
Methods: abortifacient, ambiotic, A-pill, d & c, dilation and curettage, ecbolic, hysterotomy, salt poisoning, suction
Types: partial abortion, pregnancy reduction, psychiatric abortion, saline abortion, selective reduction, selective termination, septic abortion, suction abortion, therapeutic abortion

AFTERLIFE
see Death, Immortality, Resurrection
SYN. afterworld, anagoge, beyond, consolation literature, damnation, Ekei, eternal, eternal care unit, eternal rest, everlasting life, hadephobia, hereafter, inferno, k.c., kingdom come, liebestol, life after death, life-in-death, lower world, netherworld, ouranophobia, paradise, perdition, religious immortality, restoration, silent land, tartarology, theological immortality, underworld, uranophobia, you-know-where
Christian: Abraham's bosom, anastasis, Beulah Land, blessed, blest, celestial air force, church suffering, church triumphant, eschatology, Gehenna, intermediate state, limbo, pandemonium, refrigerium, sprout wings, Tophet
Classical: Acheron, Acherusian Bog, Asphodel Meadows, Cerberus, Charon, chthonian, chthonic, Cocytus, danake, down there, Elysian Fields, Elysium, Erebus, Field of Asphodels, Field of Offerings, Fields of Punishment, Fortunate Fields, hound of hell, Isle of the Blessed, Lethe, obolus, Orcus, Phlegethon, stygian, Styx, Tartarus, there

Nonclassical: Aalu, Abaddon, Adlivun, Al-Sirat, Amentet, Amenti, Annwn, Aralu, Avalon, Bardos, Book of the Dead, Duat, Field of Reeds, Happy Hunting Ground, Hel, Jigoku, Kuthu, Kuzimo, Land of the Moon, letters to the dead, Mag Mel, Manala, Mictlam, Nai Thombo Thombo, Nenokatatsu-kuni, Neno-kuni, Niflheim, Nine Wells, Prydain, Sekhet-Aaru, Sheol, Ta-Djesart, thanatism, Tien, Tuat, Tuonela, Vaitarani, Valhalla, Xolotl, Yaaru, Yalaing, Yama, Yomi, Yomotsu-kuni

ASSASSINATION
see Crime, Murder
SYN. armed propaganda, death threat, direct action, executive action, exit plan, health alteration committee, hired gun, hit, iron out, make bones, morganize, neutralize, propaganda by deed, put out a contract, put the cross on, put the finger on, rub out, spot, target, terminate with extreme prejudice, wipe out
  Assassin: hatchet man, headhunter, highbinder, hired gun, hitman, international disposal man, long knife, mbt, mechanic, murder for hire, sicarian, torpedo, triggerman
  Investigation: A.A.R.C., AIB, assassrep, C.I.A., Congressional Assassination Act, death threat, P.C.A.P.J.F.K.

AUTOPSY
see Corpse
SYN. autop, complete autopsy, human dissection, medical-legal autopsy, necropsy, necroscopy, necrotomy, pm, post, postmortem, postmortem examination
  Examination: algor mortis, bullet entrance wound, bullet exit wound, cadaveric spasm, hypostasis, instantaneous cadaveric spasm, livor mortis, post-mortem changes, rigor mortis, suggillation, trocar
  Investigation: accidental death, coroner's jury, DOS, forensic odontology, hospital autopsy rate, inquest, psychological autopsy, skeletochronology
  Medical examiner: cor., coroner, crowner, death profession, diener, FCAP, forensic medicine, I.A.C.M.E., ME, M.E., medical examiner, mortuary diener, N.A.M.E., N.B.M.E., necroscience, preparation room, S.B.M.E.
  Morgue: anatomy room, cold room, deadhouse, decomposed room, five-day case, ice box, Old Mr. Grim's house, slab

BURIAL
See Corpse, Cremation, Funeral, Grave
SYN. aged in wood, basketed, beneath, box, boxed up, bur., cold-meat party, committal, committal service, count worms, crate, d&b, deep six, deposit, deposited with the parent earth, disposition, earth bath, entombment, give the last compliment, go to grass, ground sweat, have a gar-

den on the stomach, hold up the Bermuda grass, inhume, insarcophagusment, inter, interment, in the dustbin, intumulate, landowner, lay one's bones, lay to rest, measured for a new overcoat, packed up, pat on the face with a spade, plant, planting, potted, put one to bed with a shovel, put under, put under glass, put under hatches, reburial, s., salt away, salt down, send home in a box, send home via the rod route, send to glory, send to one's future home, send west, sepulture, sewed in a blanket, six feet under, take a dirt nap, throw in the dustbin, tumulate, with a garden on the stomach

Associations: C.A.F.M.S., C.H.M.A., C.M.A.A., C.W.G.C., H.F.B.A., I.W.G.C., L.A.F.S., M.S.A.C., N.C.B.V.A., P.A.I.A.A.

Chamber: arcosolium, catacombs, charnel house, cist, columbarium, confessio, cromlech, crypt, cubiculum, dromos, entomb, finestra, golden room, house of eternity, house of the ka, hypogeum, immure, loculus, marabout, mastaba, mausoleum, ossuary, oven, pyramid, pyramidology, ra-stau, rock-cut tomb, sacellum, sepulcher, sepulchral, sepulture, serdah, skullbox, tomb, undercroft, vault

Exhumation: disentomb, disinter, reburial, resume, soil silhouette

Mound: barrow, cairn, cist, montjoy, tola, tumulus

Premature: defossion, life signals, taphephobia, vivisepulture

Preparation for: acroteriazein, bier, burial goods, burial guild, burial laws, burial programs, casketed, catafalque, cere, decani, direct disposers, embalm, f.c., foot candle, f.t.c., funeral furniture, funeral merchandise, funerary furniture, funerary offerings, GR, grave-finds, grave gifts, GrReg, grreg, GRS, laid out, lay out, lay up in lavender, memorial estate, memorial society, mortuary fee, plot, preneed, prothesis, quarterage, S.D.M.S., S.F.B.C.S., shawabti, soul shot, U.S.G.R.S., ushabti, wake

Receptacle: anthropoid coffin, baldachin, bedside coffin, bone box, bone house, bone-vase, box, burial case, burial casket, burial enclosure, burial safe, C, canopic jar, canopus, casket, casket-burial case, casket-case, Chicago overcoat, coffin, coffin-case, coffin furniture, coffin-maker, coffin-plate, cold meat box, cold-meat crate, encoffin, end sealer, enshrine, eternity-box, govi, grave liner, half-couch, HRC, human remains case, ice coffin, kimona, man box, mort, mort-safe, mummy-case, mummy-coffin, outside enclosure, pall, peach-blossom cave, pine box, pine overcoat, planting crate, prison coffin, rental casket, repository, sarcophagus, sealer casket, six-foot bungalow, vault, willow coffin, wooden jacket, wooden kimono, wooden overcoat, wooden suit

Shroud: burial bundle, burial clothing, burial robe, cerecloth, cerements, enshroud, mort cloth, sindon, sindonology, slumber robe, swaddling clothes, winding-sheet

Types: bundle burial, burial at sea, catacomb burial, chested, deep 6, dry burial, earth burial, ground burial, hydriotaphia, immurement, intramural burial, multiple burial, organic burial, scaffold burial, secondary burial, second burial, ship burial, sky burial, stacking, tree burial, vertical burial, winter bodies

CANNIBALISM
see Human sacrifice
SYN. androphagous, anthro, anthropophagus, ghuls, man-eater, necrophage, taking the fruit, Thyestean banquet, touching the flesh, Windigo
  Consumption: bakolo, blood, long pig, two-legged mutton
  Types: endocannibalism, endophagy, exophagy, necrophagy, nonrecurrent cannibalism, omophagic rites, societal cannibalism, teknophagy, vakatoga, wiitiko psychosis

CAUSES
see Abortion, Assassination, Autopsy, Crucifixion, Death, Euthanasia, Execution, Murder, Terminal Illness
SYN. bane, be death on, deathblow, death-dealing, death threat, put in one's grave
  Air injection: air injec, bubbling
  Asphyxia: autoerotic asphyxia, gasphyxiation
  Choking: cafe coronary, pnigophobia, quackle, quirk
  Crib Death: D.S.F., FSIDSP, N.S.I.D.S.C., N.S.I.D.S.F., SID, sid, SIDS, sudden infant death, sudden infant death syndrome, W.A.P.S.D.
  Disease: Black Death, Black Plague, CA, DOD, dod, Great Death, loimic, loimology, pestilence, plague, scourge, Typhoid Mary, virulent, widow-maker
  Dismemberment: artuate, decollate, rest in pieces, white death
  Drowning: feed the fishes, gone for a Burton, make a hole in the water, noyade, spilled in the drink, take one's last drink
  Electrocution: burn, juice, shocked to death, take the juice
  Exposure: starve, winterkill
  Fire: holocaust, SHC, spontaneous human combustion
  Impalement: ganch, poleax
  Poison: alc, bane, black-bottle, bomb, fd50, hot shot, iafd, inheritance powder, iophobia, LD, ld, ld50, least fatal dose, lethal dosage, lethal dose, level four, LFD, lfd, minimun fatal dose, MFD, mfd, mithridatize, MLD, mld, mld50, morph injec, overjost, pizen, poi., pois., strych injec, tox., toxicant, toxicophobia, toxin, toxiphobia, toxophobia, venenation
  Shooting: be stopped, blast off, blow one's head off, blow one's lights out, blow one's top off, blow out, blow the gizzard out of, burn off, cannon, castored, chop off, crack down, crack off, feed a fatal pill, go down blazing, had one's name on it, iron out, lead-poison, pick off, pump off, rod out, smoke out, stop, torch out, via the rod route, well-holed

Starvation: do a perisher, peg
Strangulation: autoerotic strangulation, burke, jugulate, masturbatory strangulation, neck, pull a score, strangle, strangulate, wring one's neck
Suffocation: burke, forlie, hypoxemia, overlaying, pnigerophobia, quackle, smother, smotheration, snuffocation, stifle, strangle, stuffocation, suffoc.
Transportation accident: donor-cycle, fatal accident, grease the track, hobo short line, teenicide

CEMETERY
see Burial, Grave
SYN. A.N.C., bone factory, bone-orchard, boneyard, boothill, burial ground, burial place, burying-ground, cem., cement city, churchyard, city of the dead, city of the silent, F.L.M.P., future home, God's Acre, God's field, Golgotha, graveyard, hell's half-acre, last abode, last home, laystall, Marble City, marble orchard, memorial park, mortuary estate, necropolis, N.M.C.P., ossuary, permanent rest camp, rest camp, sacred land, Skeleton Park, Stiffville, underground jungle, village of the dead
   Associations: A.A.C., A.A.C.S., A.C.A., A.C.C.M., A.C.M.C., C.C.S.C., C.S.C.A., C.S.C.A.S., I.C.S.A., N.A.C., N.C.A., N.C.B.V.A., N.C.C.C., N.C.S., S.C.A.
   Care of: brambling, cemeterians, cemetery reform, C.S.I.I., C.W.G.C., death profession, Memorial Services, National Cemetery System, perpetual care, sexton
   Gods of: Baron Samedi, Cecrops, Seker
   Structures/Sections: cemetery lot, corpse gate, cross of the cemetery, cross of the dead, D.O.M., exedra, hud, lich gate, lich stone, lich way, lychgate, monument lot, tax of the dead, vertical cemetery
   Types: architectural cemetery, forest cemetery, gallery 13, landscape cemetery, park cemetery, potter's field, prison cemetery, rural cemetery

CORPSE
see Autopsy, Grave
SYN. atomy, body, broken pitcher, cad., cadav, cadaver, cadaveric, carcass, carrion, cdv., charogne, clay, cold meat, cold pig, corp, corpus, corse, croaker, crowbait, db, dead body, deader, dead goner, dead meat, defunct, dog meat, filling for a casket, flybait, food for worms, goner, John R. Corpse, khet, landowner, lich, lych, meat, megacorpses, morgue-aged property, necr-, necro-, pork, relics, remains, remnants, roast, roast meat for worms, Signal 7, silent passenger, specimen of humanity, stiff, 10-18, terminal expression, transi, uncoffined, unconscious person, worm food
   Blood of: cruentation, exsanguinate, gore, grisly, hypostasis, sanguinary, sanguineous

Decay of: adipocere, autolysis, caseation, decompose, dessication, grave wax, livor mortis, miasma, molder, Rainbow Body, sapon., saponification, spoil, transi, turn into wind

Disposal of: burial, burial position, CDC, compound disposal, concealment of birth, cremation, disposition, dokhma, encharnelled, final disposition, grave, primary disposal, secondary disposal, simple disposal, sky burial

Dissection of: bioemporium, biological philanthropy, body bequest program, burking mania, burkiphobia, burkism, dissecting fee, donor, donor-cycle, eyebank, neomort, paunch, resurrection days, rolfincked, sack-'em-up men, U.A.G.A.

Preservation of: adipocere, artificial mummification, auto-icon, C.C.M.S., cooling board, corpse cooler, corpse preserver, cutter, E.C.M.A., embalm, embalming fluid, five-day case, house of vigor, house of vitality, hypoinjection, ice coffin, incorruptibles, intentional natural mummification, mummify, mummy, mummy unrolling, natural mummification, sanitary embalmer, sapon., saponification, scribe, self-mummification, slicer, suspended animation, trade embalmer, trocar, tsantsa, wi

Skeleton: anthropolite, anthropolith, articulated, bones, calvarium, crossbones, Dance of Death, danse macabre, death's-head, disarticulate, extended, flexed, Jolly Roger, ossature, osteobiography, paleopathology, physical anthropology, skel, skel., skeletalized, skeletochronology, skeletonization, skull, skull and crossbones

Storage of: A.C.S., A.L.E.F., B.A.C.S., C.A., cryogenic interment, cryonaut, cryonics, cryonic suspension, cryopreservation, C.S.S.D., dormantory, freezee, frozen death, human cold storage, in cold storage, I.S., L.E.S., neural preservation, post-suspension counseling, resuscitee

Transport of: bear, body bag, body cot, meat wagon, removal cot, remove, stretcher

CREMATION

see Burial

SYN. balefire, crem., crematist, crematorium, funeral pyre, incineration, pyre

Associations: C.A.A., C.A.NA.A., C.S.N.A., I.C.F.

Remains: ashes, cinerary, cremains, remains

Disposal: cinerarium, columbarium, cremo., dial-a-mation, Doms, incinerator, inurnment, niche, urn

CRIME

see Assassination, Mortality, Murder

Life threat: abwik, ADW, adw, aggravated assault, armed robbery, assault with a deadly weapon, assault with intent to kill, attempted murder, cwik, dangerous weapon, ddw, deadly weapon, death

threat, DWA, Make my day!, mug, noiseless assassin, ransom, reckless disregard, Russian roulette, shoot-out, sterile arms, trigger-happy
Organized: brains, button man, cement coffin, concrete overcoat, contract, drop-dead list, gang hit, hatchet man, headcrusher, headhunter, hit list, hitman, hit murder, hot shot, id racket, laundered man, mechanic, merchant of death, put out a contract, put the finger on, trigger
Punishment of: abatement by death, natural life sentence, wrongful death statute
Types: capital, capital crime, grave crime

CRUCIFIXION
see Execution, Martyrs, Resurrection
SYN. anamnesis, carry a tree, exactor mortis, lifted up, quaternio, stretch out the hands
  Cross: crouch, crux commissa, crux decussata, crux humilis, crux immissa, patibulum, rood, staurolatry, staurophobia, stipes crucis, suppedanem, three-sides cross
  Of Christ: anamnesis, Calvary, Easter, Golgotha, madonna della febre, Mater Dolorosa, mortorio, Passion, pietà, Stations of the Cross, stigmata, Via Dolorosa

DEAD
see Death, Die, Dying, Soul
SYN. absent from the body, across the river, amort, asleep in the deep, at home with the Lord, at rest, basketed, behind the scenes, belly up, bloodless, blooey, blown away, bound for glory, called away, called home, ceased, cold, content, cooked, crestos, cut adrift, d., d'd, dead and gone, dead as a doornail, dead as a herring, death-struck, dec., decd., deceased, decedent, def., defunct, departed, dished, diw, dog meat, done for, doubled up, down for the long count, easy, e vev. disc., exanimate, extinct, feeling no pain, finished, flattened, flattened out, flummoxed, flunked out, folded, folded up, free, gest, go down, gone, gone beyond, gone pffft, gone phut, goner, gone the way of all flesh, gone to a better place, gone to Davey Jones's locker, gone to glory, gone to heaven, gone to one's maker, gone to Riga, gone under, gone up Salt River, gone west, good, grounded for good, hasn't come back for his or her cap, heros, home, in cold storage, installed in furnace No. 10, in storage, in the dustbin, in the hereafter, Kami, kaput, kicked off, knocked off, knocked out, knocked over, k.o.'d, Kwei, laid out, laid to rest, late, licked, lifeless, liquidated, makarios, makarites, missing, napoo, now picking at the coverlet, ob., obiit, obt., one's hash is settled, one's race is run, on ice, on the cooling board, on the shelf, out, outed, out for the long count, out like a light, out of it, out of one's misery, out of the game, out of the picture, out of the running, out of the

way, overboard, p, petered out, Pitaras, playing one's harp, pushing the clouds around, ran the good race, resting, resting easy, rubbish, safely gathered in, sewed up, shuffled out of the deck, six feet under, soul aloft, stiff, stone dead, taken, 10-18, that one, thrown for a loss, toes up, trumped, t.u., under daisies, up the flue, used up, washed up, wasted, west, westerners, winked out, with God

DEATH
see Abortion, Casualties, Dead, Die, Disaster, Dying, Hospital, Soul, Terminal illness
SYN. abiosis, all bets off, all off, all up, all washed up, back door parole, back-gate exit, big jump, biocide, blowoff, bow out, bump off, call, call all bets off, call it a day, call it a job, call it quits, call of God, cold, croak act, curtain call, curtains, deanimation, debt of nature, deep end, demise, done on toast, dood, end, end of life, end up, EOL, expr., extreme penalty, fadeout, final call, final curtain, final kickoff, final kiss-off, final payoff, final push-off, final summons, finis, finish, fold, fold-up, funeral in one's family, getaway, gone cold, gone for a Burton, great out, heavy fall, kibosh, kick-off, kifo, kiss-off, knock-off, konk-out, kuolema, last bow, last call, last cue, last debt, last go-off, last muster, last oblivion, last rattler, last roll call, last roundup, last send-off, Libitina, lights out, loss of life, mati, moarte, mort, morte, morto, muerte, necr-, necro-, obit, one-way ride, one-way ticket, pale horse, payday, pay-off, push-off, quietus, rest, reward, send-off, shove-off, shuffle off, sleep, smrt, stiff racket, supreme penalty, take-off for eternity, taps, Thanatos, 30, Tod, ultimate penalty, washout, wash-up, way of all flesh, windup
   Accidental: A., Ack, act of God, ad&d, autocide, autoerotic asphyxia, blow across the creek, blue glow, criminal negligence, DAI, double indemnity, fatal, fatal accident, fatality, negligent manslaughter, non-negligent manslaughter, perish, tragedy, wrongful death statute
   Angels of: Azrael, Gabriel, St. Michael, Valkyries
   Announcements of: banns, bidder, biography, death crier, death notice, death watch, elogy, funeral achievement, hatchments, heriot, Inviter to Funerals, necrol., necrologist, necrologue, necrology, next of kin, NNK, notification, obit, obituarian, obituarist, obituary, pronounce
   Associations: A.D.E.C., C.E.D.
   Averted: basic thanatomimetic narrative, borrowed time, close call, close shave, I.A.N.D.S., keep body and soul together, N.D.E., near and certain, but averted death, near-death encounter, near death experience, nondeath, out of the woods, pulmonary resuscitation, reanimation, relict, save, S.R.F., survival, survive, within an inch of one's life, zombi savane
   Demons of: Ammit, Charontes, Chihuateteo, Citipati, Culsu, Eurynomous, Galla, ghoul, Ghuls, Ke'lets, Lamia, Lelwani, Nari,

Nidhoggr, nosferatu, Pey, Rusalka, Sri, talamaur, undead, vamp., vampire, vampirism, Vetalas, Vodnik, Vrykolakas, zombi astral, zombi cadavre, zombie

Descriptions of: abatement by death, acerbitas mortis, agonal, à la mort, A.M., à outrance, backdoor parole, back-gate parole, bioscopy, capital, C.D.E.R., consolation literature, coup de grace, death day, deathlike, death-related, d in a, d in b, distant and certain death, distant and uncertain death, dn, doi, dormitio, DOW, dow, kba, liebestod, necrography, nominal marriage, PM, POD, pod, post-death, postmortal, postmortem, post-obit, rite of passage, telos, thanatognomonic, thanatography, thanatopsis, tremore et reverentia, untimely, vitalism

Fear of: agonal, annihilation anxiety, antidysthanasia, awareness of finitude, ballistophobia, bell the cat, Burking Mania, Burkiphobia, Burkiphoby, coimetrophia, death anxiety, death-capitulator, death fear, death-welcomer, earthquake fever, hadephobia, Hine-Nui-Te-Po, iophobia, necrophobia, nucleomitaphobia, ouranophobia, placophobia, pnigerophobia, pnigophobia, premonition, taphephobia, thanatophobia, traumataphobia

Ghosts of: di Manes, ekephalos, Etemmu, ghost, give up the ghost, haint, Lemures, Lemuria, manes, Nari, necrolatry, necromancy, Preta, psychomancy, revenant, sciomancy, shade, spiritualism, taisch, Vily, Vodnik, wraith

Gods/Goddesses of: Abatur, Adapa, Aecus, Aesculapius, Ahriman, Aiakos, Aker, Ala, Alignak, Allatu, Amentet, Amenti, Ameretat, Anaitis, Anubis, Apis, Arawn, Ares, Arimanius, Armaiti, Asto Vidatu, Ataecina, Atropos, Baiame, Barastir, Beletseri, Beli, Bhagwan, Branab Llyr, Charun, Chontamenti, Cihuateto, Clotho, Coatlicue, Crnobog, Crnoglav, Dagda, Dagde, Dagodevas, Danu, Daramulun, Diancecht, Dis Pater, Di-zang, Dong-yo Da-di, Ekimmu, Emma-O, Eochaid Ollathair, Ereshkigal, Erinyes, Erlik, Erra, Fatit, Februus, Furies, Gaea, Giltine, Guede, Gula, Gun, Gwynn, Ha, Hades, Harendotes, Haros, Hathor, Haurvatat, Hecate, Hel, Hermes, Heros, Hine-nui-te-po, Holle, Horae, Hotep, Hsi-Wang-Mu, Hunhau, Igau, inferiae, Isdes, Ixtab, Izanami, Jarri, Jumala, Jurojin, Kapu mate, Keres, Lachesis, Libitina, Lord of the Cave Mouth, Lord of the Divine Hall, Maat, Mahuika, Mamitu, Mamtar, Mars, Mayin, Meresger, Mictlantecutli, Minos, Moma, Morrigan, Mot, Mutu, Ndjambi, Ndyambi-Karunga, Nebthet, Nehebkau, Nephthys, Nergal, Nga, Ninazu, Nirrti, Nurundere, Nyia, Orcus, Osiris, Pachacamac, Pakheth, Pancaraksa, Persephone, Petbe, Picullus, Pluto, Proserpina, Pusan, Pwyll, Ran, Rasnu, Rhadamanthus, Ruad Ro-fhessa, Ruti, Saosyant, Seker, Selket, Selkis, Serapis, Serquet, Sesmu, Shou Lao, siren, Sokar, Spandarament, Sridevi, Sulmanu, Supay, T'ai Shan, Thanatos, Todote, Tonatiuh, Turms, unseen one, Ursanabi, Vanth, Veles,

Velu mate, Whiro, Xipe totec, Xi-wang-mu, Xolotl, Yama, Yan-lo, Yen-lo-wang, Yen-Wang, Zagreus, Zemes mate, Zhong-li Quan
Mimicry of: amort, anabiosis, death feigning, depersonalization, necromimesis, necromorphous, play opossum, play possum, thanatomimesis, thanatosis, tonic immobility
Omens of: anthropomancy, banshee, barghest, blue glow, burculacas, deathbell, death-fire, death knell, death-token, fetch, fetch-light, Jolly Roger, necromancy, Nekker, Nikker, taisch
Personification of: bold one, bony one, buck-toothed, clean and peeled one, Dance of Death, danse macabre, Death, equalizer, Flat-nosed, frugal one, grave one, Great Leveller, Great Whipper, Grim Monarch, Grim Reaper, Mr. Mose, Old Floorer, Old Man Mose, Old Mister Grim, pale horse, reaper man, shaky one, skinny, totentanz
Premature: angelitos, angel makers, A.R.L.S., C.G.I.S., chrisom, cut off, deadborn, die before one's time, early fetal death, fetal death, I.C.I.S., intermediate fetal death, killing nurses, late fetal death, L.O.S.S., M.C.P.L., miscarriage, Nav, N.C.R.F.Y.S., neonatal death, N.P.B.A., P.C.C.Y.D., perinatal death, sds, S.I.D.S., spontaneous abortion, stillbirth, stillborn, sudden infant death, sudden infant death syndrome, suid., untimely
Study of: death education, eschat., eschatology, I.I.S.D.I., L.D.P., meanings of death, mechanics of death, social thanatology, thanat., thanatology, thanatosophy
Types: accidental death, anesthesiological death, anthropological death, apparent death, appropriate death, artificial death, autoerotic death, biological death, brain death, cardiac death, cellular death, cellular/molecular death, cellu-vegetative death, cerebral death, civil death, clinical death, constructive death, creative death, dormition, ego death, equivocal death, fetal death, heart death, intentional death, interruption, legal death, line-of-duty death, living dead, medical death, megadeath, metabolic death, metaphorical death, mort bon Dieu, N, natural death, needless death, neonatal death, obiit sine prole, omnicide, operative death, organ death, organismal death, perinatal death, permanent vegetative state, presumptive death, pseudo-death, psychic death, psychological death, psychosomatic death, puppet death, PVS, ritual death, second death, social death, somatic death, spiritual death, subintentional death, sudden death, surgical death, suspended animation, symbolic death, taphonomy, technological death, temporary death, termination, theoktony, theological death, trauma death, unintended death, vegetative death, voodoo death

DIE
see Dead, Death, Dying, Terminal illness
SYN. be all washed up, be bound for glory, be cancelled, become a

landowner, become filling for a casket, be cut down, be put to bed with a shovel, be salted away, be thrown for a loss, bite the dust, bow off, bow out, box, break it off, break one's clay pipe, breathe one's last, burn slowly, buy the farm, cancel one's account, cash in one's checks, catch the tide, cheat the gallows, check out, click it, close up one's accounts, cock up one's toes, coil up one's cable, coil up one's rope, conflummox, conk, conk out, count daisies, crap out, croak, cross over, curl up and die, curl up one's toes, cut one's cable, cut one's stick, decease, depart, die all at once, die by inches, die game, die in harness, die in one's boots, die in one's shoes, die off, die out, die with one's boots on, die without issue, do a blackout, do a croak, do a fadeout, do a fold, do a fold-up, do the croak act, douse, draw a blank, drop everything, drop off, drop off the hook, drop one's leaf, drop the curtain, d.s.p., d.u., d.v.m., d.v.p., eat dandelions by the root, ebb out, escape, evaporate, exit, expire, expr., fade out, fan out, fire one's last shot, fizz, fizzle out, flatten out, flicker out, flunk out, fly off the handle, get one's everlasting, get one's ticket punched, get out from under, get paid off, get the call, give in, give life the go-by, give life the slip, give up, give up the ghost, give up the ship, give up the struggle, go across, go across the river, go belly up, go bung, go cuckoo, go dead, go home feet first, go into eclipse, go into the shadows, go Lethewards, go off the handle, go out, go over, go the way of all flesh, go to grass, go to kingdom come, go to one's account, go to one's ka, go to one's last reward, go to the last roundup, go to the races, go under, go up the flue, go west, grow stiff, hand in one's chips, hand in one's dinner pail, hang up, hang up one's harness, head for Cloud Nine, hear the final call, hit the rocks, honk out, hop a twig, hop off, hop off the perch, hop the last rattler, join the immortals, join the majority, jump the last hurdle, keel over, kick, kick off, kick the bucket, kick up one's heels, kick up one's toes, kiss off, kiss the dust, launch into eternity, lay down one's knife and fork, lay down one's shovel and hoe, lay down on the job, lay 'em down, leave feet foremost, lose breath, lose the decision, make a die, make one's final exit, meet, meet one's allotted day, ob, o.b., obt., pack up, pass away, pass in one's chips, pass on, pass out, pass out of the picture, pass over, pay one's last debt, pay St. Peter a visit, pay the debt of nature, pay the last debt, peg out, perish, pike, pip out, play one's last card, play one's last hand, pop off, pop off the hook, predecease, pull in at the last terminal, put one's checks back in the rack, put out one's nightlight, quit, rejoin one's ka, rest in Abraham's bosom, ring down the curtain, ring off, ring out, rot, run down, run out, say goodbye to this world, sell out, set as the sun, settle one's account, shut up shop, sign off, slam off, sleep, slide into last oblivion, slip off, slip off one's cable, slip one's breath, slip one's cable, slip one's wind, snuff it, snuff out, sough, sound off, sprout wings, stall, step into one's last bus, step off, step off the carpet, step off the curb, step out, step out of the picture, strike out, swallow one's birth certificate, take a dirt nap, take off for eternity, take oneself away, take the count, take the easy way out, take the final count, take the jump, take the last cue from life's stage, take the last jump, take the long count, throw sixes, throw up the cards, throw up the sponge, tip off, toss in one's marbles, transfer one's rifle to the left side, tube, turn belly up, turn it in, turn one's toes, turn one's toes to daisies, turn one's toes up, turn up one's toes, wink out

DISASTER
see Causes
SYN. accidental death, act of God, annihilation, calamity, catastrophe, D, damnum fatale, destroy, holocaust, trag., vis major
  Types: acute disaster, chronic disaster
  Victims of: accounted for, bite the dust, body count, bought it, buy it, buy the farm, cas., cascan, cascor, civil defense, commorient, cop, cop it, death roll, death toll, earthquake fever, fatality, gone across the creek, identification, kd., knocked cold, lay down one's life, lay down one's mess, pip, scuppered, toll, written off, zap

DYING
see Dead, Death, Die, Hospital, Terminal illness
SYN. amort, ante mortem, at death's door, at the end of one's rope, cessation, charopalevi, circle the drain, death agony, deathbed, death by degrees, death sentence, done for, done under, done up, eleventh hour, emergent, final decline, gone, goner, had it, in articulo mortis, in extremis, in peril, near and certain death, one foot in the grave, one foot in the grave and the other on a banana peel, one's days are numbered, one's number is up, on one's last leg, on one's last pegs, on the spot, perimortem, played one's last card, preagony, predeath, soon-to-terminate, under sailing orders
  Descriptions of: agathanasia, agonal breath, agonal heartbeat, ante mortem, antethumous, ars moriendi, booked, cadaverous, cold-bed, deathbed hallucinations, deathbed visions, deathbed words, death-chill, death-damp, death gurgle, death rattle, death room, death scene, death-sough, death-throe, deathwatch, death with dignity, dying day, dying words, last breath, last days, last laugh, last words, lead apes in hell, life review, like death warmed over, long goodbye, no more chance than a rabbit, resistance, ride one out, slated for a fancy epitaph, swan song, thanatropism, This is it!, transcendence, washed up
  Last rites of: A.A.D.N.C., anele, anointing of the sick, deathbed confession, deathbed marriage, dying declarations, extreme unction, Kiss of Peace, last anointing, P.U.S.J.D., P.U.S.J.D.S., pyx, viaticum

EUTHANASIA
see Terminal illness

SYN. death control, death with dignity, euthanize, marantology, mercy death, mercy killing, orthothanasia, pessimism, pull the plug, self-deliveration, suicide by proxy
Associations: A.E.F., C.D., C.F.D., E.A.C., E.E.C., E.E.F., E.S.A., H.L.F., H.S., I.A.E.J.F., right to die, S.R.D., V.E.S.
Types: active euthanasia, active voluntary euthanasia, benemortasia, geronticide, indirect involuntary euthanasia, indirect voluntary euthanasia, involuntary euthanasia, medicide, misericorde, negative euthanasia, non-voluntary euthanasia, passive euthanasia, positive euthanasia, put out of one's misery, quietus, senicide, voluntary euthanasia

EXECUTION
see Crime, Crucifixion, Murder
SYN. capital punishment, capun, cruel and unusual punishment, death penalty, die with one's boots on, ex., exec., execution in effigy, extreme penalty, judicial murder, lifeboat, lynch law, public murder, social killing, social suppression, supreme penalty, theater of terror
Associations: A.L.A.C.P., C.A.L.M., C.P.P., L.L., N.C.A.D.P., N.E.A.N., P.A.D.P.
Beheading: block, decap, decapitate, decollate, head-chopping, high block, low block
Burning at the stake: auto-da-fé, burning in effigy, philotheopareptesism, quemadero
Condemned: all up with, attainder, C., cc, cd., cheat the gallows, civil death, cold meat shed, corruption of blood, dance hall, dead man, death cell, death chamber, executee, execution chamber, execution ground, execution sermon, gallows bird, gallows literature, get the works, give short shrift to, hand of glory, hangman's meal, last confession, last meal, last mile, last waltz, last wish, lead away, long goodbye, mourning cart, pre-execution chamber, roue, short shrift, tumbrel, tumbrilitis, UDS, wry-neck day, X'd
Dismemberment: drawing and quartering, godly butchery
Drowning: keelhauling, keelraking, noyade, walk the plank
Electric chair: America's Hot Seat, barbecue stool, burn, chair, cheat the chair, cook, dance hall, death switch, die in the hotseat, electric cure, electrocute, electrocution chamber, electrolethe, fry, give a permanent wave, hair curler, hot seat, hummingbird, juice, manufactured lightning, old smoky, old sparky, ol' sparky, ride the lightning, shock, shocked to death, sit in the hotseat, sizzle, sizzle seat, social killing, squat, strapped, take the juice, thunderbolt, wired works
Executioner: bourreau, carnifex, carnificial, choker, death profession, deathsman, dempster, execution squad, galgenmeister, gallows man, hangman, headsman, hereditary hangman, Jack Ketch, John Ketch, Esq., lockman, loon-slatt, Lord High Executioner, master of high

works, mazzatollo, monsieur de Paris, scragsman, staffman, state chemist, state electrician, valet, William Boilman

Exposure: la fossa, last suit, scaphism

Firing squad: blindfold act, die of lead poisoning, firing wall, military execution, wall

Gas chamber: Big Sleep, chamber, gas, gassing, smogged, smokehouse

Guillotine: bascule, Blade of Eternity, declic, French blade, headbreaker, heads will roll, Lady Guillotine, little window, louisette, louison, lunette, mirabelle, national razor, national shortener, patriotic shortener, people's avenger, photographer, saint, Saint Guillotine, sword of justice, traveling bag, widow

Hanging: airdance, air jig, air polka, air rhumba, blindfold act, cottonwood blossom, dance, dance of death, dance on air, dangle in the sheriff's picture frame, decorate a cottonwood, derrick, die in a horse's nightcap, die of throat trouble, do a dance in midair, drop, dry tree, execution box, execution shed, gallows, gallowstree, get it in the neck, gibbet, gimmaces, half-hanged, halter, hand of glory, hanging, drawing and quartering, hanging in effigy, hempen, hempen cravat, hempen four-in-hand, hemp fever, hoist, human fruit, judicial hanging, kitchen, look through cottonwood leaves, lynch, lynch-execution, lynch-murder, lynch victim, Maiden, masshanging, neck-cracking, necktie, necktie hanger, necktie party, noose, noosed, nubbing-cheat, patent drop, patibulary, patibulate, rope, shuggie-shue, slip-string, stretch, stretch a neck, stretch hemp, string up, supercollate, suspensus per collum, sus. per coll., swing, Texas cakewalk, throat trouble, throw from the cart, triple tree, twist in the wind, twist slowly in the wind, Tyburn tree, under a cottonwood limb, waghalter, widdy, yardarm

Impalement: ganch, placed on the stake

Lethal injection: e by i, execution by injection

Pressing: pein forte et dure

Sentencing: black cap, clemency, commutation, commutation of sentence, condemn, death sentence, death warrant, hanging judge, Hangman's Day, Ius Gladii, mercy, necking verse, pollice verso, posthumous exoneration, posthumous pardon, reprieve, splicing the rope, stay, stay of execution, summary execution

Stoning: lapidate, mazzatello

Strangulation: garrotte

FUNERAL
see Burial

SYN. carry out, cold-meat party, deader, death rite, exequies, feral, fun., funeralization, funeral rite, funeral service, Grandchildren's New Year, memorial service, mortuary behavior, mortuary rites, obsequies, rite of passage, solemnities

Associations: A.B.F.S.E., A.B.F.S.E.C., A.C.M.C., A.F.D.A., A.F.D.E.A., A.F.D.S., A.F.D.S.I., A.P.F.S.C., A.P.F.S.P., C.A.F.M.S., C.F.S.E.B.U.S., E.F.D.A., F.S.C.A.P., I.F.A., I.M.R., J.C.M.E., N.F.D.A., N.F.D.M.A., N.F.F.S., N.N.F.D.M.A., N.S.M.
Director: belly puncturer, Blackhead, casketeer, crapehanger, curbstone undertaker, death profession, designator, dismal trade, funeral functionary, funeral furnisher, funeral manager, funeral service practitioner, funeral upholder, furnishing undertaker, herald, Inviter to Funerals, layer out of the dead, libitinarius, mort., mortician, mortuary priest, necroponent, pollinctores, praeco, sem, sem-priest, undertaker, undtkr., upholder, vulture
Home: bi-unit method, chapel, death room, display room, dormitory facilities, functional method, funeral direction, funeral establishment, funeral parlor, funeral service, funeral service education, funeral service room, itemization, M.D.I., mort., mortuary, mortuary education, mortuary science, multi-unit method, preparation room, register book, removal, selection room, slumber room, tri-unit method, undertaking, unit method, visitation room
Procession: automorguemobile, bear, bearers, bier, Black Master, bone box, caisson, casket bearers, cortege, ekphora, featherman, feather-page, flower car, funeral car, funeral coach, funeral procession, funeral train, funeral trolley car, funeral vehicle, hatchment, hearse, lich way, motorcade, mute, pallbearer, representation, service car, shillibeer, tamashiro, underbearers
Services: altarage, committal service, cult of the dead, D.A.D., death-bell, death-duties, death knell, death money, death toll, death vigil, direct disposition service, F.T.S., full-couch, funeral customs, funeral etiquette, funeral expenses, funeral hymn, funeral industry, funeral music, funeral oration, funeral sermon, funeral tasks, graveside services, half-couch, Kiss of Peace, knell, knoll, last offices, last respects, last rites, laudation, laying out, libera, lich bell, lie in state, lychweake, Mass of Christian Burial, memorial cards, memorial music, mortuary, mortuary cult, mortuary practice, offering table, panegyrize, parentate, parentation, passing-bell, placebo, position, praeco, puppet death, repose, requiem, return home, ritual service, sin-seater, spiritual bouquet, streeking, taphophilia, taps, thanatousia, toll, viewing, viewing the remains, visitation period, wake
Types: dry funeral, green funeral, military funeral, total funeral

GRAVE
see Burial, Cemetery, Memorial
SYN. bed of clay, coffin silhouette, cold mud, corpse silhouette, deep-six, dustbin, earth bath, final resting place, future home, great divide, ground sweat, in cold storage, last abode, last home, last lodging, lich

rest, long home, narrow home, narrow house, neat oblong hole in the ground, public grave
  Associations: A.B.M.C., A.G.S., A.I.C.A., A.M.A., C.G., K.W.V.M.A., M.B.A., M.B.N.A., M.C.A., N.C.K.W.M.
  Epitaph: b.q., Dis manibus, DM, e.p.d., epit., hic jac, hic jacet, H.J., H.J.S., h.j.s., H.R.I.P., HRIP, H.S., i.h., inscription, lie like an epitaph, M.I., monumental inscription, monument poet, Q.I.P., requiescat in pace, rest in peace, RIP, R.I.P., sermon in stone, STTL
  Markers: bale-tomb, bed-board, bed-head, beggar's cross, body-snatcher's stone, body-stone, cenotaph, deadboard, ebenezer, exedra, flush marker, footstone, gabled cross, gravepost, grave rails, gravestone, hatted cross, hell-stone, hic jacet, hogback, horizontal memorial, jankers, leaping-board, ledger stone, mem., meml., memorial tablets, M.I.P.F., mon., monument, motif, placophobia, ringed cross, saddled cross, sheep-board, shingled cross, slabstone, slant marker, slat, stela, stone, tablestone, table tomb, tomb, tombstone, trophy, upright monument
  Plots: common grave, companion spaces, dismal trade, family plot, fossarian, fossor, gravedigger, grave orientation, grave recycling, gravesite, haunt a grave, overburden, pit grave, poor hole, sexton, shaft grave, stone pillow, taphephobia, tenant
  Robbers: bodysnatcher, coffin torpedo, ghoul, grave robber, gravewatchers, mort-safe, plunder, resurrectionist, resurrection men, sack-'em-up men, spoil, stiff hunter
  Underwater: burial at sea, Davey Jones's Locker, death ship, deep-six

GRIEF
see Mourning, Widowhood
SYN. bereave, dole, dolor, gloom, lose, loss, lovelorn, mourn, mourning, mourning process, niobean, pine, plaintive, plangent, regret, shibah, shiva, sorrow, viduous, wailful, winter, woe, woebegone, woeful
  Associations: B.P., C.C., C.F., C.F.D., G.G.P., G.P.G., P.O.M.C., P.O.S., S.C.F., S.S.B.
  Expressions of: bemoan, caoine, ceremonial weeping, comploration, conclamatio mortis, cry, dirge, dolent, doloroso, elegy, epicede, epicedium, jeremiad, Kaddish, keen, klama, lachrymatory, lament, memory place, moan, moirologist, monody, myriologue, professional mourner, reciprocal ritual weeping, requiem, threnetic, threnody, tristisonous, ululate, waesuck, wail, weep, weeper, wirra, yomer, yowl
  Lack of: dedolence, nepenthe, unknelled, unmourned, unwept
  Stages of: bereaved, bereavement counseling, C.S.H.C.S.B., denial, depression, grief psychology, grief resolution, griefwork, identity reconstruction, motherless, orphan, postvention, removal, renewal, resuscitation, separation anxiety, shock, survivor

Sympathy: acknowledgement cards, B, B.C., B.C.P., bereavement team, C.L.L.T., commiserate, condolence, console, C.S.L., death profession, E.K.R.C., G.E.I., get it out, grief counselor, I.L.B., minister of consolation, orphanage, orphanotrophy, ruth, solace, solacement, wreath
Types: anniversary phenomenon, anomic grief, anticipation, anticipatory bereavement, anticipatory grief, childhood bereavement, high grief death, improper grief, low grief death, private grief, public grief, shadow grief

HOSPITAL
see Causes, Terminal illness
Death in: abortion, anesthesiological death, autopsy, check out, clinical death, code, constructive death, critical illness, die on one, go out, go under, negative patient care outcome, operative death, O-sign, out of one's pain, Q-sign, technological death, vitalism
Designations: BID, bid., chronic care, CL, CMO, CPR, critical list, danger list, dead on arrival, DL, DNR, DOA, D.O.A., emergent, EOL, E.R., extraordinary means, FDN, life support equipment, life support system, LSS, marantology, no code, OD, O.D.
Resuscitation: anabiosis, CPR, cryonics, living dead, redivivus, resurrect, undead, zombie
Staff: CCRN, closed awareness, death profession, dire, distancing, emergent, open awareness
Wards: benign, CCU, CICU, critical care, death bed, death valley, dire, emergency care, ER, ICU, intensive care, terminal care

HUMAN SACRIFICE
see Cannibalism, Martyrdom, Suicide
SYN. immolate, lay down one's life, mactation, martyrdom, protomartyr, self-immolation
Gods/Goddesses of: Camaxtli, Juggernaut, Moloch, Tlaloc, Xipe
Practitioners of: headhunting, morestschiki, ritual death, ritual murder, Soshigateli, thug, voodoo
Types: anthropomancy, autosacrifice, devotio, foundation sacrifice, happy dispatch, hara-kiri, kamikaze, retainer sacrifice, seppuku, snuff film, suttee, tzompantlis, vivisepulture

IMMORTALITY
see Afterlife
SYN. apotheosis, athanasia, athanasy, big sleep, ensky, eternity, posth., posthumous, significant survival
Gods of: nectar, Savitri, scarab
Types: biological immortality, biosocial immortality, conditional immortality, creative immortality, immortalism, legacy, natural immortality, posthuma, religious immortality, social heir, social

184 Thesaurus

immortality, sponsoring, symbolic immortality, theological immortality

LIFE INSURANCE
see Vital statistics, Will
Descriptions of: actuary, beneficiary, death benefits
Types: burial allowance, burial insurance, double indemnity, term life insurance, whole life insurance

MARTYRDOM
see Crucifixion, Human sacrifice
SYN. win one's glorious palm
Relics: brandea, confessio, feretory, halidom, lipsanotheca, phylactery, rel., relic, reliquary, secondary treatment, second-class relic, stupa, tabernacle, third-class relic, translation
Types: BM, cephalophore, E.M., incorruptibles, mart., martyr, MM, Mm, protomartyr, v. and m., V & M
Veneration of: beatification, canonization, consistory, koimesis, martyrolatry, martyrology, martyry, menology, saint's day

MEMORIAL
see Cemetery, Funeral, Grave
SYN. commemoration, eloge, eulogy, in mem., in memoriam, mem.
Associations: H.S.M.F., N.S.J.W.D.
Monuments: cenotaph, durgah, epitaph, feretory, K.W.M., mastaba, tomb, tomb-dimensions, tomb-location, xat
Portraits: death mask, gisant, memory picture, mourning picture
Rites: Decoration Day, Memorial Day, Mind Day, requiem service, Year Day

MORBID
SYN. ghastly, grim, lugubrious, macabre, winter
Humor: black comedy, black humor, gallows humor
Preoccupations: automania, autophonomania, death cult, gallows literature, grave-dancer, Graveyard School, lypemania, medical vampirism, murder sheet, necrolatry, necromania, necrophilia, necrophilism, nonsexual necrophilia, sexual necrophilia, shoot-'em-up, snuffer, snuff film, snuff movie, taphophilia, thanatomania, thanatophile, thanatophilia, vulture

MORTALITY
see Causes, Crime, Murder, Vital statistics
SYN. borrowed time, critical, deadly, deathly, fatal, fatiferous, fell, funest, imperil, killing power, lethal, lethality, lethiferous, life-or-death, mort., mortal, mortal., mortiferous, nail in one's coffin, near and uncertain death, nonviable, occupational mortality, peril, perinatal mortality,

pernicious, pestilent, pestilential, poi., pois., poison, POS, pthartic, Sic transit gloria mundi, SSKP, terminal, thanatize, thanatoid, tox., toxic, upasian, virulent, walk onto a spot, widow-maker
  Awareness of: anticipation, awareness of finitude, memento mori, pda, personal death awareness, psychothanatic, thanatopsis
  Denial of: death-ignorer, death-initiator, denial, distant and uncertain death
  Types: death-chancer, death-darer, death-experimentor, death trap, kiss of death, kj, kk, murder merchandise, psychoweaponry, vanities

MOURNING
see Grief, Widowhood
  Dress: black, crape, don filial pity, doole, mourning clothing, mourning costume, mourning etiquette, mourning wear, weed, weepers, widow's weeds
  Signs of: door badges, funeral gloves, hatchment, hired mourner, mourner, plangorous, saulie
  Types: deep mourning, Nine-Day, shiva

MURDER
See Assassination, Autopsy, Causes, Crime, Vital statistics
SYN. abbreviate, bang off, baste, battue, be cancelled, bilge, blast, blast off, blood, bloodbath, bloodletting, bloodshed, blot, blot off the map, blot out, blotting, blow away, blow one's head off, blow one's lights out, blow one's top off, blow out, blow the gizzard out of, bottle up, brush off, buggy ride, bump off, burn off, bury, butcher, butchery, cancel one's Christmas, cannon, chill, chop off, -cide, clean up on, clip, commit, cook one's goose, corpse, count out, crackdown, crack off, crease, croak, cut down, cut off, decimate, deep six, destroy, dim one's lights, dish, dispatch, do, do away with, do business for, do for, do in, do one's business for, do the job for, douse, douse one's lights, douser, draw the curtain, drive rivets into the coffin of, drop, drop into Kingdom-Come, drop the curtain on, dump, dust, dusting, dust-off, dust off, erase, erasure, escalated interpersonal altercation, exit plan, extermish, extinguish, fake, feed a fatal pill, fell, finish, finish off, fix, flatten out, fordo, foul play, free ticket, get, get rid of, give one's everlasting, give one the works, give the ax, give the bump, give the Grand Bounce, give the push, give the push-off, give the rap, give the shuffle, go for the jugular, Grand Bounce, H, handle, head-hunting, hit, huff, ice, iron out, kd, kick into the beyond, kick the bucket out from under, kill, killing spree, kill off, kiss off, knock, knock cold, knock off, knock out, knock-over, knock over, knock the daylights out of, lay on the shelf, lay out cold, lead-poison, lead poisoning, leave one leaning, liquidate, lose, make a corpse of, make dead, make meat of, make mincemeat of, make one easy, make one "go cool," make out of the

186 Thesaurus

way, make short work of, martyrize, massacre, measure out, meat-axe, mop up, morganize, mummified, murderous assault, murdrum, murther, napoo, necation, nuke, off, 187, one-way ride, one-way ticket, out, outed, out of the way, pay one's respects to, pick off, plant, prey on, prey upon, pull a score, put a lily in one's hand, put away, put down, put easy, put it to, put on a marble slab, put on a slab, put one easy, put on the extinguisher, put on the spot, put out, put out of one's misery, put out of the way, put out one's light, put the brakes to, put the chill on, put the finger on, put the finisher on, put the rollers under, put the settler on, put the skids under, put to bed, put to bed with a shovel, put to sleep, queer, quirk, redlight, reward, ripoff, rod out, rub out, saw off, scrag, send across, send across the river, send home, send to glory, send to Jericho, send to Jesus, send to kingdom come, send up Salt River, set easy, settle one's hash, ship, shove across, shove off, Sicilian vespers, silence, skrag, slay, slay ride, slip the bump, slip the works, slough, smoke out, snub out, snuff, spifflicate, spiflicate, spill, spoil, stall one's engine, stop, stop in one's tracks, stop one's clock, take a life, take care of, take down the pike, take off, take one for a ride, take out, tell the bad news, the business, the works, top, torch out, touch home, trucidation, turn off, ultimate crime, used up, violent death, wash away, wash out, waste, whack out, wipe, wipe off the map, wipe out, work off, X-out, zap, zotz

Associations: C.S.C.M., P.O.M.C., S.C.M.

Investigation: corpus delecti, homicide city, homicide report, HomRep, murder capital, Murder City, murderologist, solve rate, victimol, victimological, victimology

Methods: blow away, crawl one's hump, death ship, defenestration, drown, dry-gulch, jugulate, killer judo, killer karate, murder kit, poleax, shoot, snipe, stifle, strangle, thropple, throttle, wring one's neck

Murderer: accessory to murder, alcoholic murder, androphomania, angel makers, avenging murderer, bloodstained, bloodthirsty, bloody-minded, Bluebeard, butcher, Cain, carbon-copy killer, child-killer, cop-killer, copycat killer, cutthroat, dacnomania, death wish, genocide, group killer, homicidal maniac, homicidomania, homo necans, husband-killer, iceman, in cold blood, killer, killer by persuasion, killing nurses, lust killer, malice aforethought, manqueller, manslayer, motiveless killer, multicide, murderee, murderess, murderholic, murder sheet, murder trial, nonmurderer, normal murderer, out for blood, parent-killer, phonomania, premeditation, prenticecide, psychopathic murderer, recreational killer, serial murderer, sex killer, sicarian, silencer, sociopathic murderer, spouse-murderer, spree killer, thanatomania, thug, wife-killer

Retribution: blood guilt, blood money, capital offense, cruentation, deodand, duel, eric, Erinyes, finger, kelchyn, ordeal of the bier, regret, rue, ruth, ruthful, wergild

Types: aggravated murder, alleged murder, amicicide, axe-murder, Brahminicide, Burkism, carbon-copy killing, chance-medley, child destruction, child-murder, Christicide, copy-cat killing, crime of passion, criminal agency, criminal homicide, czaricide, deicide, dirtbag murder, domestic homicide, double murder, episcopicide, excusable homicide, execution-style killing, felonious homicide, felonious murder, felony murder, femicide, filicide, first degree manslaughter, first degree murder, fratricide, genocide, geronticide, ghettocide, giganticide, gun-murder, gynaecide, gynecide, hereticide, heretocide, hericide, high-profile murder, hit murder, homicide, hosticide, infanticide, justifiable homicide, kfo, legal intervention, lust murder, lynch, lynch-murder, man. one, manslaughter, man. two, marital homicide, mariticide, mass murder, matricide, modernicide, multiple homicide, multiple murder, mundicide, murder in the first degree, murder in the second degree, murder one, murder spree, murder-suicide, neonaticide, nepoticide, non-capital homicide, non-capital murder, nonsexual homicide, parenticide, parricide, patricide, perfect murder, petit treason, petty treason, philosophicide, police murder, populicide, prison homicide, professional murder, prolicide, pseudautochiria, rape-murder, rape-slaying, regicide, ritual murder, sadistic murder, second-degree murder, self-defense, senicide, serial murder, sex murder, sexual homicide, sororicide, sparticide, spouse murder, stranger murder, suspected murder, thrill murder, triangle murder, trunk murder, tyrannicide, uxoricide, vaticide, vehic manslgtr, vehicular manslaughter, victim-precipitated homicide, viricide, voluntary manslaughter, v-p homicide, willful homicide

Victim: blown away, can't ever get well, catch it where the chicken got it, Chicagoed, come to a sticky end, corpsed, corpus delecti, cruentation, die of lead poisoning, die of the measles, disappear, done to death, do the Houdini, drag a lake, dumping, eliminated, end up, found in the bay, fratricide, get a free ticket, get a one-way ticket, get a permanent, get one's comeuppance, get one's everlasting, get one's gruel, get one's ticket punched, get pooped, get the ax, get the business, get the skids, get 30, go down blazing, go out in the country, have a funeral in one's family, have a permanent, have one's goose cooked, have one's gruel, kayoed for the long count, kiboshed, kilt, lick the dust, lost, mark, matricide, off the pigs, sell out, stonkered, take a long walk off a short pier, take one's gruel, take the checkers, wasted, wear cement shoes, X'd out

SOUL
see Afterlife, Death, Memorial
SYN. akh, astral body, ba, celestial air force, esprit, ghost, ghost-soul, Hun-soul, ka, Kwei, Po-soul, psychosophy, spirit
 Guides/Receivers of: Holle, Mayin, psychopomp, Psychopompos,

Pushan, refrigerium, soul rescue, Sraosha, Valkyrie, Vayu, Yamadutas
Judgment of: Abatur, Aeacus, Aiakos, Amam, Amenti, Ammit, ascension of the soul, Bhagwan, day of judgment, day of reckoning, Dies Irae, Di-zang, doom, doomsday, Emma-O, Isdes, Judgment Day, Last Day, last judgment, Mamitu, Minos, Mithra, mortal sin, pantocrator, particular judgment, perdition, psychostasia, psychostasis, Ragnarok, Rasnu, Rhadamanthus, Saint Michael, Sridevi, Valley of Jehoshaphat, Yama, Yincao
Prayer for: All Souls' Day, altarage, chantry, deesis, Dessounin, Lemuria, Nine-Night, requiescat, trental
Transmigration of: canari, Great Transfer, metamorphosis, metempsychosis, palingenesis, psychopannychism, psychorrhagy, reincarnation, samsara, translation to heaven
Types: Amkihiu, Ciuapipiltin, Ekimmu, lares, larvae, lemures, manes

SUICIDE
see Euthanasia, Human sacrifice
SYN. automania, autophonomania, brodie, bump oneself, check out, commit sideways, croak oneself, death instinct, death-seeker, death wish, die by one's own hand, do away with oneself, do oneself in, douse oneself, douse the lights, Dutch act, Dutch cure, Dutch route, end it all, felo-de-se, gamble with death, go without a passport, kiss oneself goodbye, lay violent hands on oneself, libido moriendi, pain principle, planned termination, play solitaire, quaff the cup, quitter, selfcide, self-deliverance, self-destruction, self-destructive behavior, self-execution, self-homicide, self-imposed death, self-inflicted death, self-termination, solitaire, suicidal, suicidal behavior, suicidal ideation, suicidal impulse, suicidal tendencies, suicidogenic, suikaput, suirep, suiterm, swing oneself, take a powder, take a rope, take hemlock, take one's own life, take the coward's way out, take the gas pipe, take the pipe, take the rope cure, thanatomania, thanatos, todestrieb, turn out the lights, undo nature's work, wipe oneself out, zonk oneself
Associations: A.A.S., I.A.S.P., N.S.A.L.L., P.O.S., S.S.B.
Gods/Goddesses of: Ixtab, Llorona
Methods: apocarteresis, autocide, autosacrifice, blow one's brains out, blow one's top, catabythismomania, defenestration, gilette one's way out, Hall of Odin, hara-kiri, hari-kari, hobo short line, kamikaze, make a hole in the water, psychological autopsy, Russian roulette, suicide airplane, suicide note, suicide shrine
Prevention: C.S.S.L.T.B., gatekeeper, I.S.D.B., N.C.Y.S.P., presuicidal, resilient cell, S.I.E.C., S.P.C., suicide prevention, suicide prevention center, suicidology, 3-Ds, Y.S.N.C.
Types: acute suicide, altruistic suicide, anomic suicide, attempted suicide, chronic suicide, cluster suicides, completed, compulsory suicide, defusion, Donatist, egoistic suicide, gradual suicide, mass

suicide, medicide, murder-suicide, mutual suicide, parasuicide, partial suicide, performance suicide, pseudophonia, self-immolation, self-mummification, self-poisoning, self-starvation, shinju, successful suicide, suicide epidemic, suicide gesture, suicide pact, suicide season, unconscious suicide, Werther effect

TERMINAL ILLNESS
see Causes, Dying, Hospital
SYN. deathly ill, doomed, fatal illness, in peril, living dead, near and certain death, social death, space, terminal care
  Hospice: bereavement team, C.H.I., C.R.T.I., freestanding hospice, H.E.I., hospital-based hospice, nursing home-based hospice
  Stages of: acceptance, bargaining, closed awareness, closure, denial, depression, disengagement, durable power of attorney, established disease, first-order denial, life-support system, LSE, LSS, M.T.C., mutual pretense, open awareness, primary recognition, rage and anger, rehabilitation, resistance, responsible conduct, resurrection syndrome, second-order denial, social disengagement, suspected awareness, suspicion awareness, third-order denial
  Types: biological survival, competent behavior, population, stance

VITAL STATISTICS
see Causes, Mortality
  Death Rate: age-specific death rate, crude death rate, death rate, d/t, fatality rate, I.M.R., infant mortality rate, kp, NDI, neonatal death rate, PcK, PK, postneonatal death rate, SCR, smr, vk, volume of death
  Life span: a.v., biometry, death day, DOD, dod, dying day, first life cycle, floruit, life, life expectancy, life expectancy at birth, life extension, life history, life-prolonging, live, living-dying interval, longevity, longevous, macrobian, macrobiosis, quick, register of death, surv., survive, time of death, v.a., yod
  Statistics: actuary, burial statistics, character of death, death certificate, death-point, death statistics, homicide city, id racket, megacorpses, megadeath, mortality revolution, mortuary statistics, murder capital, Murder City, Necropolis of the South, vital events, X-17, z-table

WAR
see Disaster, Murder
SYN. annihilation, AOW, AW, bellicism, belligerent, bellipotent, blood bath, butchery, carnage, casus belli, centesimation, decimate, declaration of war, genocide, hecatomb, holocaust, internecine, massacre, mass killing, necation, nuke, obliviate, pogrom, Reign of Terror, vegesimation, w., warfare, war-time, WT, WWI, WWII
  Associations: A.C.W.A., A.N.W.P.P., AWWWWII, C.A.N.W.,

C.A.W.A.W.L., C.I.N.W., C.P.N.W., N.A.P.N.W., S.S.A.N.W., S.T.O.P.N.W., U.C.P.N.W.

Battle: aceldama, annihilate, batt., blitz, Blitzkrieg, CCS, clean-out, decimate, FEBA, first strike, first use, fusillade, guerrilla, land of Badb, M.A.D., mop up, occision, pacification, typewriter party

Casualties of: A.B.C.C., accounted for, b-c kit, bite the dust, body count, bought it, buy a packet, buy it, buy the farm, CACO, cannon fodder, cas., cascan, cascor, Cas Reps, C.C.S., cold meat ticket, combat fatality, COMEX, confirmed kill, cop, cop a packet, cop it, CVN, death camp, death toll, do one's bit, ed, expendable, fatal casualties vulnerability number, fatality, FCVN, final solution, fire one's last shot, frag, get his or hers, go home in a box, gold star mother, gone for a Burton, Graves Registration, Hibakusha, identification, kamikaze, kd., kha, KIA, kia, killed in action, knocked cold, lay down one's life, lose the number of one's mess, massacree, megadeath, M.M.P.N.C., mow down, old Newton got him or her, overkill, ovk, pip, present at the last muster, present at the last roll call, promoted to glory, sanguinary, sanguineous, SCR, scuppered, shellshock, slaughter, slaughterhouse, smabbled, snabbled, suicide airplane, take out, thud, toll, trucidation, ultimate sacrifice, USLA, war crime, wr, written off, zap

Deterrence: conditional restraint, EWP, I.W.P.S., misopolemical, mutual assured destruction, nucleomitaphobia, P.A.W.M, U.S.C.A.N.W., W.W.W.C.

Gods/Goddesses of: Adrasta, Andarta, Aralez, Aray, Ares, Athena, Badb, Badb Catha, Beg-tse, Belatu-Cadros, Bellona, Camaxtli, Cariociecus, Ch'i-you, Cocidius, Guan Di, Gwydyon, Hachiman, Hathor, Huitzilopuchtli, Inanna, Ishtar, Karttikeya, Kottavei, Kuan-Ti, Lug, Mahasakti, Mars, Mentu, Meslamta'ea, Mithra, Morrigan, Morrigu, Neith, Nergal, Odin, Ogun, Oro, Quirinus, Reshef, Rugevit, Sachmet, Scanda, Segomo, Sekhmet, Shango, Skanda, Sulmanu, Svantevit, Svetovid, Teutates, Tiu, Tonatiuh, Tu Tyr, Valkyrie, Verethraghna, Xocotl, Zaba

Study of: A.C.H.S.W., C.W.C., C.W.P.S., I.C.H.S.W.W., N.W.E.P.A.P., N.W.S.G., S.A.N.S.

Types of: abcw, antisubmarine warfare, ASW, asw, asw/aaw, bacteriological warfare, biological warfare, biowar, BW, bw, bw-cw, BWL, BWRC, cbrw, CBW, cbw, cebar, chemical warfare, chem war, coin., conventional warfare, CW, cw-bw, desert warfare, electronic warfare, EW, ew, guerrilla warfare, GW, gw, jungle warfare, limited war, mountain warfare, nonnuclear warfare, nuclear warfare, omnicide, psychological warfare, psywar, PW, radiological warfare, radwar, RW, rw, space warfare, submarine warfare, unconventional warfare, USW, usw, UW, WW

WIDOWHOOD
see Grief, Mourning, Will
SYN. ace of spades, consort, dow, dowager, feme sole, relict, seneucia, ve, ved, vid., viduage, viduity, viduous, Vve, W, w., Wed, wid, wid., widowerhood, widowhood, Wwe
Associations: A.W.W.I.I., F.C.W., I.A.W.P., I.N.A.W.P., J.W.W., N.A.M.W., N.A.M.W.M.W., N.A.W.P., S.M.W., T.F., W.P.S., W.W.W.I.
Rights of: deuterogamy, digamy, dower, dowry, Enoch Arden, karao, levirate, levirate marriage, quarantine, W.C.C.

WILL
see Widow, Life insurance
SYN. ancient writings, attestation, bequeath, devise, endow, holographic, last will and testament, olographic, testament, testamentary disposition
Administration: administer, administration, administration cum testamento annexo, administration de bonis non, administration durante in absentia, administration durante minore aetate, administrator, administratrix, admix., admx., death duties, de bonis non administratis, decree of distribution, exec., executor, executress, executrix, exor., exr., exrx., extrx., exx., letters of administration, letters testamentary, necroponent, personal representatives
Estate: conditional estate, conditional fee, curtesy, demise, devise, disposition, dower, entail, fee simple, fee tail, gross estate, heritage, inchoate dower, loom, net estatem nonage, personal property
Inheritance: abatement of a legacy, ancestor, antilapse statute, beneficiary, beneficiary under the will, beqt., bequeath, bequest, bfcy., borough English, cleronomy, co-heir, collateral inheritance tax, collation, come into, communal property, conditional bequest, coparcener, corruption of blood, damnosa hereditas, death tax, descent, disinherit, eigne, election under the will, escheat, executory bequest, exheredrate, favored beneficiary, fee tail, first devisee, forisfamiliate, gavelkind, h., hand down, heir, heir apparent, heirdom, heiress, heir presumptive, heirship, her., heredipity, hereditament, hereditaments, hereditary succession, hereds., heriot, heritable, heritor, heritress, inherit, inheritance, inheritance tax, intestate succession, inventory, jointress, jointure, legacy, legatee, legator, matriherital, next of kin, parcenary, parcener, patrimony, pecuniary legacy, per capita, per stirpes, post-obit bond, postremogeniture, primogeniture, profectitious, real property, residuary bequest, residuary clause, residuary estate, residuary legacy, residuary legatee, scion, secundogeniture, specific bequest, specific legacy, succession, survivorship, tenant by the curtesy, testator, testatrix, tontine, ultimogeniture
Validity: ademption, animo testandi, attest, caducity, causa mortis,

codicil, codl., construction proceeding, c.t.a., dead hand, decedents' debts, die without issue, disinherit, disinheritance, dower right, dying declarations, execute, executory devise, failure of issue, HLS, in extremis, inofficious, in terrorem, intestacy, intestate, litigation, m.s.p., o.s.p., preterition, prob., probate, statue of wills, testacy, testamentary causes, testate, widow's election, w.w.a.

Types: holographic will, holograph letter, joint wills, multiple wills, mutual and reciprocal wills, mutual will, noncupative, nuncupative, olographic will

BIBLIOGRAPHY

Ammer, Christine. *It's Raining Cats and Dogs . . . and Other Beastly Expressions.* New York: Dell, 1989.

Baumgartner, Anne S. *A Comprehensive Dictionary of the Gods.* New York: Carol Communications, 1984.

Bergman, Peter M. *The Concise Dictionary of 26 Languages in Simultaneous Translations.* New York: New American Library, 1968.

Berrey, Lester V. and Melvin Van Den Bark. *The American Thesaurus of Slang.* New York: Thomas Y. Crowell, 1952.

Burek, Deborah M. *Encyclopedia of Associations 1991 (25th Edition).* Detroit: Gale Research, 1990.

Byrne, Josefa Heifetz. *Mrs. Byrne's Dictionary of Unusual, Obscure, and Preposterous Words.* Secaucus, New Jersey: Citadel Press, 1974.

Claiborne, Robert. *Loose Cannons and Red Herrings: A Book of Lost Metaphors.* New York: W.W. Norton, 1988.

De Sola, Ralph. *Abbreviations Dictionary.* New York: American Elsevier Publishing, 1974.

———. *Crime Dictionary.* New York: Facts on File, 1982.

Douglas, Auriel. *Webster's New World Dictionary of Eponyms.* New York: Simon and Schuster, 1990.

Drever, James. *A Dictionary of Psychology.* Middlesex, England: 1971.

Edwardes, Marian and Lewis Spence. *A Dictionary of Non-Classical Mythology.* New York: E.P. Dutton, 1923.

Enright, D.J. *Fair of Speech: The Uses of Euphemism.* New York: Oxford University Press, 1985.

Evans, Bergen, Editor. *Dictionary of Quotations.* New York: Delacorte Press, 1968.

Funk, Charles Earle. *Heavens to Betsy! and Other Curious Sayings.* New York: Harper & Row, 1955, 1983.

———. *A Hog on Ice and Other Curious Expressions.* New York: Harper & Row, 1948.

———. *Thereby Hangs a Tale: Stories of Curious Word Origins.* New York: Harper & Row, 1950.

194 Bibliography

———— and Charles E. Funk, Jr. *Horsefeathers and Other Curious Words.* New York: Harper & Row, 1958.

Gifis, Steven H. *Law Dictionary.* New York: Barron's Education Series, 1975.

Goldstein, Milton. *Dictionary of Modern Acronyms and Abbreviations.* New York: Howard W. Sams, 1963.

Habenstein, Robert W. and William M. Lamers. *The History of American Funeral Directing.* Milwaukee: National Funeral Directors Association, 1955.

Hellweg, Paul. *The Insomniac's Dictionary: The Last Word on the Odd Word.* NY: Ivy Books, 1986.

Hill, Robert H. *A Dictionary of Difficult Words.* New York: Gramercy Publishing, 1989.

Hunt, Cecil. *Word Origins: The Romance of Language.* New York: Philosophical Library, 1962.

Kaster, Joseph. *Putnam's Concise Mythological Dictionary.* New York: Perigee Books, 1963.

Kling, Samuel G. *The Legal Encyclopedia and Dictionary.* New York: Pocket Books, 1970.

Leming, Michael R. and George E. Dickinson. *Understanding Dying, Death and Bereavement.* New York: Holt, Rinehart & Winston, 1984.

Long, Kim and Terry Reim. *Fatal Facts: A Lively Look at Common and Curious Ways People Have Died.* New York: Arlington House, 1985.

Lucaire, Ed. *Phobophobia: The Fear of Fear Itself.* New York: Perigee Books, 1988.

Lurker, Manfred. *Dictionary of Gods and Goddesses, Devils and Demons.* New York: Routledge & Kegan Paul, 1987.

Makkai, Adam. *Handbook of Commonly Used American Idioms.* New York: Barron's Educational Series, 1984.

Mencken, H.L., Editor. *A New Dictionary of Quotations on Historical Principles.* New York: Knopf, 1982.

Moser, Reta C. *Space-Age Acronyms: Abbreviations and Designations.* New York: Plenum Press, 1964.

Neaman, Judith S. and Carole G. Silver. *Kind Words: A Thesaurus of Euphemisms.* New York: McGraw-Hill, 1983.

Packs, John. *A Glossary of Arms Control Terms.* Washington, D.C.: Arms Control Assoc., 1979.

Partridge, Eric. *Smaller Slang Dictionary.* New York: Dorset Press, 1961.

Saussy, George Stone, III. *The Logodaedalian's Dictionary of Interesting and Unusual Words.* Columbia, South Carolina: University of South Carolina Press, 1989.

Seymour, Elizabeth, Editor. *Hobble-de-Hoy! The Word Game for Geniuses.* New York: W.W. Norton, 1984.

Bibliography 195

Shneidman, Edwin S. *Deaths of Man*. Baltimore: Penguin Books, 1974.

Spears, Richard A. *NTC's Dictionary of American Slang and Colloquial Expressions*. Lincolnwood, Illinois: National Textbook Co., 1989.

Stevenson, Burton, Editor. *The Home Book of Quotations*. New York: Dodd, Mead, 1934.

Urdang, Laurence. *The New York Times Everyday Reader's Dictionary of Misunderstood, Misused, and Mispronounced Words*. New York: Signet, 1985.

Walsh, Dermot and Adrian Poole, Editors. *A Dictionary of Criminology*. London: Routledge & Kegan Paul, 1983.

Webster, William. *Webster's Dictionary Game*. Deephaven, Minnesota: Meadowbrook, 1987.

Webster's Guide to Abbreviations. Springfield, Massachusetts: Merriam-Webster, 1985.